# ESSAYS IN THE
# METAPHYSICS OF MODALITY

# ESSAYS IN THE
# METAPHYSICS OF MODALITY

Alvin Plantinga

Edited by Matthew Davidson

OXFORD
UNIVERSITY PRESS
2003

# OXFORD
UNIVERSITY PRESS

Oxford   New York
Auckland   Bangkok   Buenos Aires   Cape Town
Chennai   Dar es Salaam   Delhi   Hong Kong   Istanbul   Karachi
Kolkata   Kuala Lumpur   Madrid   Melbourne   Mexico City   Mumbai   Nairobi
São Paulo   Shanghai   Taipei   Tokyo   Torono

Published by Oxford University Press, Inc.
198 Madison Avenue, New York, New York 10016

Oxford is a registered trademark of Oxford University Press, Inc.

Library of Congress Cataloging-in-Publication Data

Plantinga, Alvin.
Essays in the metaphysics of modality / Alvin Plantinga ; edited by Matthew Davidson.
p. cm.
A collection of previously published articles from 1969 to 1993.
Includes bibliographical references and index.
ISBN 0-19-510376-9; 0-19-510377-7 (pbk.)
1. Modality (Logic)   2. Metaphysics.   I. Davidson, Matthew, 1972–

B945.P553 M48 2001
110—dc21      2001133030

1 3 5 7 9 8 6 4 2

Printed in the United States of America
on acid-free paper

# Acknowledgments

"De Re et De Dicto" originally appeared in *Nous* 3, 1969, pp. 235–258. Reprinted with kind permission of the editor of *Nous*.

"World and Essence" originally appeared in *Philosophical Review* 79, 1970, pp. 461–492. Reprinted with kind permission of the editors of *Philosophical Review*.

"Transworld Identity or Worldbound Individuals?" originally appeared in *Logic and Ontology*, ed. Milton Munitz (New York: New York University Press 1973), pp. 193–212. Reprinted with kind permission of New York University Press.

*The Nature of Necessity*, chapter VIII reprinted with kind permission of Oxford University Press.

"Actualism and Possible Worlds" originally appeared in *Theoria* 42, 1976, pp. 139–160. Reprinted with kind permission of the editor of *Theoria*.

"The Boethian Compromise" originally appeared in *American Philosophical Quarterly* 15, 1978, pp. 129–138. Reprinted with kind permission of the editor of *American Philosophical Quarterly*.

"De Essentia" originally appeared in *Essays on the Philosophy of Roderick M. Chisholm*, ed. E. Sosa (Amsterdam: Ropoli), 1979, pp. 101–121. Reprinted with kind permission of *Grazer Philosophische Studien*.

"On Existentialism" originally appeared in *Philosophical Studies* 44, 1983, pp. 1–20. Reprinted with kind permission of Kluwer Academic Publishers.

"Reply to John L. Pollock" originally appeared in *Alvin Plantinga,* ed. James Tomberlin and Peter van Inwagen (Dordrecht: D. Reidel), 1985, pp. 313–329. Reprinted with kind permission of Kluwer Academic Publishers.

"Two Concepts of Modality: Modal Realism and Modal Reductionism" originally appeared in *Philosophical Perspectives 1, Metaphysics* (Atascadero: Ridgeview Publishing Company), pp. 189–231. Reprinted with kind permission of James Tomberlin.

"Why Propositions Cannot Be Concrete" originally appeared in *Warrant and Proper Function* (Oxford: Oxford University Press 1993), pp. 117–120. Reprinted with kind permission of Oxford University Press.

# Contents

# ESSAYS IN THE
# METAPHYSICS OF MODALITY

# Introduction

For the past thirty years, Alvin Plantinga's work in the metaphysics of modality has been both insightful and innovative; it is high time that his papers in this area were collected together in a single volume. This book contains eleven pieces of Plantinga's work in modal metaphysics, arranged in chronological order so one can trace the development of his thought on matters modal. In what follows I will lay out the principal concepts and arguments in these papers.

## "DE RE ET DE DICTO" (1969)

In this essay, Plantinga is concerned mainly with defending the notion of *de re* modality against the attacks of people like W. V. Quine and William Kneale. After looking at some plausible examples of *de re* modality, he considers some of the arguments put forth by Kneale and Quine. He notes that all these arguments trade on a *de dicto/de re* confusion in one of the premises, a confusion that stems from the belief that, as Quine puts it, "necessity resides in the way we talk about things, not in the things we talk about." The following Quinean argument will serve nicely as an example of the sort of attack that Kneale, Quine, and others level against *de re* modality.

(1) Mathematicians are necessarily rational but not necessarily bipedal.
(2) Cyclists are necessarily bipedal but not necessarily rational.
(3) Paul J. Swiers is both a cyclist and a mathematician.

3

(4)  Swiers is necessarily rational but not necessarily bipedal (from
     (1) and (3)).
(5)  Swiers is necessarily bipedal and not necessarily rational.
     (from (2) and (3)).

(4) and (5) contradict each other, so the essentialist, who presumably
would accept both (1) and (2), is in trouble.

The problem with the Quincan argument is that, like the other
arguments Plantinga considers, it rests on a *de re/de dicto* confusion.
How are we to understand (1) and (2)? The only way that (4) and
(5) follow from (1) and (2) (and (3)) is if the necessity is read *de re*
in both (1) and (2). But when read *de re* (1) and (2) surely are false.
Why should we think that it is true *de re* of each mathematician that
he is necessarily rational, or true *de re* of each cyclist that he is necessarily bipedal? These *de re* claims are false, but there are *de dicto*
truths lurking in the neighborhood here which give (1) and (2) the
appearance of truth. For example, we may grant that the proposition
*mathematicians are rational* is necessarily true and the proposition *mathematicians are bipedal* is contingently true. But on this sort of *de dicto*
reading, we're not able to reach our contradictory conclusions. So
this argument trades on a *de re/de dicto* confusion. The other arguments he considers against *de re* modality founder on the same rock.

In the rest of the essay, Plantinga attempts to show how any *de re*
modal claim is equivalent to a *de dicto* modal claim. People like Quine
and Kneale seem to be much more sanguine about modality *de dicto*
than about modality *de re*; dialectally it would be significant if one
could show this *de re-de dicto* equivalence. Plantinga spends many pages
chisholming out a formula that will allow for a *de re* to *de dicto* trans-
formation. The reasoning is far too intricate to try to summarize here,
but I will say this. It is clear to Plantinga that as far as modality goes,
there is an important difference between proper names and definite
descriptions. Plantinga's account relies heavily on proper names. Post-
Kripke, the differences between the two in modal contexts seems very
clear: Names are rigid designators while most definite descriptions
are not. But it should be noted that Kripke certainly wasn't alone in
the late 1960s and early 1970s in his recognition of important facts
about the way names and descriptions behave in modal contexts.


"WORLD AND ESSENCE" (1970)

"World and Essence" is an extremely important essay in the development of Plantinga's thought in the metaphysics of modality. In it he
works out many of the core notions he embraces both in his main
work in the metaphysics of modality, *The Nature of Necessity*, and in his
present thinking. Also, Quentin Smith claims it's the first place where

the necessary *a posteriori* shows up in the philosophical literature. Plantinga begins this essay where "De Re et De Dicto" stops, with a formula for translating *de re* modal claims into *de dicto* modal claims. As the reader will note, it is a fairly complex-looking formula. But the core concepts are easily grasped. To say that an object x has a property p essentially is to say that x has p and it is necessarily false that x has the complement of p. Note that the last clause is satisfied when it is true that x exists in a world and lacks the complement of p and when x doesn't exist in a world (supposedly because all predications of properties of an object in a world in which it doesn't exist are false— this assumption amounts to a view Plantinga will defend in great detail later, serious actualism).

Plantinga introduces his notion of a state of affairs, the sort of entity that is expressed by phrases like "Socrates' being snubnosed" and "Gore's winning the election." As Plantinga later will stress, all states of affairs exist necessarily, yet only some of them are actual or obtain. Immediately after introducing states of affairs, he uses them to say what a possible world is, a maximal (or as he puts it here, "fully determinate") state of affairs, such that for every state of affairs A it either includes or precludes A. A state of affairs S includes a state of affairs A just in case it's not possible that S obtain and A fail to obtain, and a state of affairs S precludes a state of affairs A just in case it's not possible that S obtain and A obtain.

For each world, there will be a *book* on that world. A book is a maximal set of propositions, all of which are true in the world of which it is a book. Maximality here is analogous to maximality in the case of states of affairs: A set of propositions is maximal just in case for every proposition p the set either includes p or its complement p'.

Furthermore, Plantinga introduces the concepts of truth in a world and having properties in a world. A proposition p is true in a world W just in case necessarily, were W actual, p would be true. An object x has a property p in a world W just in case necessarily, were W actual, x would have p.

Finally, he introduces the notion of an *essence* or *haecceity*. Here he seems to think that they are equivalent notions; later he will claim that a haecceity is a type of essence, a primitive identity property expressed by phrases like "being Socrates" or "being identical with Socrates". To be sure, in this essay Plantinga includes these sorts of properties as essences. But it appears as though he isn't thinking of haecceities as a separate type of essence here. An essence or haecceity of an object x is a property that is essentially exemplified by x that entails all of x's essential properties and isn't possibly exemplified by anything distinct from x. Late in the essay, Plantinga points out that each of us has innumerably many essential properties. Consider any property p that is exemplified by an object x in a world W. It will be essential to x that it has the property *having p-in-W*; in every world in which x exists, it has the property of *having p-in-W*. In addition, consider a property p that is uniquely exemplified by an object x in a world W. Then not only is *having p-in-W* essential to x, *having p-in-W* is an essence of x. That is, it is a property that is had essentially by x and is necessarily such that nothing distinct from x has it. Plantinga calls these sorts of properties "world-indexed properties."

The above metaphysical machinery lays the groundwork for Plantinga's thinking on issues in the metaphysics of modality to this day. However, there is still more in this essay. Plantinga addresses what he calls "the problem of transworld identification" and what others sometimes call "the problem of transworld identity" (Plantinga's terminology is better given the nature of the problem—though neither term is apt, given the meaning of the prefix "trans"). The difficulty is this. Suppose we say that Socrates possibly has p, though he actually lacks p. Then there is a nonactual possible world W in which Socrates has p. But how are we able to pick out Socrates from the myriad of other entities that inhabit W? What "empirically manifest" property will allow us correctly to identify the individual in W who is Socrates? This was a problem that those who are suspicious of modality, like Quine, used to great rhetorical effectiveness against those serious about modality, such as Plantinga. But as Plantinga points out, it is difficult to see what the problem *is*. Which individual in W is Socrates? Why, it's Socrates, that's who. Why does it matter whether in W Socrates has any sort of empirically manifest property (e.g., a sweatshirt that says in bright orange letters "I Am Socrates!") that will let us pick him out from other individuals in the world? We've stipulated that Socrates exists in W. Why must we do anything more?

There is one more item of considerable philosophical interest I'll address in introducing this essay. Plantinga, following Descartes in Meditation VI, develops a modal argument for dualism. That is, he moves from a modal claim like "Possibly I exist and there are no physical objects" to the conclusion that he is distinct from any material object. One may question the validity of the inference (and Plantinga does) from the premise to the conclusion in this case. It appears as though some additional premise is needed to make the argument valid. Plantinga supplies it: Necessarily, if x is material then x is essentially material. This will allow us to move from the possibility of the immateriality of an object to its actual immateriality, which is just what the argument does. It is worth noting that modal arguments for dualism (like this one) have received much scrutiny in the past thirty years; Plantinga in this essay thirty years ago helped to fuel the volume of work on modal arguments for dualism that came after his paper.

## "TRANSWORLD IDENTITY OR WORLDBOUND INDIVIDUALS?" (1973)

Plantinga begins where he left off in "World and Essence" by laying out the basic metaphysical framework he developed there and from which he will pursue further issues in the metaphysics of modality. In this paper he wants to focus on two topics, the "Theory of Worldbound Individuals" (TWI) and the Problem of Transworld Identification (or Identity). The former is the claim that individuals exist in only one world; it's not possible for an individual to have any different properties than she actually has. A way of seeing the significance of this claim is to note that if anything about the world were different, nothing that actually exists would exist. The latter problem, the Problem of Transworld Identity we encountered before in "World and Essence."

Intuitively it seems as if I could have lacked any number of properties. I could have had blond hair or I could have been taller than I am. So what is the motivation for holding to TWI, a thesis that *prima facie* looks clearly to be false? Plantinga sets out two arguments, one from the absolute idealists and one from Leibniz. Both arguments are seen to rest on a misunderstanding of the Indiscernibility of Identicals (or "Leibniz's Law"). The principle normally is stated in such a way that it's easy to see how one might misapply it and conclude that TWI is true. Put in simple terms, Leibniz's Law is the claim that if x and y differ in any property, then x and y are distinct. Or conversely, if x and y are identical, then x has a property p iff y has p. Both arguments fail to appreciate that one must be careful when applying it to individuals across worlds (and across times). That is, the principle really should be thought of as applying to a given x and y at the same time in the same world.

Having shown two arguments for TWI to be wanting, Plantinga sets his sights on the allegedly intractable Problem of Transworld Identity. The "problem" seems to arise from a certain picture of possible worlds. Many people who champion the problem talk as if we're to imagine we're peering into other possible worlds and looking for the individual in question. As I noted in "World and Essence," it is as if the proponent of the Problem of Transworld Identity is demanding some sort of manifest property by which we can discern which individual is the one in question. But this is just an example of taking a sometimes-useful picture and abusing it. Do you want to know which person in W is Socrates? It's Socrates, that's who. Plantinga cleverly draws out an analogy between modality and time and points out that we don't demand some sort of empirically manifest property when we're judging transtemporal identity. Socrates no doubt looked quite different when he was a baby than when he was drinking hemlock at the end of his life. Yet we've no problem claiming that baby Socrates is identical with old, bearded Socrates. The Problem of Transworld Identity is a problem that arises from confused thinking brought about by using a certain picture of possible worlds.

Having looked at arguments for TWI and noted that they are wanting, Plantinga turns to giving positive arguments against TWI. He notes again that it entails what we might call "superessentialism": the claim that I have all my properties essentially. This has absurd entailments. It entails that any proposition predicating of me the complement of any property I have is necessarily false. It also entails that any proposition predicating existence of an individual that actually exists entails every true proposition. Consider Plantinga's example, "Socrates exists." It's true in only one world, the actual world (call it "$\alpha$"). So if it is true, then $\alpha$ is actual, which of course entails that every proposition that is true in $\alpha$ is true *simpliciter*. Thus, TWI appears to have some serious defects.

However, the proponent of TWI can enlist the aid of counterpart theory, an alternative semantic picture for modal discourse. On this theory, a sentence of the form "a is possibly F" is true iff one of a's counterparts is F. The counterpart relation is one of similarity; x is a counterpart of mine in W iff x is similar enough to me in the right sorts of ways. What sorts of ways are those? It depends on the context of the discussion and the interests of those involved in the modal discourse. An individual x might be my counterpart if we're emphasizing one sort of similarity, yet he may not be my counterpart under a different similarity relation. (See Lewis 1968 and 1986 for a detailed development of counterpart theory for modal discourse. See Plantinga 1974 for criticism of counterpart theory.)

So, though an individual only exists in one world (as per TWI), it is still possible for that individual to have different properties than she actually has. It just needs to be the case that she has counterparts in other worlds with the requisite properties. But problems lurk in the neighborhood. Consider the property *being identical with Socrates*. This clearly ought to be something that Socrates has essentially. But on counterpart theory, it's not had essentially by Socrates. Each of Socrates' counterparts lacks this property; TWI entails this in claiming that individuals are worldbound.

There are more problems that Plantinga brings out. TWI entails that I exist only in this world, $\alpha$. So if things had gone any differently than they actually did go, I wouldn't have existed, for another world would be actual. If Castro had chosen to refrain from his morning cigar yesterday, I wouldn't have existed. Surely this consequence is absurd.

One might respond to this latter point that if the sentence "if Castro had chosen to refrain from his morning cigar yesterday, I wouldn't have existed" in the above objection is being read through the lens of a standard semantics for modal discourse, and if one reads it through a counterpart-theoretic semantics, the sentence winds up expressing a false proposition. Let us suppose that this sentence would express a false proposition were we to evaluate it with counterpart semantics. Is it illegitimate to read it with a standard semantics, as the objection does? I think it is not. Even Lewis has to have some recourse to the standard semantics, at the very least in stating his theory. For instance, Lewis will admit that, strictly speaking (and according to a standard semantics for modal discourse) I exist in only one world. He couldn't say, for instance, that since I have a counterpart in another world who has the property *existence*, I exist in more than one world. When he gives the theory, he obviously isn't stating it in terms of itself—that is, in counterpart-theoretic terms. So, though Lewis could give a counterpart reading of the Castro sentence, strictly speaking Lewis would admit that it is true. After all, the statement simply states something that Lewis admits, that if a different world were actual, none of the concrete individuals in the actual world (read rigidly) would exist, though they might have counterparts that would. He can't totally avail himself of the standard modal semantics, and this is one point at which he can't.

There is a strong intuition that is deeply held by many philosophers who reject counterpart theory. Simply put, it is that the possession of a property by *someone else* in another world has nothing whatsoever to do with whether *I* possibly could have had that property. The proponent of counterpart theory will protest that this objection is little more than an outright denial of his theory. But for many philosophers, this very simple point—the fact that someone else in another world has a property has nothing to do with modal facts about me—gets at the heart of what is wrong with counterpart theory.

## THE NATURE OF NECESSITY, CHAPTER VIII (1974)

*The Nature of Necessity* is Plantinga's book on the metaphysics of modality. It is a terrific work, a "treasure trove," as Peter van Inwagen puts it. Much of the book works out in greater detail some of the ideas that appeared in earlier papers. However, there is much that is new, too. I have selected the central chapter on nonexistent objects from this book for inclusion in this collection of essays.

There is a standard argument that has been given for the claim that there are nonexistent objects. Plantinga characterizes it as follows:

(1) There are negative singular existential propositions.
(2) Some of them are possibly true.
(3) In any world where a singular proposition is true, there is an entity that the proposition is about.

(4) There are true negative singular existential propositions, hence there are objects which these propositions are about.

(5) Hence there are objects that don't exist.

When we say "Socrates is snubnosed," it certainly looks like what we're doing is referring to Socrates and then predicating a property of him. Consider the sentence "Socrates does not exist." If we take note of its grammar, the grammatical similarity between the first sentence and the second would lead us to think that here too, we are referring to Socrates and predicating a property of him—*nonexistence*. But if this is true, Socrates must have some sort of positive ontological status. After all, we're referring to him. Hence, one might conclude, there are objects that don't exist.

Plantinga makes a distinction between those singular propositions that predicate a property of an object (e.g., *Socrates is snubnosed*) and those that deny a property of it (e.g., *Socrates is not snubnosed*). The former he dubs "predicative" and the latter "impredicative" singular propositions. He notes that there is a *de re/de dicto* ambiguity with some impredicative propositions (and our example is one of them). *Socrates is not snubnosed* could be read *de re* as *Socrates is nonsnubnosed* (and hence is *predicative*, it predicates the property of *nonsnubnosedness*); or *de dicto* (where the negation applies to the entire proposition) *It is false that Socrates is snubnosed*. Now we are in a position to reconsider our main argument for nonexistent objects. We might revise (3) as

(3') If a predicative singular proposition is true of a subject S in a world W, then S exists in W.

Plantinga is inclined to accept (3'). (We'll see why momentarily.) Now, what does the argument look like if we replace (3) with (3')? If we do this, we need it to be the case that the negative singular propositions we're using to motivate the claim that there are nonexistent objects are predicative (e.g., *Socrates has nonexistence*). This is what is required by the antecedent of (3'). Plantinga denies that any true singular negative existential propositions are predicative. All true singular negative existential propositions are impredicative. All are of the form *It is false that S exists*. Why think this? Plantinga thinks that objects have no properties, not even *nonexistence*, in worlds in which they don't exist. This is a view which he later comes to call "serious actualism." So, the standard argument above is seen to be flawed, once we correctly understand its third premise and see the truth of serious actualism.

The rest of the chapter deals with the interesting question of the metaphysical status of fictional creatures. Here we have yet another argument for nonexistent objects—the truth of fictional propositions. It could be stated as follows. It is true that, for example, Hamlet is male. We have here a sentence that refers to an object and predicates a property of that object. But Hamlet clearly doesn't exist. Therefore, there are nonexistent objects. Plantinga rejects this argument, in part because he doesn't think that fictional names are referring terms. In some sense, this clearly is true. It is false that Hamlet exists (in the real world). "Hamlet" doesn't refer to anything in the actual world.[1] Yet, we do say it is true (in the fiction *Hamlet*) that Hamlet is male. So, if fictional terms don't refer at all, how can we account for the truth of this claim? If proper names don't refer in fictional contexts, how do they function?

Plantinga thinks that in telling a story, a storyteller directs the attention of the audience to various propositions (along with mental images and the like). In the most basic cases, the proposition expressed would be expressed by an existentially quantified sentence (e.g., "There is an x, and x=George, and x is tall. . . ."). In more complex cases there will be multiple propositions like the one above, both about George and other characters. For each character in a fiction, Plantinga thinks that there is such an existentially quantified sentence that expresses what he calls a *Story Line*. So in fictional discourse, the storyteller is directing our attention to various Story Lines. All sorts of hard questions remain, though. Does the Story Line include obvious truths, like the fact that $2+2=4$? Does it include truths not explicitly mentioned in the sentence expressing the Story Line, the fact that George was taller than a gopher? What about unmentioned facts—does George have a favorite ice cream? Plantinga suggests that with these latter sorts of cases, it's indeterminate as to what their answer is.

Now the storyteller doesn't assert that the various Story Lines are true in reality. He merely calls our attention to them and invites us to entertain them. There is some sense in which the sentences he utters express true propositions; if we affix something like "In the story" (basically a true-in-fiction operator) to these sentences, we will get sentences that express true propositions.

## "ACTUALISM AND POSSIBLE WORLDS" (1976)

This is one of Plantinga's most important and impressive essays in the metaphysics of modality. Plantinga is concerned here with setting out a metaphysics of modality in an actualist mode. Actualism, as Plantinga defines it (he gets the term from Adams 1974), is the claim that there aren't and could not be any nonexistent objects. We saw before that Plantinga wants to avoid nonexistent objects. So his commitment to actualism is nothing new; he has come to label a position he already held.

Plantinga begins by laying out very clearly the sort of metaphysical picture that standard Kripke-semantics for modal logic would suggest. I won't go into details on this picture, called by Plantinga the "Canonical Conception" of modal metaphysics, since Plantinga's lucid exposition needs no further elaboration. Of particular importance in the Canonical Conception is the union U of all individuals in α and every other world. Since it is plausible to suppose that U includes individuals not in α, the Canonical Conception leads very naturally to the view that there are nonexistent objects. Plantinga points out that we could weaken this claim and still violate actualism: we could show that it is possible that there be nonexistent objects. We do this simply by noting that surely there is some world W that is such that U contains an individual that doesn't exist in W. It's possible that the domain of all individuals, actual and possible, include at least one individual who doesn't exist in some world. This is to say that it is possible for there to be nonexistent objects, which is a violation of actualism.

Plantinga sets out his own metaphysics of modality in contrast to that of the Canonical Conception. There are noteworthy places where the two metaphysical pictures differ. Consider properties. On the Canonical Conception, properties are functions from worlds to sets of individuals (we can ignore relations for simplicity), or alternatively, sets of ordered pairs, whose first member is a world and second is a set of individuals. Usually, on this second way of looking at things, the world part of the ordered pair is dropped, and properties are thought of as sets of individuals. On this picture, we can see that properties can exist contingently. Plantinga's example is the property *being Quine*, which on the Canonical Conception just is Quine's singleton set. But it exists iff Quine does. In worlds where Quine doesn't exist, neither will his singleton, and hence neither will the property *being Quine*. This is problematic, though, because it seems quite reasonable to suppose that properties are necessarily existing entities. The problem is that sets are ontologically dependent on the existence of their members, whereas properties aren't dependent on the individuals that instantiate them.

There are other differences. On the Canonical Conception logically equivalent propositions are identical. So "2+2=4" and "No circle is a square" express the same proposition. Yet, intuitively they don't express the same proposition.[2] Also, possible worlds and propositions end up existing contingently on this picture. On the Canonical Conception possible worlds have their domain of individuals essentially. Suppose my coffee cup didn't exist. Then the domain of existing objects would be lacking one object it actually has. But then the actual world α wouldn't exist, for it has its domain of objects essentially. This quickly leads to the contingency of propositions, for if propositions are sets of worlds, were my coffee cup not to exist, neither would any proposition that contained α as a member.

Of note in this chapter is a method of "reducing" *de dicto* modal claims to *de re* modal claims. Simply put, the *res* in question will be the proposition in question, and the property ascribed to it will be some modal property (*being possible*, for instance). So we can take the *de dicto* claim *It is possible that Socrates is snubnosed* and note that it is equivalent to the claim that *Socrates is snubnosed* has the property *being possible*. Earlier in "De Re et De Dicto" we had a "reduction" that went the other way, from *de re* to *de dicto*.

Also of note in this chapter is Plantinga's acceptance of the fact that necessarily, objects have *existence* essentially. This may seem implausible at first, which is why Plantinga found the claim to be "dubious" in "De Re et De Dicto." But really, the claim is harmless and follows naturally from understanding what it is to have a property essentially. An object o has a property p essentially iff o has p in every world in which o exists. Clearly o exists in every world o exists. So o has *existence* essentially. But we must be careful to distinguish this claim from the claim that o exists necessarily, or in every possible world. Socrates has existence essentially, but exists contingently. Among necessarily existing individuals are properties, propositions, states of affairs and possible worlds, and if the Ontological Argument is sound, God. To say that possible worlds exists necessarily is to say that each world exists in every world, which paves the way for understanding the possibility relation between worlds as an equivalence relation. (S5).[3]

Plantinga, in response to an objection to actualism, makes use of individual essences to go "proxy" for nonexistent objects when making certain modal statements. This is something that most actualists today do when they need to be able to say things that *prima facie* look to commit them to the existence of nonexistent objects. (The same goes for presentism about time.) Suppose the actualist wanted to say that it's possible that there exist an object distinct from any in α. How could the actualist say this? Plantinga makes use of individual essences, which exist necessarily. To say that it is possible that there exist an individual distinct from any individual in α is to say that there is an unexemplified individual essence that is exemplified in some other world W. (An essence of an individual S is exemplified in a world W just in case necessarily, were W actual, S would exist.)

We turn now to Plantinga's main contribution to the philosophy of language.

## "The Boethian Compromise" (1978)

In this chapter Plantinga argues for a particular sort of Fregean view about names: a conception on which names express properties that determine the reference of the name. He begins by noting difficulties for the Millian about proper names. A Millian believes, with John Stuart Mill, that names don't express properties that are their contents that determine their reference; the semantic content of a proper name just is the individual to which the name refers. Classically there are four sorts of problems the Millian must confront.[4] First, if the content of a name is the object it denotes, what do we say about empty names? It would appear that they are contentless. This is problematic when we consider sentences that have empty names, for it's difficult to see how such a sentence could express a proposition. Suppose Noah never existed. Consider the sentence, "Noah built an ark." If "Noah" is empty, hence contentless on the Millian view, it is difficult to see how this sentence could express a proposition. Yet surely it does express a proposition; it's not as though such a sentence is meaningless. The Fregean is free to say that empty terms have a content (a property or properties) even if the term doesn't refer.

Second, what about true negative existentials? Suppose I utter "Hamlet doesn't exist." I'm saying something true with this statement. Yet how could I express a proposition with this utterance if "Hamlet" is empty, and hence contentless? The Fregean is free to say that "Hamlet" expresses a property or properties and can construe the true negative existential as a statement about this property or these properties (something to the effect that the property or properties in question aren't exemplified).

Third, the Millian has problems with opaque contexts. Suppose the Superman stories were true. Then Clark Kent=Superman, and on the Millian picture these names have identical contents, the man Clark/Superman. But if this is true, how can it be that Lois can believe that Superman is strong without believing that Clark Kent is strong? Both of these sentences express the same proposition; they say the same thing. The Fregean is free to say that "Clark Kent" and "Superman" express different properties and hence make different semantic contributions to the propositions expressed by the sentences in which they appear. This is to say that the two sentences can express different propositions on a Fregean view.

Last, it appears as though a Millian will have problems explaining the significance of some identity statements. "Superman" and "Clark Kent" mean the same thing on a Millian picture, so the claim "Superman is Superman" *prima facie* should be no more or less informative than the claim "Clark is Superman." Yet surely the latter can be informative while the former is not. The Fregean can explain this by claiming that the two names here express different properties and hence the two sentences above will express different propositions.

(I should note that in spite of these objections, many, perhaps most, of the philosophers of language today are Millians.)

There is a problem with the Fregean view, though. Most people think that proper names are rigid designators; they denote the same object in each world in which that object exists. The sorts of definite descriptions that express the contents of names on a Fregean picture don't appear to be rigid designators. Suppose the name "Cain" expresses the property expressed by the definite description "the man who killed Abel." It seems that this definite description can pick out different people in different counterfactual circumstances, while it seems the name "Cain" picks out the man Cain in any counterfactual circumstance. One way to see this is to note that "Cain is Cain" is necessarily true, while "Cain is the man who killed Abel" is contingently true. Other people could have killed Abel.

This point is made forcefully by Kripke (1980). However, Plantinga has the resources to solve this problem within a generally Fregean framework. Following Boethius, Plantinga claims that proper names express essences. In particular, they express world-indexed essences (or the properties expressed by $\alpha$-transforms of definite descriptions, as Plantinga puts it). So while it is a contingent matter that Cain killed Abel, it is a necessary truth that *in $\alpha$ Cain killed Abel*. Plantinga has proper names express these world-indexed properties, each of which is essential to the individual who instantiates them. In particular, there is a subclass of these properties, those whose "non $\alpha$-transformed" segment of the property is uniquely instantiated, that will be (individual) essences of the individual who instantiates them. The description "in $\alpha$ the man who killed Abel" will refer to Cain and only Cain in any world in which he exists. Hence, "Cain" will turn out to be a rigid designator on Plantinga's view. Plantinga has devised a view that inherits all the benefits of a Fregean view, and allows for names to be rigid designators. It is a clever theory indeed.

More particularly, coreferring names can express semantically and epistemically inequivalent world-indexed properties. So "Superman" might express *being the strongest man alive in $\alpha$*, "Clark Kent" might express *being the weakest man at the Daily Planet in $\alpha$*. This will allow Plantinga to account for the significance of some identity statements and the problem of opacity just the way a standard Fregean would. This view is a shift from the position he held in 1974 in *The Nature of Necessity*. There he thought that names expressed haecceities. By 1978 he thinks that they express a different sort of individual essence, one that allows for coreferring names to differ in cognitive significance.

Plantinga shows how he can incorporate intuitions that the referent of proper names is fixed causally by world-indexing a causal description and having its content function as the content of a proper name. So, being the person who *bears* R to "Socrates" in $\alpha$ where "R" designates the desired causal relation, could serve as the content of "Socrates." He also shows how one can world-index Searle's "cluster theory" of proper names. Searle believes that proper names express the property *having enough of the Si*, where Si is a cluster of descriptive properties. World-indexing this content will allow one to keep Searlean intuitions while at the same time allowing for rigid designation.

One very interesting consequence of Plantinga's view is that if a term that has a world-indexed property or properties as a content is empty, sentences that use the name as a referring term turn out to express necessary falsehoods. Suppose no one killed Abel, and the content of "Cain" is *being the man who killed Abel in* α. Then any proposition "about" Cain will be a necessary falsehood. So *Cain is tall* will turn out to be necessarily false, since no one satisfies the content of "Cain" in any world. I don't think that this tells against his view or helps it either, but it is worth noting.


## "DE ESSENTIA" (1979)

This chapter appeared in a *Festschrift* for Roderick Chisholm, and thus Plantinga spends some time dealing with issues in Chisholm's philosophy. The content of the paper makes it an ancestor of his seminal paper "On Existentialism" at which we will look next. Plantinga begins the essay by laying out his account of essences. He then takes up a claim of Chisholm's, that it is impossible for one individual to grasp another's essence. Plantinga finds this dubious, though perhaps there is more to the claim than one might think at first (see Davidson 2000b, forthcoming). He introduces the term *serious actualism* for the claim that an object has properties in a world only if it exists in that world. As we saw, this is a proposition he accepts in "World and Essence" and in chapter VIII of *The Nature of Necessity*. Now the proposition has a name. Plantinga thinks that it follows from actualism. This is a claim he will take back and then later embrace in some of his later work.[5]

Plantinga divides properties into two kinds, those that make essential reference to an individual (like *being Socrates*) and those that don't (like *being a mountain climber*). The first sort of property he calls "quidditative"; the latter he calls "qualitative."

The bulk of this paper is focused on exploring and critiquing a view Plantinga calls "existentialism." Existentialism is the view that singular propositions and quidditative properties depend for their existence on the objects they are "about." Many people (direct reference theorists in particular) hold to the claim that individuals are constituents of singular propositions. If propositions have their constituents essentially, one can see why such a person would be an existentialist. If one thinks of haecceities as "thisnesses" (see Adams 1979), it might seem natural to accept the second thesis of existentialism; if there is no "this" as it were, how could there be a thisness?

Plantinga considers whether an essence could consist wholly of qualitative properties.[6] To him it looks as if for any collection of qualitative properties, it is possible that more than one individual exemplify them (in different worlds). So he rejects the claim that an essence could be constructed of wholly qualitative properties.

It is a common existentialist maneuver to distinguish the possible from the possibly true. Consider the proposition *Socrates does not exist.* This proposition is possible, according to the existentialist, though not possibly true. It can be true only if it exists, and it exists only if Socrates exists, in which case it would be false. So "being possible" is weaker than "being possibly true." These two modalities have duals, naturally enough. The dual of weak possibility is strong necessity and the dual of strong possibility is weak necessity. These relationships will become clearer when we look at some of the uses to which the existentialist puts them. There is a third sort of possibility, possible truth in a world. This, supposedly, would be even stronger than possible truth. But for our purposes the first two senses of possibility and their duals are most important.

One reasonably might ask what it could mean to say that something is possible but not possibly true. The only sense that Plantinga can make out of this is to say that if something is possible, yet not possibly true, it is possibly non-false. *Socrates does not exist* is not possibly true, but it is possibly non-false: In worlds where Socrates does not exist, neither does this proposition, and hence it has no truth value at such worlds.

Plantinga raises some devastating counterexamples to existentialism and these varying notions of possibility. The existentialist wants to say that possible non-falsehood is possibly enough; we can use this notion to explain how it is true that it is possible that Socrates not exist. Though the proposition *Socrates does not exist* is not possibly true, neither is it necessarily false. Again, when Socrates does not exist, this proposition won't exist and hence won't be false. But there are many propositions that are "possible" in this sense. Consider the proposition *Socrates is a philosopher and Socrates is not a philosopher.* It is possible in just the same sense as *Socrates does not exist* is possible. But surely this shows that this sense of possibility, which is weaker than possible truth, is far too weak to capture the possibility involved in the proposition *Socrates does not exist.* In fact, the denial of the existentialist's own thesis comes out true on this weak sense of possibility. The existentialist wants to say that it's not possible for Socrates not to exist and either singular propositions about Socrates or Socrates' essences exist. Let E be one of these two sorts of entities. So the existentialist wants to claim that it's impossible that *E exists and Socrates does not exist.* But it is clear that this claim is possible on the existentialist's weaker sense of possibility. It is possibly non-false; in worlds where Socrates does not exist, this conjunctive proposition won't exist, either; hence it won't be false at these worlds. The existentialist appears to be hoist on his own petard.

Plantinga concludes that for propositions, the only sense of possibility is possible truth. He does concede that there might be two senses of possibility for sentence tokens. Consider the token "There are no sentence tokens." In no world is it true; however, there are worlds in which it doesn't exist and hence isn't false. It might be said to be possible, though not possibly true, because of the existence of such worlds.

## "ON EXISTENTIALISM" (1983)

Here Plantinga deepens and expands on his exploration and critique of existentialism. Again, existentialism is the view that quidditative properties and singular propositions are dependent for their existence on the objects they are "about." Plantinga considers two arguments for the thesis and one, at length, against it. The first argument for existentialism is the sort of appeal to intuition we saw in "De Essentia." Isn't it just clear that *being Socrates* or *being this person* (that is, Socrates) are dependent on the existence of the person they are about? As we expressed it earlier, "How can there be a 'thisness' if there is no 'this?'"

The second argument is that on certain views of content, concrete individuals can be constituents of propositions. Propositions presumably have their constituents essentially if they have constituents. So, were the person who is the subject of the singular proposition not to exist, neither would that proposition.

Plantinga finds neither of these arguments persuasive. His intuitions aren't in accord with the first argument, and he finds the nature of constituency to be unclear. He's not quite sure what it is to be a constituent of a proposition, and he has even less of an idea when it's a physical object that is being considered for constituenthood.

The real meat of this paper lies in his argument against existentialism. It is similar to an argument given by Fine (1977), who claims that he found the argument in Prior's work. However, as far as I know, no one else states it and examines it with the rigor Plantinga does.[7] I will state it, using the premise numbers Plantinga uses in the text.

(3)  Possibly, Socrates does not exist.
(4)  If (3) then the proposition *Socrates does not exist* is possible.
(5)  If the proposition *Socrates does not exist* is possible it is possibly true.
(6)  Necessarily, if *Socrates does not exist* had been true, then *Socrates does not exist* would have existed.

(7) Necessarily, if *Socrates does not exist* had been true, then Socrates would not have existed.

(8) (From (3), (4), and (5)) *Socrates does not exist* is possibly true.

(9) (From (6) and (7)) Necessarily, if *Socrates does not exist* had been true, then *Socrates does not exist* would have existed and Socrates would not have existed.

(10) (From (8) and (9)) It is possible that both Socrates does not exist and the proposition *Socrates does not exist* exists.

Let us consider the argument as Plantinga has presented it. He takes (4) to be relatively uncontroversial, though he very briefly addresses an objection to it. (6) follows from serious actualism; if a proposition has *being true* in a world, it exists in that world. Here Plantinga doesn't think that actualism entails serious actualism. Previously he did, and he will again in the next essay we examine. But here he thinks it doesn't follow from actualism alone, though he certainly thinks it's true.

He considers one argument against serious actualism that rests on a blurring of the predicative/impredicative distinction. It goes as follows. Consider a world in which Socrates doesn't exist. *Socrates is not tall* is true in such a world. This is to say that Socrates has the property of *being non-tall*, which contradicts serious actualism. We saw this sort of argument arise when we looked at the selection from *The Nature of Necessity*. There we noted a *de dicto/de re* ambiguity in statements like "Socrates is not tall." This sentence might express the proposition *Socrates has the property of being non-tall* or it might express the proposition *It's false that Socrates is tall*. When Socrates does not exist, we take it to express the latter proposition. So this really isn't a good objection to serious actualism, and (6) seems acceptable.

The argument with respect to (5) follows very closely the argument concerning weak possibility from "De Essentia." Plantinga examines weak possibility and its dual as a way of showing that (5) is false. But the weak sense of possibility is far too permissive, as we saw in "De Essentia," and thus the hopes of having a proposition that is possible yet not possibly true are dashed. (7) is uncontroversial, and the rest of the premises follow from previous premises.

## "REPLY TO JOHN L. POLLOCK" (1985)

This piece nicely illustrates much of Plantinga's current thinking on the metaphysics of modality. It is taken from a collection of essays on Plantinga's work (see Tomberlin and van Inwagen 1985), and this particular essay was written in response to John Pollock's contribution to the work. Since it is a response to particular objections, the piece isn't as fluid as a normal paper, and what is said about it here also will be piecemeal.

Plantinga begins by trying to make sense of the claim that there are objects that don't exist. Call this position "possibilism." Plantinga wants the first quantifier to be read as widely as one would like, so that it ranges over Meinongian possible and impossible objects and Lewisian possibilia if there are such creatures. So the possibilist is claiming something significant when he says that there are some objects that don't exist; it's not equivalent to the obvious contradiction "There exist objects that don't exist."

In his essay Pollock proposes *nonexistence* as a property that objects have in worlds where they don't exist. This would violate serious actualism, however. Plantinga gives an argument to the conclusion that necessarily, *nonexistence* is unexemplified. It proceeds as follows:

(1) Necessarily, for every property p, if p is exemplified, then there is (read this quantifier as widely as you like) something that exemplifies p.

(2) Necessarily, for every property p, whatever exemplifies p exists (from actualism).

(3) Necessarily, if *nonexistence* is exemplified, then it is exemplified by something that exists (which is impossible).

(4) Therefore, necessarily, *nonexistence* is unexemplified.

Plantinga has had a change of heart from "On Existentialism"; he thinks that there is a good argument from actualism to serious actualism. It goes as follows.

Consider a world W in which Socrates exemplifies any property p.

(5) Necessarily, if Socrates exemplifies p, he exemplifies p and *existence* or he exemplifies p and *nonexistence*.

(6) Necessarily, *nonexistence* is unexemplified (from (4) above).

(7) Therefore, necessarily, if Socrates exemplifies p, he exemplifies *existence*.

So it appears as though there is a good argument from actualism to serious actualism.[8]

In response to some arguments Pollock makes, Plantinga distinguishes between satisfying a condition *at* a world as opposed to satisfying a condition *in* a world. He argues that the condition -(x exists) is satisfied *at* many worlds, but *in* none. His argument is very similar to the one above for the conclusion that *nonexistence* isn't possibly exemplified.

He begins with a conception of what it is to satisfy a condition in a world: An object x satisfies a condition C in a world W if and only if necessarily, if W had been actual, then x would satisfy C. Then, the argument proceeds as follows.

(8) Necessarily, for any condition C, if C is satisfied there is (in as wide a sense as one likes) something that satisfies it.

(9) Necessarily, for any condition C, whatever satisfies C exists (actualism).

(10) Necessarily, If -(x exists) is satisfied, it is satisfied by something that exists (from (9)).

(11) Therefore, necessarily, -(x exists) is unsatisfied.

Plantinga distinguishes between satisfying a condition at a world and satisfying a condition *in* a world. He takes the above argument to show that Socrates satisfies -(x exists) in no world. However, he grants that he can satisfy this condition at worlds; he satisfies it at any world in which he doesn't exist. Plantinga thinks that Pollock may be confusing the two notions.

One important distinction comes out in Pollock's piece that Plantinga accepts: The states of affairs that compose a possible world must be temporally invariant (if they obtain, there is no time at which they don't obtain). Otherwise, which world is actual could change over time, and this is not desirable.


"Two Concepts of Modality: Modal Realism
and Modal Reductionism" (1987)

People often call David Lewis a modal realist (usually it's "extreme modal realist"). However, Plantinga wants to argue in this paper that Lewis is no realist about matters modal at all. So *prima facie* Plantinga is making a quite interesting claim.

Plantinga begins by laying out what he calls three grades of modal realism. Grade I is that there are necessary and contingent propositions, and objects have essential and accidental properties. Grade II is that there are possible worlds, which are temporally invariant maximal states of affairs. Grade III is that objects have properties in worlds, and there are individual essences.

He then turns to Lewis's modal metaphysics. Lewis is very similar in some regards to his teacher Quine. Like Quine, Lewis thinks that basically there are concrete objects and sets. Lewis will use these to "construct" a whole host of different entities.[9] For Lewis, possible worlds are concrete objects, each spatiotemporally unrelated to any other. Objects exist only in one world; they are worldbound. But they do have counterparts, objects distinct from them that resemble them in certain ways. Propositions are sets of worlds, properties are sets of individuals, and individual essences are sets of counterparts.

Plantinga's contention is that really all Lewis is doing is choosing entities to *model* things like propositions, properties, and possible worlds. Yet these are but weak surrogates for the real thing, Plantinga contends. For instance, intuitively propositions and properties are much more fine-grained than they are on Lewis's conceptions of them. Furthermore, propositions are supposed to be the sorts of things that are true and false, and they are supposed to be capable of being the objects of our attitudes. Yet sets are neither true nor false; nor are they the sorts of things that can be believed or entertained. So Plantinga's contention is that Lewis is at best a modal reductionist, and he's certainly no modal realist. The sorts of things he offers up as possible worlds, propositions, and properties at best partially fit the role they are supposed to play.

Lewis thinks that we have no well-defined concepts of possible worlds, propositions, or properties. We have different ways of making these concepts precise. On some ways of making these concepts precise, sets and large concrete objects will do just fine. On other ways of making them precise, for example sets might not completely fill the "proposition" role. But to insist on one precise conception of any of these entities is to miss the semantic indecision that we exhibit with respect to these terms. What we have here are rough roles, and different entities can play these roles, depending on which elements of the roles we want to stress.

Plantinga doesn't buy any of this. He's certainly willing to grant that our concepts of properties, propositions, and possible worlds may not be totally precise, but they're also not so nebulous as to allow things like sets to count as propositions and properties. Our concepts are better defined than Lewis thinks they are, and we can do better than insist that at best what we have are rough roles that different objects may play. There are several essential features of our concepts of these entities, and anything that lacks these features just can't be counted as satisfying these concepts.

So at best what Lewis is doing, according to Plantinga, is modeling certain properties of things like properties, propositions, and possible worlds. But that's *all* he's doing—modeling—and the models he proposes should not to be confused with the real things they're modeling.

## "WHY PROPOSITIONS CANNOT BE CONCRETE" (1993)

One might be tempted to identify propositions with something concrete. For instance, they might be sentences in the language of thought. Or they might be sentence tokens on a page. Plantinga wants to argue that no physical object can be a proposition.

There is an immediate problem with identifying propositions with physical objects. It certainly appears possible that there be no physical objects. If this were the case, we should want to say that the proposition *there are no physical objects* is true. But we can't say this, for the very proposition we're affirming is itself a physical object and wouldn't exist in such worlds. Because of serious actualism, this proposition couldn't be true in such worlds.

The person who wants to identify propositions with something physical can't say then that this proposition would be true if there were no physical objects. It wouldn't exist in order to be true if there were no physical objects. Supposedly it is possible for no physical objects to exist, though. So the concretist will want to say that it is possible that there are no physical objects without it being possibly true that there are no physical objects, for this would require the existence of a physical object—a proposition. Can we make sense of a notion of possibility other than possible truth? We did so in the case of existentialism. Possibility in that instance was possible non-falsity, and it looks like that will be the case here, as well. It is possible that it is not false that there are no physical objects. So we again find occasion for a weaker sense of possibility. However, we've also seen that there are serious problems with affirming that possible non-falsity is possibility enough. The proposition $2+2=5$ is possibly non-false; in a world in which there are no physical objects, it won't be false (since it won't exist). So it looks like this appeal to a weaker sense of possibility in order to rescue the intuition that it's possible that there be no physical objects fails.

We'll also have occasion for a weaker sense of necessity due to the contingency of physical objects. We can't say that what it is for a proposition to be necessarily true is for it to be true in every world, since some worlds will have no physical objects and hence no true propositions. We must weaken our notion of necessity to something like: a proposition is necessary if it is true in every world in which it exists. $2+2=4$ is true in every world in which it exists and hence is necessary. However, there are propositions that are true in every world in which they exist that appear to be contingent. Consider the proposition *There are physical objects*. If this proposition exists, it's *ipso facto* true since it itself is a physical object. Hence it's necessary. Yet intuitively this proposition is not necessary; surely it's possible that there not be physical objects.

The moral to draw from all this is that it's possible that propositions be physical objects.

*Matthew Davidson*
*California State University at San Bernardino*

NOTES

Thanks to Gordon Barnes, Tom Crisp, Dave VanderLaan, Alvin Plantinga, and an anonymous referee from Oxford University Press for helpful suggestions.
1. There are views on which fictional creatures are abstract objects, so "Hamlet" would refer. See Salmon 1998.
2. See Stalnaker 1976, 1984; and Lewis 1986 for responses to this objection.

3. See Chandler 1976 and Salmon 1981, 1986 for reasons for thinking that the possibility relation between worlds isn't S5.

4. The literature here is vast; I point the reader to Recanati 1993 for a good overview of the territory in contemporary philosophy of language. See also Davidson, forthcoming. I also should say that the responses to each of these objections are numerous. However, my role is to introduce the reader to Plantinga's thought, and giving each of these problems its due would take us too far away from Plantinga's own thought.

5. For more on serious actualism, see Bergmann 1996, 1999, Hudson 1997, and Davidson 2000a, 2000b, forthcoming.

6. See Adams 1981 for more on this.

7. See Davidson 2000a for further application and examination of this sort of argument.

8. See Bergmann 1996; 1999; Hudson 1996; and Davidson 2000a, forthcoming, for more on this.

9. See Lewis 1986, p. 64, where he states that he is undecided as to whether there are tropes or immanent universals.

## REFERENCES

Adams, Robert. "Theories of Actuality," *Nous* 8 (1974), pp. 211–31.

Adams, Robert. "Primitive Thisness and Primitive Identity." *Journal of Philosophy* 76 (1979), pp. 5–26.

Adams, Robert. "Actualism and Thisness." *Synthese* 49 (1981), pp. 3–41.

Bergmann, Michael. "A New Argument From Actualism to Serious Actualism," *Nous* 30 (1996), pp. 356–59.

Bergmann, Michael. "(Serious) Actualism and (Serious) Presentism" *Nous* 33 (1999), pp. 118–32.

Chandler, Hugh. "Plantinga and the Contingently Possible" *Analysis* 36 (1976), pp. 106–109.

Davidson, Matthew. "Direct Reference and Singular Propositions," American Philosophical Quarterly 37 (2000).

Davidson, Matthew. *Propositions, Proper Names, and Indexicals: A Neo-Fregean Approach.* Ph.D. dissertation, University of Wisconsin 2000b.

Davidson, Matthew. *Semantics; A Fregean Approach* (forthcoming).

Fine, Kit. "Plantinga on the Reduction of Possibilist Discourse," in Tomberlin and van Inwagen.

Hudson, Hud. "On a New Argument from Actualism to Serious Actualism," *Nous* 31 (1997), pp. 520–24.

Kripke, Saul. *Naming and Necessity* (Cambridge: Harvard University Press, 1980).

Lewis, David. "Counterpart Theory and Quantified Modal Logic," *Journal of Philosophy* 65 (1968), pp. 113–26.

Lewis, David. *On the Plurality of Worlds* (Cambridge: Blackwell, 1986).

Prior, A. N. and Fine, Kit. *Worlds, Times, and Selves* (Amherst: University of Massachusetts Press, 1977).

Recanati, François. *Direct Reference* (Cambridge: Blackwell, 1993).

Salmon, Nathan. *Reference and Essence* (Princeton: Princeton University Press, 1981).

Salmon, Nathan. "Modal Paradox: Parts and Counterparts Points and Counterpoints." In *Midwest Studies in Philosophy: Essentialism.* Ed. French et al. (1986).

Salmon, Nathan. "Nonexistence," *Nous* 32 (1998), pp. 277–319.

Stalnaker, Robert. "Possible Worlds," *Nous* 10 (1976), pp. 65–75.

Stalnaker, Robert. *Inquiry* (Cambridge: MIT Press, 1984).

Tomberlin, J. and van Inwagen, P. *Alvin Plantinga* (Dordrecht: D. Reidel, 1985).

# 1

# De Re et De Dicto

In *Prior Analytics i,* 9 Aristotle makes an interesting observation: "It happens sometimes that the conclusion is necessary when only one premise is necessary; not, however, either premise taken at random, but the major premise." Here Aristotle means to sanction such inferences as

(1) Every human being is necessarily rational
(2) Every animal in this room is a human being

∴ (3) Every animal in this room is necessarily rational.

On the other hand, he means to reject inferences of the following sort:

(4) Every rational creature is in Australia
(5) Every human being is necessarily a rational creature

∴ (6) Every human being is necessarily in Australia.

Aristotle would presumably accept as sound the inference of (3) from (1) and (2) (granted the truth of 2). But if so, then (3) is not to be read as

(3') It is necessarily true that every animal in this room is rational;

for (3') is clearly false. Instead, (3) must be construed, if Aristotle is correct, as the claim that each animal in this room has a certain property—the property of being rational—*necessarily* or *essentially*. That is to say, (3) must be taken as an expression of modality *de re* rather than modality *de dicto*. And what this means is that (3) is not the assertion that a certain *dictum* or proposition—*every animal in this room is rational*—is necessarily true, but is instead the assertion that each *res* of a certain kind has a certain property *essentially* or *necessarily*.

In *Summa Contra Gentiles* Thomas considers the question whether God's foreknowledge of human action—a foreknowledge that consists, according to Thomas, in God's simply *seeing* the relevant action taking place—is consistent with human freedom. In this connection he inquires into the truth of

(7) What is seen to be sitting is necessarily sitting.

For suppose God sees at $t_1$ that Theatetus is sitting at $t_2$. If (7) is true, then presumably Theatetus is necessarily sitting at $t_2$, in which case this action cannot be freely performed.

Thomas concludes that (7) is true if taken *de dicto* but false if taken *de re*; that is,

(7') It is necessarily true that whatever is seen to be sitting is sitting

is true but

(7") Whatever is seen to be sitting has the property of sitting essentially

is false. The deterministic argument, however, requires the truth of (7"), and hence that argument fails. Like Aristotle, then, Aquinas appears to believe that modal statements are of two kinds. Some predicate a modality of another statement (modality *de dicto*); but others predicate of an object the necessary or essential possession of a property; and these latter express modality *de re*.

But what is it, according to Aristotle and Aquinas, to say that a certain object has a certain property essentially or necessarily? That, presumably, the object in question *couldn't conceivably have lacked* the property in question; that under no possible circumstances could that object have failed to possess that property. I am thinking of the number 17; what I am thinking of, then, is prime and *being prime*, furthermore, is a property that it couldn't conceivably have lacked. The world could have turned out quite differently; the number 17 could have lacked many properties that in fact it has—the property of having just been mentioned would be an example. But that it should have lacked the property of being prime is quite impossible. And a statement of modality *de re* asserts of some object that it has some property essentially in this sense.

Furthermore, according to Aquinas, where a given statement of modality *de dicto*—(7'), for example—is true, the corresponding statement of modality *de re*—(7"), in this instance—may be false. We might add that in other such pairs the *de dicto* statement is false but the *de re* statement true; if I'm thinking of the number 17, then

(8) What I'm thinking of is essentially prime

is true, but

(9) The proposition *what I am thinking of is prime* is necessarily
    true

is false.

The distinction between modality *de re* and modality *de dicto* is not confined to ancient and medieval philosophy. In an unduly neglected paper "External and Internal Relations," G. E. Moore discusses the idealistic doctrine of internal relations, concluding that it is false or confused or perhaps both. What is presently interesting is that he takes this doctrine to be the claim that all *relational properties* are internal—which claim, he thinks, is just the proposition that every object has each of its relational properties *essentially* in the above sense. The doctrine of internal relations, he says, "implies, in fact, quite generally, that any term which does in fact have a particular relational property, could not have existed without having that property. And in saying this it obviously flies in the face of common sense. It seems quite obvious that in the case of many relational properties which things have, the fact that they have them is a *mere matter of fact*; that the things in question *might* have existed without having them".[1] Now Moore is prepared to concede that objects *do* have *some* of their relational properties essentially. Like Aristotle and Aquinas, therefore, Moore holds that some objects have some of their properties essentially and others non-essentially or accidently.

One final example: Norman Malcolm believes that the Analogical Argument for other minds requires the assumption that one must learn what, for example, *pain* is "from his own case." But, he says, "if I were to learn what pain is from perceiving my own pain then I should, necessarily, have learned that pain is something that exists only when I feel pain. For the pain that serves as my paradigm of pain (i.e., my own) has the property of existing only when I feel it. That property is essential, not accidental; it is nonsense to suppose that the pain I feel could exist when I did not feel it. So if I obtain my conception of pain from pain that I experience, then it will be a part of my conception of pain that I am the only being that can experience it. For me it will be a *contradiction* to speak of *another's* pain."[2]

This argument appears to require something like the following premise:

(10) If I acquire my concept of *C* by experiencing objects and all
    the objects from which I get this concept have a property *P*

essentially, then my concept of *C* is such that the proposition *Whatever is an instance of C has P* is necessarily true.

Is (10) true? To find out, we must know more about what it is for an object to have a property essentially. But initially, at least, it looks as if Malcolm means to join Aristotle, Aquinas, and Moore in support of the thesis that objects typically have both essential and accidental properties; apparently he means to embrace the conception of modality *de re.*

A famous and traditional conception, then, the idea of modality *de re* is accepted, explicitly or implicitly, by some contemporary philosophers as well; nevertheless it has come under heavy attack in recent philosophy. In what follows I shall try to defend the conception against some of these attacks. First, however, we must state more explicitly what it is that is to be defended. Suppose we describe the *de re* thesis as the dual claim that (a) certain objects have some of their properties essentially, and (b) where *P* is a property, *having P essentially* is also a property—or, as we might also put it, where *being F* is a property, so is *being F necessarily*. What is the force of this latter condition? Suppose we define the locution "has sizeability" as follows:

D₁ *x* has sizeability = def. ⌐*x*⌐ contains more than six letters.

Here the peculiar quotation-like marks around the second occurrence of 'x' indicate that it is to be supplanted by the result of quoting the singular term that supplants its first occurrence. D₁ is a definitional scheme enabling us to eliminate any sentence or phrase of the form "_____ has sizeability" (where the blank is filled by a name or definite description) in favor of a synonymous sentence or phrase that does not contain the word 'sizeability'. As such it is unobjectionable; but notice that its range of applicability is severely limited. D₁ gives no hint as to what might be meant by a sentence like "Most of the world's great statesmen have sizeability" or "Your average middle linebacker has sizeability." And accordingly, while it is true that

(11)  Pico della Mirandola has sizeability,

it would be a piece of sheer confusion to conclude

(12)  Therefore there is at least one thing that has sizeability;

for as yet these words have been given no semblance of sense. This peculiarity of D₁ is connected with another. To find out whether nine has sizeability we are directed to consider whether 'nine' contains more than six letters; since it does not, it is false that nine has sizeability. On the other hand, 'the number nine' contains more than six letters; hence the number nine has sizeability.

What this shows, I take it, is that sizeability is not a property—that is, the context "*x* has sizeability" does not, under the suggested definition, express a property. The proposition *the number nine has sizeability* is true but does not predicate a property of the number nine. For suppose this context *did* express a property: then the number nine would have it, but nine would lack it, a state of affairs conflicting with

(13) Where *P* is any property and *x* and *y* any individuals, *x* is identical with *y* only if *x* has *P* if and only if *y* has *P*.

Like Caesar's wife, this principle (sometimes called the Indiscernibility of Identicals) is entirely above reproach. (Of course the same cannot be said for

(13') Singular terms denoting the same object can replace each other in any context *salva veritate*,

a 'principle' that must be carefully distinguished from (13) and one that, for most languages, at least, is clearly false.)

(13), then, lays down a condition of propertyhood; any property is had by anything identical with anything that has it. The second clause of the *de re* thesis asserts that *P* is a property only if *having P essentially* is; part of the force of this claim, as we now see, is that if an object *x* has a property *P* essentially, then so does anything identical with *x*. The number nine, for example, is essentially composite; so, therefore, is the number of planets, despite the fact that

(14) The number of planets is composite

is not a necessary truth.

Now the *de re* thesis has been treated with a certain lack of warmth by contemporary philosophers. What are the objections to it? According to William Kneale, the view in question is based on the assumption that

properties may be said to belong to individuals necessarily or contingently, as the case may be, without regard to the ways in which the individuals are selected for attention. It is no doubt true to say that the number 12 is necessarily composite, but it is certainly not correct to say that the number of apostles is necessarily composite, unless the remark is to be understood as an elliptical statement of relative necessity. And again, it is no doubt correct to say that this at which I am pointing is contingently white, but it is certainly not correct to say that the white paper at which I am looking is contingently white.[3]

The conclusion of this argument, pretty clearly, is that an object does not have a property necessarily *in itself* or *just as an object*; it has it necessarily or contingently, as the case may be, *relative to* certain *descriptions of the object.* "Being necessarily composite," on Kneale's view, is elliptical for something like "Being necessarily composite relative to description *D*." And hence it does not denote a *property*; it denotes, instead, a three-termed *relation* among an object, a description of that object, and a property.

Kneale's argument for this point seems to have something like the following structure:

(15)  12 = the number of apostles.
(16)  The number 12 is necessarily composite.
(17)  If (16), then if *being necessarily composite* is a property, 12 has it.
(18)  The number of the apostles is not necessarily composite.
(19)  If (18), then if *being necessarily composite* is a property, the number of the apostles lacks it.
        ___
∴ (20)  *Being necessarily composite* is not a property.

But *being composite* is certainly a property; hence it is false that where *being F* is a property, so is *being F necessarily*; and hence the *de re* thesis is mistaken.

Now clearly Kneale's argument requires as an additional premise the Indiscernibility of Identicals—a principle the essentialist will be happy to concede. And if we add this premise then the argument is apparently valid. But why should we accept (18)? Consider an analogous argument for the unwelcome conclusion that *necessary truth* or *being necessarily true* is not a property that a proposition has in itself or just as a proposition, but only relative to certain descriptions of it:

(21)  The proposition that 7 + 5 = 12 is necessarily true
(22)  The proposition I'm thinking of is not necessarily true
(23)  The proposition that 7 + 5 = 12 is identical with the proposition I'm thinking of
        ___
∴ (24)  *Being necessarily true* is not a property.

This argument is feeble and unconvincing. One immediately objects that if (23) is true then (22) is false. How can we decide about the truth of (22) unless we know *which proposition it is* that I'm thinking of? But isn't the very same answer appropriate with respect to (18) and (15)? If (15) is true, then presumably (18) is false. And so the question becomes acute: why *does* Kneale take (18) to be true? The answer, I believe, is that he is thinking of sentences of the form "x has P necessarily" as defined by or short for corresponding sentences of the form "the proposition *x has P* is necessarily true."

Quine offers a similar but subtler argument:

> Now the difficulty . . . recurs when we try to apply existential generalization to modal statements. The apparent consequence:
>
> (Q30) (∃ x) (*x* is necessarily greater than 7)
>
> of

Handwritten: *Left ar.*

(Q15) 9 is necessarily greater than 7

raises the same question as did (Q29). What is this number which, according to (Q30), is necessarily greater than 7? According to (Q15), from which (Q30) was inferred, it was 9, that is, the number of planets; but to suppose this would conflict with the fact that

(Q18) the number of planets is necessarily greater than 7

is false. In a word, to be necessarily greater than 7 is not a trait of a number but depends on the manner of referring to the number. . . . Being necessarily or possibly thus and so is in general not a trait of the object concerned, but depends on the manner of referring to the object.[4]

This argument does not wear its structure upon its forehead. But perhaps Quine means to argue (a) that being necessarily greater than 7 is not a trait of a number, and hence (b) that existential generalization is inapplicable to (Q15), so that (Q30) is meaningless or wildly and absurdly false. And presumably we are to construe the argument for (a) as follows:

(25) If *being necessarily greater than 7* is a trait of a number, then for any numbers $n$ and $m$, if $n$ is necessarily greater than 7 and $m = n$, then $m$ is necessarily greater than 7
(26) 9 is necessarily greater than 7
(27) It is false that the number of planets is necessarily greater than 7
(28) 9 = the number of planets

∴ (29) Being necessarily greater than 7 is not a trait of a number.

But why does Quine accept (27)? He apparently infers it from the fact that the proposition *the number of planets is greater than 7* is not necessarily true. This suggests that he takes the context 'x is necessarily greater than 7' to be short for or explained by the proposition *x is greater than 7* is necessarily true.' Like Kneale, Quine apparently endorses

$D_2$ x has $P$ essentially = def. the proposition *x has P* is necessarily true

as an accurate account of what the partisan of the *de re* thesis means by his characteristic assertions.

Now $D_2$ is a definitional schema that resembles $D_1$ in important respects. In particular, its 'x' is a schematic letter or place marker, not a full-fledged individual variable. Thus it enables us to replace a sentence like 'Socrates has rationality essentially' by a synonymous sentence that does not contain the term 'essentially'; but it gives no hint at all as to what that term might mean in such a sentence as 'Every animal in this room is essentially rational'. And what Quine and Kneale show, furthermore, is that a context like '*x* has rationality essentially', *read in accordance with* $D_2$, resembles '*x* has sizeability' in that it does not express a property or trait. So if $D_2$ is an accurate account of modality *de re*, then indeed Quine and Kneale are correct in holding the *de re* thesis incoherent. But why suppose that it is? Proposing to look for cases of modality *de re*, Kneale declares that none exist, since 'being necessarily thus and so', he says, expresses a three-termed relation rather than a property of objects. What he offers as argument, however, is that 'being necessarily thus and so' read *de dicto*—read in the way $D_2$ suggests—does not express a property. But of course from this it by no means follows that Aristotle, Aquinas, *et al.* were mistaken; what follows is that if they were not, then $D_2$ does not properly define modality *de re*.

But are we not a bit premature? Let us return for a moment to Kneale's argument. Perhaps he does not mean to foist off $D_2$ on Aristotle and Aquinas; perhaps we are to understand his argument as follows. We have been told that '*x* has *P* essentially' means that it is impossible or inconceivable that *x* should have lacked *P*; that there is no conceivable set of circumstances such that, should they have obtained, *x* would not have had *P*. Well, consider the number 12 and the number of apostles. Perhaps it is impossible that the number 12 should have lacked the property of being composite; but it is certainly possible that the number of apostles should have lacked it; for clearly the number of apostles could have been 11, in which case it would not have been composite. Hence *being necessarily composite* is not a property and the *de re* thesis fails.

How could Aristotle and his essentialist confreres respond to this objection? The relevant portion of the argument may perhaps be stated as follows:

(30)  The number of apostles could have been 11

(31)  If the number of apostles had been 11, then the number of apostles would have been prime

Hence

(32)  It is possible that the number of apostles should have been prime

and therefore

(33)  The number of apostles does not have the property of being composite essentially.

But one who accepts the *de re* thesis has an easy retort. The argument is successful only if (33) is construed as the assertion *de re* that a certain number—12, as it happens—has the property of being composite essentially. Now (32) can be read *de dicto*, in which case we may put it more explicitly as

(32a) The proposition *the number of apostles is prime* is possible;

it may also be read *de re*, that is, as

(32b) The number that numbers the apostles (that is, the number that *as things in fact stand* numbers the apostles) could have been prime.

The latter, of course, entails (33); the former does not. Hence we must take (32) as (32b). Now consider (30). The same *de re-de dicto* ambiguity is once again present. Read *de dicto* it makes the true (if unexciting) assertion that

(30a) The proposition *there are just 11 apostles* is possible.

Read *de re* however, that is, as

(30b) The number that (as things in fact stand) numbers the apostles could have been 11

it will be indignantly repudiated by the *de re* modalist; for the number that numbers the apostles is 12 and accordingly couldn't have been 11. We must therefore take (30) as (30a).

This brings us to (31). If (30a) and (31) are to entail (32b) then (31) must be construed as

(31a) If the proposition *the number of apostles is 11* had been true, then the number that (as things in fact stand) numbers the apostles would have been prime.

But surely this is false. For what it says is that if there had been 11 apostles, then the number that in fact *does* number the apostles—the number 12—would have been prime; and this is clearly rubbish. No doubt any vagrant inclination to accept (31a) may be traced to an unremarked penchant for confusing it with

(34) If the proposition *the number of apostles is 11* had been true, then the number that *would have* numbered the apostles would have been prime.

(34), of course, though true, is of no use to Kneale's argument.

This first objection to the *de re* thesis, therefore, appears to be at best inconclusive. Let us therefore turn to a different but related complaint. Quine argues that talk of a difference between necessary and contingent attributes of an object is baffling:

Perhaps I can evoke the appropriate sense of bewilderment as follows. Mathematicians may conceivably be said to be necessarily rational and not necessarily two-legged; and cyclists necessarily two-legged and not necessarily rational. But what of an individual who counts among his eccentricities both mathematics and cycling? Is this concrete individual necessarily rational and contingently two-legged or vice versa? Just insofar as we are talking referentially of the object, with no special bias towards a background grouping of mathematicians as against cyclists or vice versa, there is no semblance of sense in rating some of his attributes as necessary and others as contingent. Some of his attributes count as important and others as unimportant, yes, some as enduring and others as fleeting; but none as necessary or contingent.[5]

Noting the existence of a philosophical tradition in which this distinction *is* made, Quine adds that one attributes it to Aristotle "subject to contradiction by scholars, such being the penalty for attributions to Aristotle." Nonetheless, he says, the distinction is "surely indefensible."

Now this passage reveals that Quine's enthusiasm for the distinction between essential and accidental attributes is less than dithyrambic; but how, exactly, are we to understand it? Perhaps as follows. The essentialist, Quine thinks, will presumably accept

> (35) Mathematicians are necessarily rational but not necessarily bipedal

and

> (36) Cyclists are necessarily bipedal but not necessarily rational.

But now suppose that

> (37) Paul J. Swiers is both a cyclist and a mathematician.

From these we may infer both

> (38) Swiers is necessarily rational but not necessarily bipedal

and

> (39) Swiers is necessarily bipedal but not necessarily rational

which appear to contradict each other twice over.

This argument is unsuccessful as a refutation of the essentialist. For clearly enough the inference of (39) from (36) and (37) is sound only if (36) is read *de re*; but, read *de re*, there is not so much as a ghost of a reason for thinking that the essentialist will accept it. No doubt he will concede the truth of

> (40) *All (well-formed) cyclists are bipedal* is necessarily true but *all cyclists are rational*, is, if true, contingent;

he will accept no obligation, however, to infer that well-formed cyclists all have bipedality essentially and rationality (if at all) accidentally. Read *de dicto*, (36) is true but of no use to the argument read *de re* it will be declined (no doubt with thanks) by the essentialist.

Taken as a refutation of the essentialist, therefore, this passage misses the mark; but perhaps we should emphasize its second half and take it instead as an expression of (and attempt to evoke) sense of puzzlement as to what *de re* modality might conceivably be. A similar expression of bewilderment may be found in *From Logical Point of View*:

> An object, of itself and by whatever name or none, must be seen as having some of its traits necessarily and other contingently, despite the fact that the latter traits follow just as analytically from some ways of specifying the object as the former do from other ways of specifying it.

And

> This means adapting an invidious attitude towards certain ways of specifying *x* . . . and favoring other ways . . . as somehow better revealing the "essence" of the subject.

But "such a philosophy," he says, "is as unreasonable by my lights as it is by Carnap's or Lewis's" (155–156).

Quine's contention seems in essence to be this: according to the *de re* thesis a given object must be said to have certain of its properties essentially and others accidentally, despite the fact that the latter follow from certain ways of specifying the object just as the former do from others. So far, fair enough. Snub-nosedness (we may assume) is not one of Socrates' essential attributes; nonetheless it follows (in Quine's sense) from the description "the snubnosed teacher of Plato." And if we add to the *de re* thesis the statement that objects have among their essential attributes certain non-truistic properties—properties, which, unlike *is red or not red*, do not follow from *every* description— than it will also be true, as Quine suggests, that ways of uniquely specifying an object are not all on the same footing; those from which each of its essential properties follows must be awarded the accolade as best revealing the essence of the object.

But what, exactly, is "unreasonable" about this? And how is it baffling? Is it just that this discrimination among the unique ways of specifying 9 is arbitrary and high-handed? But it is neither, if the *de re* thesis is true. The real depth of Quine's objection, as I understand it, is this: I think he believes that "A's are necessarily B's" *must*, if it means anything at all, mean something like "*All A's are B's* is necessary"; for "necessity resides in the way we talk about things, not in the things we talk about" (*Ways of Paradox*, p. 174). And hence the bafflement in asking, of some specific individual who is both cyclist and mathematician, whether he is essentially rational and contingently two-legged or vice versa. Perhaps the claim is finally, that while we can make a certain rough sense of modality *de dicto*, we can understand modality *de re* only if we can explain it in terms of the former.

It is not easy to see why this should be so. An object has a given property essentially just in case it couldn't conceivably have lacked that property; a proposition is necessarily true just in case it couldn't conceivably have been false. Is the latter more limpid than the former? Is it harder to understand the claim that Socrates could have been a planet than the claim that the proposition *Socrates is a planet* could have been true? No doubt for any property *P* Socrates has, there is a description of Socrates from which it follows; but likewise for any true proposition *p* there is a description of *p* that entails truth. If the former makes nugatory the distinction between essential and accidental propertyhood, the latter pays the same compliment to that between necessary and contingent truth. I therefore do not see that modality *de re* is in principle more obscure than modality *de dicto*. Still, there are those who do or think they do; it would be useful, if possible, to *explain* the *de re* via the *de dicto*. What might such an explanation come to? The following would suffice: a general rule that enabled us to find, for any proposition expressing modality *de re*, an equivalent proposition expressing modality *de dicto*, or, alternatively, that enabled us to replace any sentence containing *de re* expressions by an equivalent sentence containing *de dicto* but no *de re* expressions.

Earlier we saw that

D₂  *x* has *P* essentially = def. the proposition *x* has *P* is necessarily
true

is competent as an account of the *de re* thesis if taken as a definitional scheme with '*x*' as schematic letter rather than variable. Will it serve our present purposes if we write it as

D₂'  *x* has *P* essentially if and only if the proposition that *x* has *P*
is necessarily true,

now taking '*x*' as full fledged individual variable? No; for in general there will be no such thing, for a given object *x* and property *P*, as *the* proposition that *x* has *P*. Suppose *x* is the object variously denoted by "the tallest conqueror of Everest," "Jim Whittaker," and "the manager of the Recreational Equipment Cooperative." What will be the proposition that *x* has, for example, the property of being 6'7" tall? *The tallest conqueror of Everest is 6'7" tall? Jim Whittaker is 6'7" tall? The manager of the Recreational Equipment Coop is 6'7" tall?* Or perhaps *the object variously denoted by 'the conqueror of Everest', 'Jim Whittaker' and 'the manager of the Recreational Equipment Cooperative' is 6'7"?* Each of these predicates the property in question of the object in question; hence each has as good a claim to the title "*the* proposition that *x* has *P*" as the others; and hence none has a legitimate claim to it. There are *several* "propositions that *x* has *P*"; and accordingly no such thing as *the* proposition that *x* has *P*.

Our problem, then, in attempting to explain the *de re* via the *de dicto*, may be put as follows: suppose we are given an object *x*, a property *P* and the set S of propositions that *x* has *P*—that is, the set *S* of singular propositions each of which predicates *P* of *x*. Is it possible to state the general directions for picking out some member of S—call it the kernel proposition with respect to $x$ and $P$—whose *de dicto* modal properties determine whether $x$ has $P$ essentially? If we can accomplish this, then, perhaps, we can justly claim success in explaining the *de re* via the *de dicto*. We might make a beginning by requiring that the kernel proposition with respect to $x$ and $P$—at any rate for those objects $x$ with names—be one that is expressed by a sentence whose subject is a proper name of $x$. So we might say that the kernel proposition with respect to Socrates and rationality is the proposition *Socrates has rationality;* and we might be inclined to put forward, more generally,

> D$_3$ The kernel proposition with respect to $x$ and $P$ ('K(x, $P$)') is the proposition expressed by the result of replacing '$x$' in '$x$ has $P$' by a proper name of $x$

adding

> D$_4$ An object $x$ has a property $P$ essentially if and only if K($x$, $P$) is necessarily true.

Now of course $x$ may share its name with other objects, so that the result of the indicated replacement is a sentence expressing several propositions. We may accommodate this fact by adding that the kernel proposition with respect to $x$ and $P$ must be a member of S— that is, it must be one of the propositions that $x$ has P. (A similar qualification will be understood below in D$_5$-D$_9$.) More importantly, we must look into the following matter. It is sometimes held that singular propositions ascribing properties to Socrates—such propositions as *Socrates is a person, Socrates is a non-number* and *Socrates is self-identical*—entail that Socrates exists, that there is such a thing as Socrates. This is not implausible. But if it is true, then D$_3$ and D$_4$ will guarantee that Socrates has none of his properties essentially. For *Socrates exists* is certainly contingent, as will be, therefore, any proposition entailing it. K(Socrates, self-identity), accordingly, will be contingent if it entails that Socrates exists; and by D$_4$ self-identity will not be essential to Socrates. Yet *if anything* is essential to Socrates, surely self-identity is.

But *do* these propositions entail that Socrates exists? Perhaps we can sidestep this question without settling it. For example, we might replace D$_4$ by

> D$_5$ $x$ has $P$ essentially if and only if K($x$, existence) entails K($x$, $P$).[6]

Then Socrates will have self-identity and personhood essentially just in case *Socrates exists* entails *Socrates is self-identical* and *Socrates is a person*; and these latter two need not, of course, be necessary. D$_5$, however, has its peculiarities. Among them is the fact that if we accept it, and hold that existence is a property, we find ourselves committed to the dubious thesis that everything has the property of existence essentially. No doubt the number seven car lay legitimate claim to this distinction; the same can scarcely be said, one supposes, for Socrates. Accordingly, suppose we try a different tack: suppose we take the kernel of Socrates and rationality to be the proposition that Socrates *lacks rationality*—that is, the proposition *Socrates has the complement of rationality*. Let us replace $D_3$ by

> $D_6$  $K(x, P)$ is the proposition expressed by the result of replacing '$x$' in '$x$ lacks $P$' by a proper name of $x$,

revising $D_4$ to

> $D_4$'  $x$ has $P$ essentially if and only if $K(x, P)$ is necessarily false

Now $D_4$' is open to the following objection. The proposition

> (41)  Socrates is essentially rational

entails

> (42)  Socrates is rational.

We moved to $D_6$ to $D_4$' to accommodate the suggestion that (42) is at best *contingently* true, in view of its consequence that Socrates exists. But if (42) is contingent, then so is (41). It is plausible to suppose, however, that

> (43)  K(Socrates, rationality) is necessarily false

is, if true at all, necessarily true. But if so, then (in view of the fact that no necessary truth is equivalent to one that is merely contingent) (43) cannot be equivalent to (41); $D_4$' is unacceptable.[7] Fortunately, a simple remedy is at hand; we need only add a phrase to the right-hand side of $D_4$' as follows:

> $D_4$"  $x$ has $P$ essentially if and only if $x$ has $P$ and $K(x, P)$ is necessarily false.

(41), then, is equivalent to, according to $D_4$", to

> (44)  Socrates is rational and K(Socrates, rationality) is necessarily false.

(44) is contingent if its left-hand conjunct is. Furthermore, it no longer matters whether or not *Socrates is rational* entails that Socrates exists. Existence, finally, will not be an essential property of Socrates; for even if attributions of personhood or self-identity to Socrates entail that he exists, attributions of non-existence do not.

A difficulty remains, however. For what about this '$P$' in $D_6$ Here we encounter an analogue of an earlier difficulty. If, in $D_6$, we take '$P$' as schematic letter, then K(Socrates, Socrates' least significant property) will be

(45) Socrates lacks Socrates' least significant property

but K(Socrates, snubnosedness) will be

(46) Socrates lacks snubnosedness.

Since (45) but not (46) is necessarily false, we are driven to the un-happy result that Socrates has his least significant property essentially and snubnosedness accidently, despite the fact (as we shall assume for purposes of argument) that snubnosedness *is* his least significant property. If we take 'P' as property variable, however, we are no better off; for now there will be no such thing as, for example, K(Socrates, personhood). According to $D_6$, K($x$, $P$) is to be the proposition expressed by the result of replacing '$x$' in '$x$ lacks $P$' by a proper name of x; the result of replacing '$x$' in '$x$ lacks $P$' by a proper name of Socrates is just 'Socrates lacks $P$', which expresses no proposition at all.

Now we resolved the earlier difficulty over '$x$' in $D_2$ by requiring that '$x$' be replaced by a proper name of $x$. Can we execute a similar maneuver here? It is not apparent that 'snub-nosedness' is a proper name of the property *snub-nosedness*, nor even that properties ordinarily have proper names at all. Still, expressions like 'whiteness,' 'masculinity,' 'mean temperedness,' and the like, differ from expressions like 'Socrates' least important property,' 'the property I'm thinking of,' 'the property mentioned on page 37,' and the like, in much the way that proper names of individuals differ from definite descriptions of them. Suppose we call expressions like the former 'canonical designations'.[8] Then perhaps we can resolve the present difficulty by rejecting $D_5$ in favor of

$D_7$  K($x$, $P$) is the proposition expressed by the result of replacing '$x$' and '$P$' in '$x$ lacks $P$' by a proper name of $x$ and a canonical designation of $P$.

We seem to be making perceptible if painful progress. But now another difficulty looms. For of course not nearly every object is named. Indeed, if we make the plausible supposition that no name names uncountably many objects and that the set of names is count-able, it follows that there are uncountably many objects without names. And how can $D_4$" and $D_7$ help us when we wish to find the *de dicto* equivalent to a *de re* proposition about an unnamed object? Worse, what shall we say about *general de re* propositions such as

(47) Every real number between 0 and 1 has the property of being less than 2 essentially?

What is the *de dicto* explanation of (47) to look like? Our definitions direct us to

> (48) For every real number $r$ between 0 and 1, $K(r$, being less than 2) is necessarily false.

Will (48) do the trick? It is plausible to suppose not, on the grounds that what we have so far offers no explanation of what the kernel of $r$ and $P$ for *unnamed r* might be.[9] If we think of $D_7$ as the specification or definition of a function, perhaps we must concede that the function is defined only for named objects and canonically designated properties. Hence it is not clear that we have any *de dicto* explanation at all for such *de re* propositions as (47).

Now of course if we are interested in a singular *de re* proposition we can always name the object involved. If the set of unnamed objects is uncountable, however, then no matter how enthusiastically we set about naming things, it might be said, there will always remain an uncountable magnitude of unnamed objects;[10] and hence $D_4$" and $D_7$ are and will remain incapable of producing a *de dicto* equivalent for general propositions whose quantifiers are not severely restricted.

This argument conceals an essential premise: it is sound only if we add some proposition putting an upper bound on the number of objects we can name at a time. We might suppose, for example, that it is possible to name at most countably many things at once. But is this really obvious? Can't I name all the real numbers in the interval (0,1) at once? Couldn't I name them all 'Charley,' for example? If all Koreans are named 'Kim,' what's to prevent all real numbers being named 'Charley'? Now many will find the very idea of naming everything 'Charley' utterly bizarre, if not altogether lunatic; and, indeed, there is a queer odor about the idea. No doubt, furthermore, most of the purposes for which we ordinarily name things would be ill served by such a maneuver, if it is possible at all. But these cavils are not objections. Is there really any reason why I can't name all the real numbers, or, indeed, everything whatever in one vast, all-embracing baptism ceremony? I can't see any such reason, and I hereby name everything 'Charley.' And thus I have rendered $D_4$" and $D_7$ universally applicable.

In deference to outraged sensibilities, however, we should try to surmount the present obstacle in some other way if we can. And I think we can. Let $(x, P)$ be any ordered pair whose first member is an object and whose second is a property. Let S be the set of all such pairs. We shall say that $(x, P)$ is *baptized* if there is a proper name of $x$ and a canonical designation of $P$. Cardinality difficulties aside (and those who feel them, may restrict S in any way deemed appropriate) we may define a function—the kernel function—on S as follows:

> $D_8$ (a) If $(x, P)$ is baptized, $K(x, P)$ is the proposition expressed by the result of replacing '$x$' and '$P$' in '$x$ lacks $P$' by a proper name of $x$ and a canonical designation of $P$.

(b) If $(x, P)$ is not baptized, then $K(x, P)$ is the proposition which *would be* expressed by the result of replacing '$x$' and '$P$' in '$x$ lacks $P$' by a proper name of $x$ and a canonical designation of $P$, if $(x, P)$ *were* baptized.

And if, for some reason, we are troubled by the subjunctive conditional in (b), we may replace it by

(b') if $(x, P)$ is not baptized, then $K(x, P)$ is determined as follows: baptize $(x, P)$; then $K(x, P)$ is the proposition expressed by the result of respectively replacing '$x$' and '$P$' in '$x$ lacks $P$' by the name assigned $x$ and the canonical designation assigned $P$.

And now we may reassert $D_4$" an object $x$ has a property $P$ essentially if and only if $x$ has $P$ and $K(x, P)$ is necessarily false. A general *de re* proposition such as

(49) All men are rational essentially

may now be explained as equivalent to

(50) For any object $x$, if $x$ is a man, then $x$ is rational and $K(x,$ rationality) is necessarily false.

So far so good; the existence of unnamed objects seems to constitute no fundamental obstacle. But now one last query arises. I promised earlier to explain the *de re via* the *de dicto*, glossing that reasonably enigmatic phrase as follows: to explain the *de re via* the *de dicto* is to provide a rule enabling us to find, for each *de re* proposition, an equivalent *de dicto* proposition—alternatively, to provide a rule enabling us to eliminate any sentence containing a *de re* expression in favor of an equivalent sentence containing *de dicto* but no *de re* expressions. And it might be claimed that our definitions do not accomplish this task. For suppose they did: what would be the *de dicto* proposition equivalent to

(51) Socrates has rationality essentially?

$D_4$" directs us to

(52) Socrates is rational and K(Socrates, rationality) is necessarily false.

Now (52) obviously entails

(53) The proposition expressed by the result of replacing '$x$' and '$P$' in '$x$ lacks $P$' by a name of Socrates and a canonical designation of rationality is necessarily false.

(53), however, entails the existence of several *linguistic* entities including, e.g., 'x' and 'x lacks P'. Hence so does (52). But then the latter is not equivalent to (51), which entails the existence of no linguistic entities whatever. Now we might argue that such linguistic entities are shapes or sequences of shapes, in which case they are abstract objects, so that their existence is necessary and hence entailed by every proposition.[11] But suppose we explore a different response: Is it really true that (52) entails (53)? How could we argue that it does? Well, we *defined* the kernel function that way—i.e., the rule of correspondence we gave in linking the members of its domain with their images explicitly picks out and identifies the value of the kernel function for the pair (Socrates, rationality) as the proposition expressed by the result of replacing 'x' and 'P' in 'x lacks P' by a proper name of Socrates and a canonical designation of rationality. This is true enough, of course; but how does it show that (52) entails (53)? Is it supposed to show, for example, that the phrase 'the kernel of (Socrates, rationality)' is *synonymous with* the phrase "the proposition expressed by the result of replacing 'x' and 'P' in 'x lacks P' by a name of Socrates and a canonical designation of rationality"? And hence that (52) and (53) express the very same proposition? But consider a function F, defined on the natural numbers and given by the rule that $F(n)$ = the number denoted by the numeral denoting $n$. The reasoning that leads us to suppose that (52) entails (53) would lead us to suppose that

(54)  F(9) is composite

entails

(55)  The number denoted by the numeral that denotes 9 is composite

and hence entails the existence of at least one numeral. Now consider the identity function I defined on the same domain, so that $I(n) = n$. If a function is a set of ordered pairs, then F is the very same function as I, despite the fact that the first rule of correspondence is quite different from the second. And if F is the very same function as I, then can't I give I by stating the rule of correspondence in giving F? And if I do, then should we say that

(56)  The value of the identity function at 9 is composite

entails the existence of some numeral or other? That is a hard saying; who can believe it? Can't we simply *name* a function, and then give the rule of correspondence linking its arguments with its values, without supposing that the name we bestow is covertly synonymous with some definite description constructed from the rule of correspondence? I think we can; but if so, we have no reason to think that (52) entails (53).

Nonetheless difficult questions arise here; and if we can side-step these questions, so much the better. And perhaps we can do so by giving the kernel function as follows: Let '$x$' and '$y$' be individual variables and '$P$' and '$Q$' property variables. Restrict the substituend sets of '$y$' and '$Q$' to proper names and canonical designations respectively. Then

> D$_9$ If $(x, P)$ is baptized, K$(x, P)$ is the proposition $y$ *lacks* $Q$ (where $x = y$ and $P = Q$).
>
> If $(x, P)$ is not baptized, K$(x, P)$ is determined as follows: baptize $(x, P)$; then K$(x, P)$ is the proposition $y$ *lacks* $Q$ (where $x = y$ and $P = Q$).

Unlike D$_8$, D$_9$ does not tempt us to suppose that (52) entails (53).

D$_4$" together with any of D$_7$, D$_8$ and D$_9$ seems to me a viable explanation of the *de re via* the *de dicto*. A striking feature of these explanations is that they presuppose the following. Take, for a given pair $(x, P)$, the class of sentences that result from the suggested substitutions into '$x$ lacks $P$'. Now consider those members of this class that express a proposition predicating the complement of $P$ of $x$. These all express the same proposition. I think this is true; but questions of propositional identity are said to be difficult, and the contrary opinion is not unreasonable. One who holds it need not give up hope; he can take K$(x, P)$ to be a class of propositions—the class of propositions expressed by the results of the indicated replacements; and he can add that $x$ has $P$ essentially just in case at least one member of this class is necessarily false.

If the above is successful, we have found a general rule correlating propositions that express modality *de re* with propositions expressing modality *de dicto*, such that for any proposition of the former sort we can find one of the latter equivalent to it. Does this show, then, that modality *de dicto* is somehow more basic or fundamental than modality *de re*, or that an expression of modality *de re* is really a misleading expression of modality *de dicto*? It is not easy to see why we should think so. Every proposition attributing a property to an object (an assertion *de re*, we might say) is equivalent to some proposition ascribing truth to a proposition (an assertion *de dicto*). Does it follow that propositions about propositions are somehow more basic or fundamental than propositions about other objects? Surely not. Similarly here. Nor can I think of any other reason for supposing the one more fundamental than the other.

Interesting questions remain. This account relies heavily on proper names. Is it really as easy as I suggest to name objects? And is it always possible to determine whether a name is proper or a property designation canonical? Perhaps the notion of a proper name itself involves essentialism; perhaps an analysis or philosophical account of the nature of proper names essentially involves essentialist ideas. Suppose this is true; how, exactly, is it relevant to our explanation of the *de re via* the *de dicto*? How close, furthermore, is this explanation to the traditional understanding of essentialism, if indeed history presents something stable and clear enough to be called a traditional 'understanding'? What is the connection, if any, between essential properties and natural kinds? Are there properties that some but not all things have essentially? Obviously so; *being prime* would be an example. Are there properties that some things have essentially but others have accidentally? Certainly: 7 has the property *being prime or prim* essentially; Miss Prudence Alcott, Headmistress of the Queen Victoria School for Young Ladies, has it accidentally. But does each object have an *essence*—that is, an essential property that nothing else has? Would *being Socrates* or *being identical with Socrates* be such a property? *Is* there such a property as *being identical with Socrates*? What sorts of properties does Socrates have essentially anyway? Could he have been an alligator, for example, or an 18th-century Irish washerwoman? And is there a difference between what Socrates *could have been* and what he *could have become*? Can we see the various divergent philosophical views as to what a *person* is, as divergent claims as to what properties persons have essentially? Exactly how is essentialism related to the idea—set forth at length by Leibniz and prominently featured in recent semantical developments of quantified modal logic—that there are *possible worlds* of which the actual is one, and that objects such as Socrates have different properties in different possible worlds? And how is essentialism related to the 'problem of transworld identification' said to arise in such semantical schemes? These are good questions, and good subjects for further study.[12]

NOTES

1. *Philosophical Studies*, p. 289.
2. "Wittgenstein's *Philosophical Investigations*," *Philosophical Review*, LXIII, 1954. Reprinted in Malcolm's *Knowledge and Certainty*, (Prentice-Hall, 1963). The quoted passage is on p. 105 of the latter volume.
3. "Modality *De Dicto* and *De Re*," in *Logic, Methodology and Philosophy of Science*, ed. Nagel, Suppes, and Tarski, (Stanford University Press, 1962), p. 629.
4. *From a Logical Point of View*, 2nd ed. (New York: Harper & Row, 1963), p. 148.
5. *Word and Object* (MIT Press, 1960), p. 199.
6. This is apparently Moore's course; see above pp. 3, 4.
7. Here I am indebted to William Rowe for a helpful comment.
8. I owe this phrase to Richard Cartwright. See his "Some Remarks on Essentialism," *Journal of Philosophy*, LXV, 20, p. 631. See also, in this connection, David Kaplan's discussion of *standard names* in "Quantifying In," *Synthese*, vol. 19, nos. 1/2 (December 1968), p. 194 ff.
9. Cartwright, op. cit., p. 623.
10. Ibid., p. 622.

11. As I was reminded by David Lewis.

12. I am indebted for advice and criticism to many, including Richard Cartwright, Roderick Chisholm, David Lewis, and William Rowe. I am particularly indebted to David Kaplan—who, however, churlishly declines responsibility for remaining errors and confusions.

# 2

# World and Essence

In much traditional philosophy we meet the admonition to distinguish assertions of necessity *de dicto* from assertions of necessity *de re*. Thomas Aquinas, for example, considers whether God's foreknowledge of human behavior is inconsistent with human freedom. Pointing out that such foreknowledge of a given item of behavior simply consists in God's seeing it take place, Thomas asks whether:

>   (1) Whatever is seen to be sitting at a time *t* is necessarily sitting at *t*

is true. For suppose it is, and suppose that Albert the Great is sitting at *t*. If, at time *t*-1, God has foreknowledge of Albert's sitting at *t*, then at *t*-1 God sees that Albert sits at *t*: but if (1) is true, then, so the deterministic argument goes, Albert is necessarily sitting at *t*, in which case he is not free to stand at *t*. Thomas replies that (1) is ambiguous; we may take it *de dicto* as:

>   (2) It is necessarily true that whatever is seen to be sitting is sitting,

or *de re* as

>   (3) Whatever is seen to be sitting at *t* has the property of sitting at *t essentially* or *necessarily*.

A true assertion about a proposition, (2) predicates necessary truth of

>   (4) Whatever is seen to be sitting is sitting.

46

(3), on the other hand, does no such thing; it predicates of every object of a certain kind—those objects seen to be sitting at *t*—the essential or necessary possession of a certain property: the property of sitting at *t*. And while (2) is true, says Thomas, (3) is not; but the argument for the inconsistency of divine foreknowledge with human freedom requires the latter as a premise.

A statement of necessity *de re*, therefore, predicates of some object or group of objects the essential possession of some property—or, as we may also put it, such a statement predicates of some object the property of having a certain property essentially. Many philosophers apparently believe that the idea of *de re* modality is shrouded in obscurity, if not an utter mare's nest of confusion. The arguments they give for this conclusion, however, are by no means conclusive.[1] Indeed, I think we can see that the idea of modality *de re* is no more (although no less) obscure than the idea of modality *de dicto*; for I think we can see that any statement of the former type is logically equivalent to some statement of the latter. Suppose we let *S* be the set of ordered pairs (*x, P*) where *x* is an object and *P* a property; and suppose we say that pair (*x, P*) is baptized if both *x* and *P* have proper names. Ignoring cardinality difficulties for the moment (and those who feel them can restrict *S* in any way deemed appropriate) we may define a function—call it the kernel function—on *S* as follows:

(5) (a) If (*x, P*) is baptized, *K* (*x, P*) is the proposition that predicates $\bar{P}$, the complement of *P*, of *x* and is expressed by the result of respectively replacing "*x*" and "*P*" in "*x* has the complement of *P*" by proper names of *x* and *P*.
(b) If (*x, P*) is not baptized, then *K* (*x, P*) is the proposition that predicates $\bar{P}$ of *x* and *would be* expressed by the result of respectively replacing "*x*" and "*P*" in "*x* has the complement of *P*" by proper names of *x* and *P*, if (*x, P*) *were* baptized.

Then we may add

(6) an object *x* has a property *P* essentially just in case *x* has *P* and *K* (*x, P*) is necessarily false.

(5) and (6) enable us to eliminate any sentence containing *de re* expressions in favor of an equivalent sentence containing no expressions of that sort;

(7) If all men are essentially persons, then some things are essentially rational,

for example, goes over into

(8) If for any object *x*, *x* is a man only if *K* (*x*, personhood) is necessarily false, then there are some things *y* such that *K* (*y*, rationality) is necessarily false.

(5) and (6) provide an explanation of the *de re* via the *de dicto*; but if the explanation is apt, the former is no more obscure than the latter.

We may approach this matter from a different direction. If we are comfortable with the idea of *states of affairs*, recognizing that some but not all of them obtain, and that some that do not *could have*, we may join Leibniz and logic (the semantics of quantified modal logic, that is) in directing our attention to *possible worlds*. A possible world is a state of affairs of some kind—one which could have obtained if it does not. *Hubert Horatio Humphrey's having run a mile in four minutes*, for example, is a state of affairs that is clearly possible in the relevant sense; *his having had a brother who never had a sibling* is not. Furthermore, a possible world must be what we may call a *fully determinate* state of affairs. *Humphrey's having run a four-minute mile* is a possible state of affairs, as, perhaps, is *Paul X. Zwier's being a good basketball player*. Neither of these, however, is fully determinate in that either of them could have obtained whether or not the other had. A fully determinate state of affairs *S*, let us say, is one such that for any state of affairs *S'*, either *S includes S'* (that is, could not have obtained unless *S'* had also obtained) or *S precludes S'* (that is, could not have obtained if *S'* had obtained). So, for example, *Jim Whittaker's being the first American to reach the summit of Everest* precludes Luther Jerstad's enjoying that distinction and includes Whittaker's having climbed at least one mountain.

We may try a slightly different route to the concept of a possible world if we possess a reasonably firm grasp of the notion of a proposition. Where *S* is a set of propositions, suppose we say that *S* is *possible* if it is possible that all of *S*'s members be true; and let us say that *q* is a consequence of *S* if *S U* (not-*q*) is not possible. A *superproposition*, we shall say, is the union of some set of propositions with the set of its consequences—or, as we may also put it, a set of propositions containing all of its own consequences. Now for each superproposition *S* there is exactly one state of affairs *A* such that *A* obtains if and only if every member of *S* is true.[2] We have a 1-1 function *F*, therefore, from superpropositions to states of affairs. Let us say, furthermore, that a *book* is a maximal possible set of propositions—one that is possible and that, for any proposition *q*, contains either *q* or its denial not-*q*. A book, clearly enough, is a superproposition; and a possible world is just the value of *F* for some book. *F*-inverse, on the other hand, associates a book with each possible world; we might call it *the bookie function*.

Leibniz and logic join further in holding that propositions are properly said to be true or false *in* these possible worlds. A proposition *p* is true in a world *W* if *p* would have been true had *W* been actual; and *the book of W* is the book of which a proposition *p* is a member just in case *p* is true in *W*.[3] The actual world is one of the possible worlds; and the set of true propositions is the set of propositions true in the actual world. Necessarily true propositions are those enjoying the distinction of being true in every world; a possible proposition is true in at least one. Still further, logic and Leibniz hold that individuals, objects, *exist* in these worlds; to say that an object *x* exists in a world *W* is to say that if *W* had been actual, *x* would have existed. Some objects—the number seven, for example—grace every world, but many others are restricted to only some. Socrates, for example, exists in this and some other possible worlds, but not in all; he is a contingent being who exists in fact but need not have. A given individual, furthermore, *has properties in* at least some of these worlds. Again, to say that *x* has property *P* in *W* is to say that if *W* had been actual, *x* would have had *P*. And of course an individual may have in one world a property—snubnosedness, let us say—that he lacks in others.

We now have several plausible options as to what it is for an object to have a property *P* essentially; Socrates has *P* essentially if he has *P* in every world, or has it in every world in which he exists, or—most plausible of all—has *P* in the actual world and has its complement $\bar{P}$ in no world. The idea that an object has essential as well as accidental properties, therefore, can be explained and defended. In what follows I shall take its intelligibility for granted and ask some questions about which objects have which properties essentially.

I

Consider first such properties as *having a color if red, being something or other, being self-identical,* and *either having or lacking a maiden aunt.* Clearly everything whatever has these properties; clearly nothing has the complement of any of these properties in any possible world. Let us call such properties—properties that enjoy the distinction of being instantiated by every object in every possible world—*trivially essential properties.* While you may concede that indeed every object does have some trivially essential properties, you may think this truth somewhat lackluster. Are there any non-trivial essential properties? Certainly; the number six has the properties of *being an integer, being a number,* and *being an abundant number* essentially; Paul Q. Zwier has none of these properties and a fortiori has none essentially. Well, then, are there properties that some things have essentially and others have, but have accidentally? Surely; *being non-green* is a property seven has essentially and the Taj Mahal accidentally. *Being prime or prim* is an accidental property of Miss Prudence Allworthy, Headmistress of the Queen Victoria School for Girls; it is essential to seven.

But, you say, these fancy, cooked-up properties—disjunctive or negative as they are—have a peculiar odor. What about Socrates and such properties as being a philosopher, an Athenian, a teacher of

Plato? What about having been born in 470 B.C., having lived for some seventy years, and having been executed by the Athenians on a charge of corrupting the youth? Are any of these ordinary meat-and-potatoes properties of Socrates essential to him? I should think not. Surely Socrates could have been born ten years later. Surely he could have lived in Macedonia, say, instead of Athens. And surely he could have stuck to his stone-cutting, eschewed philosophy, corrupted no youth, and thus escaped the wrath of the Athenians. None of these properties is essential to him.

But what about their disjunction? No doubt Socrates could have lacked *any* of these properties; could he have lacked them *all*? John Searle thinks this suggestion incoherent.

> Though proper names do not normally assert or specify any characteristics, their referring uses nonetheless presuppose that the object to which they purport to refer has certain characteristics. But which ones? Suppose we ask the users of the name "Aristotle" to state what they regard as certain essential and established facts about him. Their answers would be a set of uniquely referring descriptive statements. Now what I am arguing is that the descriptive force of "This is Aristotle" is to assert that a sufficient but so far unspecified number of these statements are true of this object. Therefore, referring uses of "Aristotle" presuppose the existence of an object of whom a sufficient but so far unspecified number of these statements are true. To use a proper name referringly is to presuppose the truth of certain uniquely referring descriptive statements, but it is not ordinarily to assert these statements or even to indicate which exactly are presupposed.[4]

So there are what we might call "identity criteria" associated with a name such as "Aristotle" or "Socrates"; these are what the users of the name regard as essential and established facts about him. Suppose we take these criteria to be properties of Socrates rather than facts about him. Then among them we should certainly find such properties as *having been born about 470 B.C., having married Xantippe, being a Greek philosopher, being the teacher of Plato, having been executed by the Athenians on a charge of corrupting the youth*, and the like. The disjunction of these properties, Searle says (and this is the point at present relevant), is essential to its owner:

> It is a contingent fact that Aristotle ever went into pedagogy (though I am suggesting it is a necessary fact that Aristotle has the logical sum, inclusive disjunction, of properties commonly attributed to him; any individual not having at least some of these properties could not be Aristotle). (1958, p. 172)

If $S_1, S_2, \ldots, S_n$, are the identity criteria associated with the name "Socrates," therefore, then Socrates has the disjunction of these properties essentially. But why so, exactly? Searle does not explicitly say, no doubt because the focus of his piece is not on just this point. One possibility is this: we might be tempted to believe that if the $S_i$ are the identity criteria for "Socrates," then to suppose that Socrates could have lacked most of these properties is tantamount to thinking it possible that the man who has most of the $S_i$ does not have most of them—tantamount, that is, to endorsing

(9) Possibly, the man who has most of $S_1, S_2 \ldots, S_n$ lacks most of $S_1, S_2, \ldots, S_n$.

But (9) appears to be false and indeed necessarily false;[5] hence Socrates could not have lacked the disjunction of the $S_i$. To yield to this temptation, however, is to commit the error of confusing (9), a false *de dicto* assertion, with the assertion *de re* that

(10) The person who has most of the $S_i$ might conceivably have lacked most of them.

(9), indeed, is necessarily false; that (10) is false does not follow. Suppose all I know about Paul B. Zwier is that he is the redheaded mathematician seated in the third row. *Being redheaded, being a mathematician*, and *being seated in the third row* are, then, presumably, my identity criteria for the name "Paul B. Zwier"; it scarcely follows that Zwier is essentially redheaded or that he could not have been standing or seated elsewhere, or that "Paul B. Zwier is not a mathematician" expresses a necessary falsehood. These properties are ones that I may use to get you to see about whom it is I am talking; if I say, "My, isn't Paul B. Zwier distinguished-looking!" and you say, "Who?," these characteristics are the ones I cite. They enable my interlocutor to identify the subject of my remarks; that these properties are essential to him does not follow.

Searle recognizes this objection and replies as follows:

> But is the argument convincing? Suppose most or even all of our present factual knowledge of Aristotle proved to be true of no one at all, or of several people living in scattered countries and in different centuries? Would we not say for this reason that Aristotle did not exist after all, and that the name, though it has a conventional sense, refers to no one at all? On the above account [i.e., the one according to which the $S_i$ serve merely to identify the subject for discussion], if anyone said that Aristotle did not exist, this must simply be another way of saying that "Aristotle" denoted no objects, and nothing more; but if anyone did say that Aristotle did not exist he might mean much more than simply that the name does not denote anyone. (1958, p. 168)

And further:

> We say of Cerberus and Zeus that neither of them ever existed, without meaning that no object ever bore these names, but only that

certain kinds (descriptions) of objects never existed and bore these names. (Ibid., p. 169)

I am not clear as to the exact structure of this argument; I do not see just how it bears on the suggestion it is designed to refute. What is fairly clear, however, is that it is to be construed as an argument for the conclusion that

(11) Socrates lacks most (or all) of the $S_i$

is necessarily false, where the $S_i$ are the identity criteria for "Socrates." But the prospects for this argument are not initially promising. Different people associate different identity criteria with the same name, even when using it to name the same person (no doubt the criteria mentioned above for "Paul B. Zwier" are not the ones his wife associates with that name). Indeed, at different times the same person may associate different criteria with the same name; are we to suppose that the properties essential to Aristotle vary thus from time to time and person to person? Nevertheless, suppose we take a closer look at the argument. How, exactly, does it go? Perhaps we can fill it out as follows. The $S_i$ are the identity criteria for "Socrates." In (11) we have a referring use of this name; this use, therefore, presupposes the existence of an object that has a sufficient number of the $S_i$. (11), therefore, entails

(12) Someone has enough of the $S_i$.

But surely it is necessarily true that

(13) If anyone has enough of the $S_i$, Socrates does.

So if (11) is true, it follows that Socrates has enough of the $S_i$—that is, that (11) is false; (11) therefore, is necessarily false.

But why suppose that (11) entails (12)? That is, why suppose that if $S_1, S_2, \ldots, S_n$ are the identity criteria for the name "Socrates"—the properties we employ to locate and identify Socrates—then "Socrates lacks enough of the $S_i$" must express a proposition entailing that someone or other *has* enough of them? Perhaps the argument goes as follows. If we discovered that no one had enough of the $S_i$, we should say (and say quite properly) that there never was any such person as Socrates—that he did not exist.

(14) No one had enough of the $S_i$,

therefore, entails

(15) Socrates did not exist.

(11), on the other hand—the assertion that Socrates had the complement of most of the $S_i$—entails

(16)  There really was such a person as Socrates—that is, Socrates did exist.

(16) is inconsistent with (15); it is also inconsistent, therefore, with (14); (11), too, therefore, is inconsistent with (14) and entails its denial—namely (12).

But is it really true that (14) entails (15)? Why so? The answer, according to Searle, is that (14) and (15) make the same assertion; (15), despite appearances, is not a singular statement predicating a property of Socrates but a general statement to the effect that no one has enough of $S_1, S_2, \ldots, S_n$ (1958, p. 172). And, of course, on this view the statement "Socrates does (did) exist" and its variants do not predicate of Socrates the dubious property of existence; they assert instead that some object does (or did) have enough of the $S_i$.

But why should we think *that* true? Suppose, says Searle, we discovered that no one had enough of the $S_i$; then what we should normally say is not "Oddly enough, as it turns out, Socrates did not have enough of the $S_i$: no one did"; what we should say is that Socrates never really existed. Is this correct? I think it is. Suppose all we know about Homer is that he was the blind bard of Chios who was born about 835 B.C. and composed the *Iliad* and *Odyssey*, so that these properties are the identity criteria associated with the name "Homer." Now imagine that a historian says, "I have discovered that no one had those properties; Homer himself had 20-20 vision, never lived in Chios, and did not compose either the *Iliad* or the *Odyssey*; they were class projects in Xenophon's School for Rhetoric." We should be justifiably perplexed. If he goes on to add, "Furthermore, his name wasn't Homer—it was Alfred E. Neuman—and actually he was an illiterate thirteenth-century French peasant," we should no doubt think him crazed with strong drink. In discovering that no one had these properties, what he discovered is a fact we should ordinarily put by saying "Homer never really existed"; and his further allegations allegedly about Homer are utterly unintelligible. By "Homer" we mean to refer to the man who had the above properties; in answer to the question "Who was Homer?" these are the properties we should mention. If he tells us, therefore, that Homer *lacks* all these properties, we no longer have any idea whom he is talking about.[6]

So

(17)  No one had (enough of) $H_1, H_2 \ldots, H_n$

entails what we should ordinarily express by saying

(18)  Homer never existed.

But the way to show that Homer really did exist, conversely, is to show that there really was a person who had most of the above properties; so (18) also entails (17). A pair of classicists might have a dispute as to whether Homer really existed. It would be incorrect to represent them as each referring to the same person—the one who had $H_1$, $H_2$ ..., $H_n$—one of them attributing to him the property of existence and the other the property of nonexistence; and this is so even if existence and nonexistence are properly thought of as properties. Searle is right in taking that dispute to be instead about whether enough of these properties are instantiated by a single person.

Ordinarily, then, when someone says, "Socrates really existed," he is to be understood as affirming that some one person had enough of $S_1$, $S_2$, . . . , $S_n$. But of course he could be affirming something quite different; out of sheer whimsy, if for no other reason, he could be referring to the man who satisfies the identity criteria associated with "Socrates" and predicating existence of him. The fact that people do not ordinarily do this scarcely shows that it cannot be done. A man might point to the Taj Mahal and say, "That really exists."[7] If he did, he would be right, though his assertion might be pointless or foolish. Bemused by Cartesian meditations, De Gaulle might say, "I really do exist." Nor would he then be saying that enough of the identity criteria associated with some word ("De Gaulle"? "I" in some particular use?) are satisfied by someone; he might be talking about himself and saying of himself that he really exists. Furthermore, the sentence, "Socrates does not exist" ordinarily expresses the proposition that no one has enough of the $S_i$, but it can also be used to express a proposition predicating of Socrates the complement of the property of existence. This proposition is false. Perhaps, furthermore, no one can believe it; for suppose someone did: how could he answer the question "Whom do you mean by 'Socrates'? Which person is it of whom you are predicating nonexistence?" It is nonetheless a perfectly good proposition.

Now suppose we rehearse Searle's argument.

(11) Socrates lacks most of the $S_i$

was said to entail

(12) Someone has most of the $S_i$.

But necessarily

(13) If anyone has the $S_i$, Socrates does

from which it follows that (11) entails its own denial. Why does (11) entail (12)? Clearly (11) entails

(16) Socrates does (did) exist.

But (16) is the contradictory of

(15) Socrates did not exist;

since the latter is equivalent to

(14) No one has (had) enough of the $S_i$,

the former must be equivalent to the contradictory of (14)—namely, (12). (11), therefore, entails (16), which is equivalent to (12); so (11) entails (12).

But (16), as we have seen, turned out to be ambiguous between (12) and a proposition predicating existence of Socrates. This argument turns on that ambiguity. For it is plausible to suppose that (11) entails the latter (presumably any world in which Socrates has the complement of most of the $S_i$ is a world in which he has the property of existing); but we have no reason at all for thinking that it entails the former.

What we have seen so far is that

(16) Socrates does exist

and

(15) Socrates does not exist

normally express statements to the effect that a sufficient number of $S_1, S_2, \ldots, S_n$ are (are not) instantiated by the same person; but each of them can also be used to express a proposition predicating existence (nonexistence) of Socrates. Let us call these latter propositions (15') and (16'). It is important to see the difference between the primed and unprimed items here. Let us say that a subset $A$ of $(S_1, S_2, \ldots, S_n)$ is *sufficient* just in case the fact that each member of $A$ is instantiated by the same person is sufficient for the truth of (16); and let $S$ be the set of sufficient sets. Call the property a thing has if it has each property in some member of $S$ a *sufficient* property. Then if the disjunction of the sufficient properties is not essential to Socrates it is possible that (15) be true when (15') is false. That is, if it is possible that Socrates should have lacked each sufficient property, then (15) does not entail (15'). And indeed this is possible. Socrates could have been born ten years earlier and in Thebes, let us say, instead of Athens. Furthermore, he could have been a carpenter all his life instead of a philosopher. He could have lived in Macedonia and never even visited Athens. Had these things transpired (and if no one else had had any sufficient property), then (15) but not (15') would have been true. Similarly, it is conceivable that Socrates should never have existed and that someone else—Xenophon, let us say—should have had most of $S_1, S_2, \ldots S_n$. Had this transpired, (15) but not (15') would have been false.

The old saw has it that Homer did not write the *Iliad* and the *Odyssey*: they were written by another man with the same name. Although this has a ring of paradox, it is in fact conceivable; there is a possible world in which the person denoted by "Homer" in this world (supposing for the moment that there is only one) does not exist and in which someone else writes the *Iliad* and the *Odyssey*.

## II

Searle is wrong, I believe, in thinking the disjunction of the $S_i$ essential to Socrates. But then what properties does he have essentially? Of course he has such trivially essential properties as *the property of having some properties* and *the property of being unmarried if a bachelor*. He also has essentially some properties not had by everything: *being a non-number* and *being possibly conscious* are examples. But these are properties he shares with other persons. Are there properties Socrates has essentially and shares with some but not all other persons? Certainly; *being Socrates* or *being identical with Socrates* is essential to Socrates; *being identical with Socrates or Plato*, therefore, is a property essential to Socrates and one he shares with Plato. This property is had essentially by anything that has it. *Being Socrates or Greek*, on the other hand, is one Socrates shares with many other persons and one he and he alone has essentially.

Socrates, therefore, has essential properties. Some of these he has in solitary splendor and others he shares. Among the latter are some that he shares with everything, some that he shares with persons but not other things, and still others that he shares with some but not all other persons. Some of these properties, furthermore, are essential to whatever has them while others are not. But does he have, in addition to his essential properties, an *essence* or *haecceity*—a property essential to him that entails each of his essential properties and that nothing distinct from him has in any world?[8] It is true of Socrates (and of no one else) that he is Socrates, that he is identical with Socrates. Socrates, therefore, has the property of *Socrates-identity*. And if a property is essential to Socrates just in case he has it and there is no world in which he has its complement, then surely *Socrates-identity* is essential to him. Furthermore, this property entails each of his essential properties; there is no possible world in which there exists an object that has *Socrates-identity* but lacks a property Socrates has in every world in which he exists. But does it meet the other condition? Is it not possible that something distinct from Socrates should have been identical with him? Is there no possible world such that, had it obtained, something that in *this* world is distinct from Socrates would have been identical with him? And is it not possible that something in fact identical with Socrates should have been distinct from him? In this world Cicero is identical with Tully; is there no possible world in which this is not so? Hesperus is in fact identical with Phosphorus; is there no possible world in which, in the hauntingly beautiful words of an ancient ballad, Hesperus and Phosphorus are entities distinct?

I think not. Cicero is in fact Tully. Cicero, furthermore, has the property of being identical with Cicero; and in no world does Cicero have the complement of that property. Cicero, therefore, has *Cicero-diversity in no possible world*. But if an object *x* has a property *P*, then so does anything identical with it; like Calpurnia, this principle (sometimes called the Indiscernibility of Identicals) is entirely above reproach. Tully, therefore, has *Cicero-diversity in no possible world.*

*Socrates-identity*, therefore, is essential to anything identical with Socrates. But this does not suffice to show that this property is an *essence* of Socrates. For *that* we must argue that nothing distinct from Socrates could have had *Socrates-identity*—that is, we must argue that an object distinct from Socrates in this world nowhere has *Socrates-identity.* This (together with the previous conclusion) follows from the more general principle that

(19) If *x* and *y* are identical in any world, then there is no world in which they are diverse.[9]

Is (19) true? I think we can see that it is. Recall that a possible world is a state of affairs that could have obtained if it does not. Here "could have" expresses, broadly speaking, logical or metaphysical possibility. Now are there states of affairs that *in fact* could have obtained, but would have lacked the property of possibly obtaining had things been different in some way? That is, are there states of affairs that in *this* world have the property of obtaining in some world or other, but in *other* worlds lack that property? Where it is metaphysical or logical possibility that is at stake, I think we can see that there are no such worlds. Similarly, we may ask: are there states of affairs that are *in fact* impossible, but would have been possible had things been different? That is, are there states of affairs that in fact have the property of obtaining in no possible world, but in some possible world have the property of obtaining in some possible world or other? Again, the answer is that there are no such worlds. Consider, therefore,

(20) If a state of affairs *S* is possible in at least one world *W*, then *S* is possible in every world.

This principle may be false where it is causal or natural possibility that is at stake; for logical or metaphysical possibility, it seems clearly true. In semantical developments of modal logic we meet the idea that a possible world *W* is possible *relative to* some but not necessarily all possible worlds,[10] where a world *W* is *possible relative to* a world *W'* if *W* would have been possible had *W'* obtained. As an obvious corollary of (20) we have

(20') Where *W* and *W'* are any possible worlds, *W* is possible relative to *W'*.

Given the truth of (20), however, we can easily show that (19) is true. For let *x* and *y* be any objects and *W* any world in which *x* is identical with *y*. In *W*, *x* has *x-identity* (that is, the property a thing has just in case it is identical with *x*); and clearly there is no world possible with respect to *W* in which *x* has *x-diversity*. By (20'), therefore, it follows that there is no world at all in which $x$ has *x-diversity;* in $W$, therefore, $x$ has the property of being nowhere $x$-diverse. Now by the Indiscernibility of Identicals, $y$ also has this property in $W$; that is, in $W$ $y$ has the property of being nowhere $x$-diverse. Therefore, $y$'s *being x-diverse* is an impossible state of affairs in $W$; accordingly, by (20) it is impossible in every world; hence, there is no world in which $x$ and $y$ are diverse. (19), therefore, is true. But then *Socrates-identity* is an essence of Socrates (and of anything identical with him); for (19) guarantees that anything distinct from Socrates in this or any world is nowhere identical with him.

Socrates, therefore, has an essence as well as essential properties. But here the following objection may arise. In arguing that Socrates has an essence I made free reference to such alleged properties as *being identical with Socrates in no world, being everywhere distinct from Socrates,* and the like. And is there even the slightest reason for supposing that there *are* any such properties as these? Indeed, is there any reason to suppose that "being identical with Socrates" names a property? Well, is there any reason to suppose that it does not? I cannot think of any, nor have I heard any that are at all impressive. To be sure, one hears expressions of a sort of nebulous discomfort; when asked to believe that there is such a property as *being identical with Socrates,* philosophers often adopt an air of wise and cautious skepticism. But this does not constitute an objection. Surely it is true of Socrates that he is Socrates and that he is identical with Socrates. If these are true of him, then *being Socrates* and *being identical with Socrates* characterize him; they are among his properties or attributes. Similarly for the property of being nowhere Socrates-diverse: a thing has the property of being Socrates-diverse in a given world $W$ if that thing would have been diverse from Socrates had $W$ obtained; it has the property of being nowhere Socrates-diverse if there is no possible world in which it is Socrates-diverse. So these are perfectly good properties. But in fact the argument does not really depend upon our willingness to say that *Socrates-identity* is a property. We may instead note merely that *that he is identical with Socrates* is true of Socrates, that *that he is diverse from Socrates in some world* is not true of Socrates in any world, and that anything true of Socrates is true of anything identical with him.

But if we propose to explain Socrates' essence and his essential properties by means of properties he has in every world in which he exists, then do we not encounter a problem about identifying Socrates across possible worlds? What about the celebrated Problem of Transworld Identification?[11] Well, what, exactly, *is* the problem? David Kaplan puts it as follows.

> I'll let you peek in at this other world through my Jules Verne-o-scope. Carefully examine each individual, check his finger prints, etc. The problem is; which one, if any, is Bobby Dylan? That is, which one is our Bobby Dylan—of course he may be somewhat

changed, just as he will be in our world in a few years. But in that possible world which ours will pass into in say 30 years, someone may ask "Whatever happened to Bobby Dylan?" and set out to locate him. Our problem is similarly to locate him in *G* (if he exists there).[12]

But have we really found a problem? Here, perhaps, there is less than meets the eye. For what, exactly, is our problem supposed to be? We are given a world *W* distinct from the actual world, an individual *x* that exists in the actual world, and asked how to determine whether *x* exists in *W* and if so which thing in *W* is *x*. We might like to know, for example, whether Raquel Welch exists in *W*; and (supposing that she does) which thing in *W* *is* Raquel Welch. But the answer to the first question is easy; Raquel Welch exists in *W* if and only if Raquel Welch would have existed had *W* been actual. Or to put the matter bibliographically, she exists in *W* if and only if *W*'s book contains the proposition *Raquel Welch exists*. Granted, we may not know enough about *W* to know whether its book *does* contain that proposition; we may be told only that *W* is some world in which, let us say, Socrates exists. Whether we can determine if *W*'s book contains this proposition depends upon how *W* is specified; but surely that constitutes no problem for the enterprise of explaining Socrates' essence in terms of properties he has in every world he graces.

Similarly with the second question. Consider a world—call it *RW<sub>f</sub>*—in which Raquel Welch exists and weighs 185 pounds, everything else being as much like the actual world as is consistent with that fact. Which individual, in *RW<sub>f</sub>*, is Raquel Welch? That is, which of the persons who would have existed, had *RW<sub>f</sub>* been actual, would have been such that, if *the actual world* had obtained, she would have been Raquel Welch? The answer, clearly, is Raquel Welch. But such an easy answer may lead us to suspect that we have misidentified the question. Perhaps we are to think of it as follows. How shall we determine which of the individuals we see (through the Verne-o-scope, perhaps) sporting in *RW<sub>f</sub>* is Raquel Welch? (Can you be serious in suggesting she is that unappetizing mass of blubber over there?) Put more soberly, perhaps the question is as follows. We are given a world *RW<sub>f</sub>* in which we know that Raquel Welch exists. We are given further that *RW<sub>f</sub>* contains an individual that uniquely meets condition $C_1$, one that meets condition $C_2$, and the like. Now which of these is Miss Welch? Is it the individual meeting $C_1$, or is it some other? To have the answer we must audit the book of *RW<sub>f</sub>*; does it contain, for example, the proposition *Raquel Welch meets $C_1$*? If so, then it is the person who meets $C_1$ that is Raquel Welch. Of course our information about *RW<sub>f</sub>* may be limited; we may be told only that *Raquel Welch exists* and *Raquel Welch weighs 185 pounds* are in its book; we may not know, for any other (logically independent) proposition predicating a property of her, whether or not it is in the book. Then, of course, we may

be unable to tell whether the thing that meets condition $C_i$ in $RW_f$ is
or is not identical with Raquel Welch.

This is indeed a fact; but where is the problem? (We need not
step outside the actual world to find cases where identification requires more knowledge than we possess.) Is the suggestion, perhaps,
that for all we can tell there is *no* world (distinct from the actual) in
which Raquel Welch exists? But to make this suggestion is to imply
that there is no book containing both *Raquel Welch exists* and at least
one false proposition. That is, it is to suggest that the conjunction of
*Raquel Welch exists* with any false proposition *p*—for example, *Paul I.
Zwier is a good tennis player*—is necessarily false; and hence that *Raquel
Welch exists* entails every true proposition. Obviously the assets of Raquel Welch are many and impressive; nonetheless they scarcely extend
as far as all that.

I therefore do not see that the Problem of Transworld Identification (if needed it is a problem) threatens the enterprise of explaining the essence of Socrates in terms of properties he has in every
world in which he exists. But what about the following difficulty? If
(as I suggested above) for any object *x*, the property of *x*-identity (the
property a thing has just in case it is identical with *x*) is essential to
*x*, then the property of being identical with the teacher of Plato is
essential to the teacher of Plato. Furthermore, *being identical with the
teacher of Plato* is essential to anything identical with the teacher of
Plato—Socrates, for example. Hence, *identity with the teacher of Plato* is
essential to Socrates. But surely

(21)  If a property *P* is essential to an object *x*, then any property
      entailed by *P* is also essential to *x*

where, we recall, a property *P* entails a property *Q* if there is no world
in which there exists an object that has *P* but not *Q*. Now whatever
has the property of *being the teacher of Plato* in a given world surely has
the property of *being a teacher* in that world. But the former property
is essential to Socrates; so, therefore, is the latter. And yet this is absurd; the property of being a teacher is not essential to Socrates.
(Even if you do not think that is absurd, we can show by an easy
generalization of this argument that any property Socrates has is essential to him—and *that* is patently absurd.) What has gone wrong?
(21) certainly has the ring of truth. Must we conclude after all that
such alleged properties as *being identical with the teacher of Plato* are a
snare and a delusion?

That would be hasty, I think. Consider a world *W* in which Socrates exists but does not teach Plato; let us suppose that in *W* Xenophon is the only teacher Plato ever had. Now in *W* Socrates is not
identical with the teacher of Plato—that is, Socrates is not identical
with the person who *in W* is Plato's only teacher. He is, however,
identical with the person who *in the actual world* is the only teacher of

Plato. Here a certain misunderstanding may arise. If *W* had transpired, then *W* would have been the actual world—so is it not true that in *W* it is *Xenophon*, not Socrates, who has the property of being the person who is the only teacher of Plato in the actual world? *Being actual* is a peculiar property; this is a property that in any given world is had by that world and that world only. Accordingly in *W* it is Xenophon who is the teacher of Plato in the actual world. We may forestall this *contretemps* as follows. Suppose we give a name to the actual world—the one that does in fact obtain; suppose we name it "Kronos." Then this property of being identical with the teacher of Plato—the property Socrates has essentially according to the above argument—is the property of being identical with the person who in fact, in the actual world, is the teacher of Plato. It is the property of being identical with the person who *in Kronos* is the teacher of Plato. But *that* property—*identity with the person who in Kronos is the teacher of Plato*—does not entail *being a teacher*. For a thing might have that property in some world distinct from Kronos—a world in which Socrates teaches no one, for example—without having, in that world, the property of being a teacher.

But now still another query confronts us. Consider the well-known facts that Cicero is identical with Tully and that Hesperus is the very same thing as Phosphorus. Do not these facts respectively represent (for many of us, at least) historical and astronomical *discovery*? And hence are not the counterfacts *Hesperus and Phosphorus are entities distinct* and *Tully is diverse from Cicero*, though counterfacts indeed, *contingently* counterfactual? Historical and astronomical science have been known to reverse themselves; might we not sometime come to discover that Cicero and Tully were really two distinct persons and that Hesperus is not identical with Phosphorus? But if so, then how can it be true that *being identical with Phosphorus* is an essence of Hesperus, so that *Hesperus is diverse from Phosphorus* is necessarily false?

The argument here implicit takes for granted that the discovery of necessary truth is not the proper business of the historian and astronomer. But this is at best dubious. I discover that Ephialtes was a traitor; I know that it is Kronos that is actual; accordingly, I also discover that Kronos includes the state of affairs consisting in Ephialtes' being a traitor. This last, of course, is necessarily true; but couldn't a historian (*qua*, as they say, *historian*) discover it, too? It is hard to believe that historians and astronomers are subject to a general prohibition against the discovery of necessary truth. Their views, if properly come by, are a posteriori; that they are also contingent does not follow.

On the other hand, when I discovered that Kronos contained *Ephialtes' being a traitor*, I also discovered something contingent. Is there something similar in the case of Venus? Exactly what was it that the ancient Babylonians discovered? Was it that the planet Hesperus has the property of being identical with Phosphorus? But *identity with Phosphorus* is in fact the very same property as *identity with Hesperus;* no doubt the Babylonians knew all along that Hesperus has *Hesperus-identity;* and hence they knew all along that Hesperus has *Phosphorus-identity.* Just what was it the Babylonians believed before the Discovery, and how did this discovery fit into the total economy of their belief? Perhaps we can put it like this. The Babylonians probably believed what can be expressed by pointing in the evening to the western sky, to Venus, and saying "*This* is not identical with" (long pause) "that" (pointing to the eastern sky, to Venus, the following morning). If so, then they believed of Hesperus and *Phosphorus-identity* that the latter does not characterize the former; since *Phosphorus-identity* is the same property as *Hesperus-identity*, they believed of *Hesperus-identity* that it does not characterize Hesperus. No doubt the Babylonians would have disputed this allegation; but of course one can easily be mistaken about whether one holds a belief of this kind. And the quality of their intellectual life was improved by the Discovery in that thereafter they no longer believed of Hesperus that it lacked the property of Hesperus-identity. Of course we can scarcely represent this improvement as a matter of discovering that Hesperus *had Hesperus-identity*; they already knew that. Their tragedy was that they knew that, and also believed its contradictory; the Discovery consisted in part of correcting this deplorable state of affairs.

Still, this is at best a partial account of what they discovered. For they also believed that there is a heavenly body that appears first in the evening, and another, distinct from the first, that disappears last in the morning. This is a contingent proposition; and part of what they discovered is that it is false. Or, to put things just a little differently, suppose the identity criteria for "Hesperus"—such properties as *appearing just after sundown, appearing before any other star or planet, being brighter than any other star or planet that appears in the evening*—are $H_1, H_2, \ldots, H_n$; and suppose the identity criteria for "Phosphorus" are $P_1, P_2, \ldots, P_n$. Then what the Babylonians discovered is that the same heavenly body satisfies both the $P_i$ and the $H_i$. They discovered that the planet that satisfies the $P_i$ also satisfies the $H_i$. And of course this is a contingent fact; there are possible worlds in which the thing that in fact has the distinction of satisfying both sets of criteria satisfies only one or neither. The Babylonian discovery, therefore, was a complex affair; but there is nothing in it to suggest that *being identical with Phosphorus* is not essential to Hesperus.

## III

Socrates, therefore, has an essence—being *Socrates* or *Socrateity.* This essence entails each of his essential properties. And among these we have so far found (in addition to trivially essential properties) such items as *being Socrates or Greek, being a non-number,* and *being possibly conscious.* But what about the property of having (or, to beg no questions, being) a body? Could Socrates have been disembodied? Or could he have had a body of quite a different sort? Could he have been an alligator, for example? That depends. We might think of an alligator as a composite typically consisting in a large, powerful body animated by an unimpressive mind with a nasty disposition. If we do, shall we say that any mind-alligator-body composite is an alligator, or must the mind be of a special relatively dull sort? If the first alternative is correct, then I think Socrates could have been an alligator (or at any rate its personal or mental component); for I think he could have had an alligator body. We have no difficulty in understanding Kafka's story about the man who wakes up one morning to discover that he now has the body of a beetle; and in fact the state of affairs depicted there is entirely possible. In the same way I can imagine myself awakening one morning and discovering, no doubt to my chagrin, that I had become the owner of an alligator body. I should then give up mountain climbing for swimming and skin diving. Socrates, therefore, could have had an alligator body; if this is sufficient for his having been an alligator, then Socrates could have been an alligator.

On the other hand, we might think, with Descartes, that an alligator is a material object of some sort—perhaps an elaborate machine made of flesh and bone. Suppose that is what an alligator is; could Socrates have been one? Descartes has a famous argument for the conclusion that he is not a material object:

> I am therefore, precisely speaking, only a thinking thing, that is, a mind (*mens sive animus*), understanding, or reason—terms whose signification was before unknown to me. I am, however, a real thing, and really existent; but what thing? The answer was, a thinking thing. The question now arises, am I aught besides? I will stimulate my imagination with a view to discover whether I am not still something more than a thinking being. Now it is plain I am not the assemblage of members called the human body; I am not a thin and penetrating air diffused through all these members, or wind, or flame, or vapour, or breath, or any of all the things I can imagine; for I supposed that all these were not, and, without changing the supposition, I find that I still feel assured of my existence.[13]

How shall we construe this argument? I think Descartes means to reason as follows: it is at present possible both that I exist and that there are no material objects—that is,

(23) Possibly, I exist and there are no material objects.

But if so, then

(24) I am not a material object.

But is the premise of this argument true? I think it is. The proposition that there are no material objects does not entail, it seems to me, that I do not exist. Furthermore, Descartes could have employed a weaker premise here:

(23') Possibly, I exist and no material object is my body.

But even if these premises are true, the argument is at the best unduly inexplicit. We might well argue from

(25) Possibly, I exist and no brothers-in-law exist

to

(26) I am not a brother-in-law.

What follows from (23) is not (24) but only its possibility:

(27) Possibly, I am not a material object.

What the argument shows, therefore, is that even if human beings are in fact physical objects, they are only contingently so. But something else of interest follows from the possibility of (23) and (23'); it follows that there are worlds in which I exist and not only *am* not a body, but do not *have* a body. *Being embodied,* therefore, is not essential to human persons. Here we might be inclined to object that

(28) All human persons have bodies

is necessarily true. Perhaps it is and perhaps it is not; in neither case does it follow that human persons are essentially embodied. What follows is only that, if they are not, then *being a human person* is not essential to human persons, just as *being a brother-in-law* is not essential to brothers-in-law. The property of being a human person (as opposed to that of being a divine person or an angelic person or a person *simpliciter*) may entail the possession of a body; it may be that whatever, in a given world, has the property of being a human person has a body in that world. It does not follow that Socrates, who is in fact a human person, has the property of having a body in every world he graces.

As it stands, therefore, Descartes's argument does not establish that he is not a body or a material object. But perhaps his argument can be strengthened. G. H. von Wright suggests the following principle:

> If a property can be significantly predicated of the individuals of a certain universe of discourse then either the property is necessarily present in some or all of the individuals and necessarily absent in the rest or else the property is possibly but not necessarily (that is, contingently) present in some or all individuals and possibly but not necessarily (contingently) absent in the rest.[14]

We might restate and compress this principle as follows:

> (29) Any property *P* had essentially by anything is had essentially by everything that has it.

Is (29) true? We have already seen that it is not; *being prime or prim, being Socrates or Greek* constitute counterexamples. Still, the principle might hold for a large range of properties, and it is plausible to suppose that it holds for the property of being a material object as well as for the complement of that property. It seems to me impossible that there should be an object that in some possible world is a material object and in others is not. That is to say, where "*M*" names the property of being a material object and "$\bar{M}$" names its complement,

> (30) Anything that has *M* or $\bar{M}$, has *M* essentially or has $\bar{M}$ essentially.

And armed with this principle, we can refurbish Descartes's argument. For if I am not essentially a material object, then by (30) I am not one at all. And hence Descartes is right in holding that he is not a material object. But if I do not have the property of being a material object, I have its complement, and by another application of the same principle it follows that I have its complement essentially. Descartes, therefore, is correct; he is an immaterial object and, indeed, is such an object in every world in which he exists. What Descartes's argument establishes is that persons are essentially immaterial; Socrates, therefore, could have been an alligator only if alligators are not material objects.

## IV

Socrates' essence, accordingly, contains or entails trivially essential properties, the property of being immaterial, the property of being Socrates or Greek, and the like. But aren't these—except perhaps for immateriality—pretty drab properties? What about such everyday properties as qualities of character and personality—being a saint or a sinner, wise or foolish, admirable or the reverse; are none of these essential to him? I think the answer is that none are. But if the essence of Socrates has no more content than this, isn't it a pretty thin, lackluster thing, scarcely worth talking about? Perhaps; but it is hard to see that this is legitimate cause for complaint. If indeed Socrates' essence is pretty slim, the essentialist can scarcely be expected to pretend otherwise. To complain about this is like scolding the weatherman for the lack of sunshine. Still it must be conceded that the present conception of essence might seem a bit thin by comparison, for example, with that of Leibniz:

This being so, we are able to say that this is the nature of an individual substance or of a complete being, namely, to afford a conception so complete that the concept shall be sufficient for the understanding of it and for the deduction of all the predicates of which the substance is or may become the subject. Thus the quality of king, which belonged to Alexander the Great, an abstraction from the subject, is not sufficiently determined to constitute an individual, and does not contain the other qualities of the same subject, nor everything which the idea of this price includes. God, however, seeing the individual concept, or haecceity, of Alexander, sees there at the same time the basis and the reason of all the predicates which can be truly uttered regarding him; for instance, that he will conquer Darius and Porus, even to the point of knowing *a priori* (and not by experience) whether he died a natural death or by poison—facts which we can learn only through history.[15]

Might *seem* a bit thin, I say; in fact it is not thin at all. And while what Leibniz says sounds wildly extravagant if not plainly outrageous, it, or something like it, is the sober truth.

Return to the property of being snubnosed. This is a property Socrates has in this world and lacks in others. Consider, by contrast, the property of being snubnosed in this world, in Kronos. Socrates has this property, and has it essentially. This is perhaps obvious enough, but we can argue for it as follows. What must be shown is that (*a*) Socrates has the property of being snubnosed in Kronos in the actual world, and (*b*) there is no world in which Socrates has the complement of this property. (*a*) is clearly true. Now Kronos includes the state of affairs—call it "*B*"—consisting in Socrates' being snubnosed: that is, the state of affairs consisting in *Kronos' obtaining and B's failing to obtain* is impossible. By (20), therefore, this is impossible in every world; hence, Kronos includes *B* in every world. But clearly Socrates exists in a given world *W* in which Kronos includes *B* only if, in that world, he has the property of being snubnosed in Kronos. Accordingly, Socrates has this property in every world in which he exists; hence, there is no world in which he has its complement.

We may also put the matter bibliographically. It suffices to show that Kronos' book contains *Socrates is snubnosed* in every world. But it is evident, I take it, that

(31) For any proposition *p* and book *B*, *B* contains *p* if and only if *p* is a consequence of *B*

is necessarily true. Now clearly *Socrates is snubnosed* is a consequence of Kronos' book: Kronos' book *U* (*it is false that Socrates is snubnosed*) is an impossible set. By (20), therefore, this set is impossible in every world—that is, *Socrates is snubnosed* is a consequence of Kronos' book in every world. Hence Kronos' book contains that proposition in every world.

The property of being snubnosed in Kronos, therefore, is essential to Socrates. And (presuming that in fact Socrates was the only teacher Plato ever had) while there are worlds and objects distinct from Socrates such that the latter *teach Plato* in the former, there is no such object that in some world has the property of *teaching Plato in Kronos*. The property of teaching Plato in Kronos, therefore, entails the property of being Socrates; accordingly, this property is an essence of Socrates. Clearly we can find as many more essences of Socrates *as we wish*. Take any property he alone has—*being married to Xantippe*, for example, or *being the shortest Greek philosopher* or *being A. E. Taylor's favorite philosopher*. For any such property *P, having P in Kronos* is an essence of Socrates. Take, more generally, any property *P* and world *W* such that in *W* Socrates alone has *P*; the property of having *P* in *W* will be an essence of Socrates.

According to Leibniz, "God, however, seeing the individual concept, or haecceity, of Alexander, sees there at the same time the basis and the reason of all the predicates which can be truly uttered regarding him." Arnauld was shocked and scandalized when he read this suggestion—no doubt in part because of the bad cold he claimed he had when he received the *Discourse* from Count von Hessen Rheinfels. But in fact what Leibniz says, or something similar, is correct. We can see that this is so if we take a closer look at the notion of *essence*, or *individual concept*, or *haecceity*. An essence *E* of Socrates, as we have seen above, is a property that meets three conditions. First of all, it is essential to Socrates. Secondly, for any property *P*, if Socrates has *P* essentially, then *E* entails *P*. And finally, the complement of *E* is essential to every object distinct from Socrates. Suppose we investigate some of the consequences of this definition. We might note, first, that for any world *W*, either Socrates exists in *W* or Socrates does not exist in *W*. Take any world *W*, that is; either Socrates would have existed, had *W* obtained, or Socrates would not have existed had *W* obtained. And that he exists in *W*, if he does, is, by the argument above, a matter of his essence; for any world *W*, either *exists in W* is essential to Socrates or *does not exist in W* is. Accordingly, if *E* is an essence of Socrates, then for any world *W*, either *E* entails *exists in W* or *E* entails *does not exist in W*.

Secondly, notice that for any property *P* and world *W* in which Socrates exists, either Socrates has *P* in *W* or Socrates has *P̄* in *W*. This, too, is a matter of his essence; so for any such world and property, any essence of Socrates either entails *has P in W* or entails *has P̄ in W*. But what about those worlds in which Socrates does *not* exist? Does he have properties in *those* worlds? Take, for example, the property of being snubnosed, and let *W* be any world in which Socrates does not exist. Are we to suppose that if *W* had obtained, Socrates would have had the property of being snubnosed? Or that if *W* had obtained, he would have had the complement of that property? I should think that neither of these is true; had *W* obtained, Socrates would have had neither snubnosedness nor its complement. I am inclined to think that Socrates has no properties at all in those worlds in which he does not exist. We cannot say, therefore, that if $E$ is an essence of Socrates, then for just any world $W$ and property $P$, either $E$ entails *the property of having P in W* or $E$ entails *the property of having $\bar{P}$ in W*; Socrates has neither $P$ nor $\bar{P}$ in a world where he does not exist. Still, in *this* world, in Kronos, Socrates has, for any world $W$ and property $P$, either *the property of having P in W* or *the property of not having P in W*. For either

(32) If $W$ had obtained, Socrates would have had $P$

or

(33) If $W$ had obtained, Socrates would not have had $P$.

More generally, an essence of Socrates will entail, for any property $P$ and world $W$, either the property of having $P$ in $W$ or the property of not having $P$ in $W$.

An essence $E$ of Socrates, therefore, meets three conditions: (*a*) for any world $W$, $E$ entails *exists in W* or *does not exist in W;* (*b*) for any world $W$ such that $E$ entails *exists in W*, $E$ also entails, for any property $P$, *has P in W* or *has $\bar{P}$ in W*, and (*c*) for any world $W$ and property $P$, $E$ entails *has P in W* or *does not have P in W*. In addition, of course, $E$ is essential to Socrates and its complement is essential to everything distinct from him. We might therefore characterize an essence, or haecceity, or individual concept as follows:

(34) $E$ is an *individual concept*, or *essence*, or *haecceity* if and only if (*a*) *has E essentially* is instantiated in some world, (*b*) for any world $W$ and property $P$, $E$ entails *has P in W* or *does not have P in W*, (*c*) for any world $W$, $E$ entails *exists in W* or *does not exist in W*, (*d*) for any world $W$ such that $E$ entails *exists in W*, $E$ also entails, for any property $P$, *has P in W* or *has $\bar{P}$ in W*, and (*e*) in no world is there an object $x$ that has $E$ and an object $y$ distinct from $x$ that has $E$ in some world or other.

But if existence is a property, clause (*c*) will be redundant in that it is entailed by (*b*). Furthermore, it is necessarily true that an object $x$ exists only if it has, for any property $P$, either $P$ or $\bar{P}$; hence clause (*d*) is also redundant. Still further, (*e*) is redundant. For let $W$ be any world in which there exists an object $x$ that has $E$. Now clearly enough it is not possible that two distinct objects share all their properties; in $W$, therefore, there is no object distinct from $x$ that has $E$. But further, $W$ contains no object $y$ distinct from $x$ that has $E$ in some world $W'$. For suppose it does. $E$ then entails *exists in W'*; hence both $x$ and $y$ exist in $W'$. But in $W'$ there is at most one object that has $E$; hence in $W'$ $x$ is identical with $y$. Accordingly in $W$, $y$ is diverse from $x$ but possibly identical with $x;$ and this is impossible.

Shorn of redundancy, our present characterization goes as follows:

(35) *E* is an essence if and only if (*a*) *has E essentially* is instantiated in some world or other, and (*b*) for any world *W* and property *P*, *E* entails *has P in W* or *does not have P in W*.[16]

By way of conclusion, then, let us return to Leibniz and his claims about God and Alexander. What we see is that he was right, or nearly right. God has a complete knowledge of Alexander's essence; hence for any property *P* and world *W*, God knows whether or not Alexander has *P* in *W*. He knows, furthermore, that it is Kronos that has the distinction of being the actual world. From these two items he can read off all the properties—accidental as well as essential—that Alexander does in fact have. So what we have here is surely no paucity of content; an essence is as rich and full-bodied as anyone could reasonably desire.

## APPENDIX

Can we make a further simplification in our account of essencehood? Yes. Suppose we say that a property *P* is *world-indexed* if there is a world *W* and a property *Q* such that *P* is equivalent to the property *of having Q in W* or to its complement—the property of *not having Q in W*. *Being snubnosed in Kronos*, for example, is a world-indexed property. Let us say further that a property *Q* is *large* if for every world-indexed property *P*, either *Q* entails *P* or *Q* entails *P̄*. *Being Socrates* or *Socrateity*, as we have seen, is a large property. Now where *Q* is a large property, there may be a large property *P* distinct from *Q* that *coincides with Q on world-indexed properties*—that is, a property that, for each world-indexed property *R*, entails *R* if and only if *Q* entails *R*. *Being Socrates*, for example, and *being Socrates and snubnosed* are distinct large properties that coincide on world-indexed properties. Accordingly, let us say that a property is *encaptic* if it is large, and is entailed by every property that coincides with it on world-indexed properties. Roughly, we may think of an encaptic property as a property equivalent to some conjunctive property *Q* each conjunct of which is a world-indexed property, and such that for each world-indexed property *P*, either *P* or *P̄* is a conjunct of *Q*. We should note that an encaptic property may entail properties that are not world-indexed; if an encaptic property *Q* entails *has P in W* for every world *W* for which it entails *exists in W*, then *Q* entails *P*. So, for example, *Socrateity* entails the property of being possibly conscious and the property of not being a number, neither of which is world-indexed. (Of course, any such non-world-indexed property entailed by an encaptic property *Q* will be essential

to whatever instantiates *Q*.) Given these definitions, then, we may say
that

> (36) An essence is an encaptic property that is instantiated in
>      some world or other.

I think we can see that (35) and (36) equivalently characterize the
idea of essence. Let us note first that any instantiated encaptic property meets the conditions for essencehood laid down by (35). Obviously, any such property will entail, for any world-indexed property
*P*, either *P* or *P̄*. But further, whatever instantiates an encaptic property *Q* has *Q* essentially. For let *W* be any world in which there exists
an object *x* that has *Q*, and let *W\** be any world in which *x* exists.
What must be shown is that *x* has *Q* in *W\**. It suffices to show that
in *W\** *x* has every world-indexed property entailed by *Q*. But an interesting peculiarity of world-indexed properties, as we have seen, is
that nothing in any world has any such property accidentally. Accordingly, since in *W* *x* has each world-indexed property entailed by *Q*, *x*
has each such property in *W\** as well; and hence *x* has *Q* in *W\**.

On the other hand, any property that meets conditions (*a*) and
(*b*) of (35) is an encaptic property that is somewhere instantiated.
Obviously, if *E* is any such property, *E* is instantiated in some world.
But it is also encaptic. *E* entails, for any world-indexed property *P*, has
*P* or has *P̄*. Accordingly, *E* entails some encaptic property *Q*. Let *W\**
be any world in which there is an object *x* that has *Q*. *E*, as we know,
is essentially instantiated; so there is a world *W'* in which there exists
an object *y* that has *E* and has it in every world in which it exists. Now
*Q* (and hence *E*) entails *exists in W\**; accordingly *y* exists in *W\**, has
*E* in *W\**, and has *Q* in *W\**. Now clearly there is no world in which
two distinct objects share an encaptic property; if, for every property
*P*, *x* has *P* in *W* if and only if *y* has *P* in *W*, then *x* is identical with *y*.
In the present case, therefore, *x* and *y* are identical in *W\**, since each
has *Q* there. But *y* has *E* in *W\**; hence so does *x*. Accordingly, *Q but
not E* is not instantiated in *W\**; hence *E* both entails and is entailed
by *Q*, and is itself, therefore, encaptic.

## NOTES

1. See chapter 1 of the present volume.
2. If we take it that if a state of affairs *S* includes and is included by a state of
affairs *S'*, then *S* and *S'* are the same state of affairs. Alternatively, we may introduce
the idea of a *super state of affairs* (analogous to a superproposition) and take the range
of *F* to be the set of super states of affairs.
3. Here I am taking it for granted that the proposition *Socrates is wise* would have
been true or false even if Socrates had not existed. The contrary view—that *Socrates
is wise* is neither true nor false in those worlds in which Socrates does not exist—is
not unreasonable and can easily be accommodated. Nothing I say below essentially
depends upon choosing between these two.

4. "Proper Names," *Mind*, LXVII (1958), 171. Henceforth, page references to this article will be given in the text.

5. If we suppose, as I do, that a modal statement—one predicating necessity or possibility of some statement—is either necessarily true or necessarily false.

6. I do not mean to deny, of course, that the pressure of historical discovery could cause a change in the identity criteria for "Homer."

7. See G. E. Moore, "Is Existence a Predicate?" *Philosophical Papers* (London, 1959).

8. Where a property *P* entails a property *Q* if there is no world in which there exists an object that has *P* but not *Q*.

9. Where the variables "*x*, and "*y*" range over objects that exist in the actual world.

10. See, e.g., Saul Kripke's "Some Semantical Considerations on Modal Logic," *Acta Philosophia Fennica* (1963). To accept (20'), of course, is to stipulate that *R*, the alternativeness relation Kripke mentions, is an equivalence relation; the resulting semantics yields as valid the characteristic axiom of Lewis's $S_5$, according to which a proposition is necessarily possible if possible.

11. See R. Chisholm, "Identity through Possible Worlds: Some Questions," *Nous*, I (1967), 1–8; J. Hintikka, "Individuals, Possible Worlds and Epistemic Logic," *Nous*, I (1967), 33–63; D. Kaplan, "Trans-World Identifications" (presented to an APA symposium, Chicago, 1967, but unpublished); L. Linsky, "Reference, Essentialism and Modality," *Journal of Philosophy*, LXVI (1969), 687–700; R. Purtill, "About Identity through Possible Worlds," *Nous*, II (1968); and R. Thomason, "Modal Logic and Metaphysics," in *The Logical Way of Doing Things*, ed. K. Lambert (New Haven, 1968).

12. Kaplan, 1967, p. 7.

13. Descartes, *Meditations*, Meditation I.

14. G. H. von Wright, *An Essay in Modal Logic* (Amsterdam, 1951), p. 27.

15. Leibniz, *Discourse on Metaphysics* (La Salle, Ind., 1945), pp. 13–14.

16. See appendix to this chapter.

# 3

# Transworld Identity or Worldbound
# Individuals?

The idea of *possible worlds* has seemed to promise understanding and insight into several venerable problems of modality—those of essence and accident, for example, necessary and contingent truth, modality *de dicto* and *de re*, and the nature of subjunctive conditionals. But just what is a possible world? Suppose we take it that a possible world is a *state of affairs* of some kind—one which either obtains, is real, is actual, or else *could have* obtained. But then how shall we understand "could have" here? Obviously no *definition* will be of much use: Here we must give examples, lay out the connections between the concept in question and other concepts, reply to objections, and hope for the best. Although I cannot do this in detail here,[1] I do wish to point out that the sense of possibility in question is wider than that of *causal* or *natural* possibility—so that *Agnew's swimming the Atlantic Ocean*, while it is perhaps causally or naturally impossible, is not impossible in the sense under discussion. On the other hand, this sense is narrower than that captured in first-order logic, so that many states of affairs are necessary, in the sense in question, although their corresponding propositions are not provable in first-order logic. Examples of such states if affairs would include those corresponding to truths of arithmetic and mathematics generally, as well as many more homely items such as *Nobody's being taller than himself, red's being a color*, (as well as *a thing's being colored if red*), *Agnew's not being a composite number*, and the like. Other and less homely candidates include *every person's being conscious at some time or other, every human person's having a body at some time during his career,* and *the existence of a being than which it's not possible that there be a greater.*

In the sense of necessity and possibility in question, furthermore, a pair of states of affairs $S$ and $S'$ may be so related that it is not possible that both obtain, in which case $S$ *precludes* $S'$; and if it is impossible that $S$ obtain and $S'$ *not* obtain, then $S$ *includes* $S'$. So, for example, *Agnew's having swum the Atlantic* includes *Agnew's having swum something or other* and precludes *Agnew's not being able to swim.* Still further, a state of affairs $S$ may be such that for any state of affairs $S'$, $S$ either includes or precludes $S'$, in which case $S$ is *maximal.* Now we may say that a possible world is just a maximal possible state of affairs. Corresponding to each possible world $W$, furthermore, there is a unique class of propositions, $C$, of which a proposition $P$ is a member just in case it is impossible that $W$ be actual and $P$ be false. Call this class *the book on W.* Like possible worlds, books too have a maximality property: each book contains, for any proposition $P$, either $P$ or the negation of $P$. And the book on the actual world, obviously, is the set of true propositions.

Now it is plausible and natural to suppose that the same individual exists in various different states of affairs. There is, for example, the state of affairs consisting in *Paul R. Zwier's being a good tennis player;* this state of affairs is possible but does not in fact obtain. It is natural to suppose, however, that if it *had* obtained, Zwier would have existed and would have been a good tennis player. That is, it is natural to suppose that Zwier *exists in* this state of affairs. But, of course, if he exists in this state of affairs, then he exists in every possible world including it; that is, every possible world including *Zwier's being a good tennis player* is such that, had it been actual, Zwier would have existed. So Zwier exists in many possible worlds. I say it is natural to make this supposition; but many philosophers otherwise kindly disposed toward possible worlds are inclined toward its denial. Among them, there is, for example, Leibniz, whose credentials on this subject are certainly impeccable; Leibniz apparently held that each object exists in just one world.[2] The idealists, furthermore, in arguing for their doctrine of internal relations, were arguing in essence that an object exists in exactly one possible world—indeed, some of them may have thought that there is only one such world. More recently, the view that individuals are thus confined to one world—let's call it The Theory of Worldbound Individuals—has been at least entertained with considerable hospitality by David Kaplan.[3] Roderick Chisholm, furthermore, finds difficulty and perplexity in the claim that the same object exists in more than one possible world.[4] Still further, The Theory of Worldbound Individuals is an explicit postulate of David Lewis's Counterpart Theory.[5] In what follows I shall explore this issue. Now perhaps the most important and widely heralded argument for the Theory of Worldbound Individuals (hereafter 'TWI') is the celebrated

*Problem of Transworld Identification,* said to arise on the supposition that the same object exists in more than one world. Accordingly I will concentrate on these two topics: TWI and the problem of Transworld Identity.

Why, then, should we suppose that an individual is confined to just one world—that you and I, for example, exist in this world and this world only? According to G. E. Moore, the idealists, in arguing for their view that all relations are internal, were really arguing that all relational properties are essential to the things that have them. The argument they gave, however, if it is sound, establishes that *all* properties—not just relational properties—are thus essential to their owners. If this is correct, however, then for no object *x* is there a possible state of affairs in which *x* lacks a property that in fact it has; so *x* exists only in the actual world, the world that does in fact obtain.

Now an argument for a conclusion as sweeping as this must pack quite a punch. What did the idealists come up with? A confusion, says Moore. What the idealists asserted is

(1) If *P* be a relational property and *A* a term to which it does in fact belong, then, no matter what *P* and *A* may be, it may always be truly asserted of them, that any term which had *not* possessed *P* would necessarily have been other than numerically different from *A* . . . [6]

Perhaps we may put this more perspicuously as

(1') If *x* has *P*, then for any object *y*, if there is a world in which *y* lacks *P*, then *y* is distinct from *x*

which clearly entails the desired conclusion. What they suggested as a reason for accepting (1), however is

(2) If *A* has *P* and *x* does not, it *does* follow that *x* is other than *A*.[7]

If we restate (2) as the claim that

(2') For any object *x* and *y*, if *x* has *P* and *y* does not, then *x* is distinct from *y*

holds in every world, we see that (2) is just the thesis that the Indiscernibility of Identicals is necessarily true. This thesis seems accurate enough, but no reason at all for (1) or (1'). As Moore, says, (1) and (2) are easily conflated, particularly when they are put in the idealists' typically opaque and turgid prose; and the idealists seized the opportunity to conflate them.

Initially, then, this argument is unpromising. It has a near relative, however, that we may conceivably find in Leibniz and that often surfaces in contemporary discussion. Leibniz writes Arnauld as follows:

Besides, if, in the life of any person and even in the whole universe anything went differently from what it has, nothing could prevent us from saying that it was another person or another possible universe which God had chosen. It would then be indeed another individual.[8]

This is on its face a dark saying. What Leibniz says here and elsewhere, however, may suggest the following. Suppose Socrates exists in some world $W$ distinct from the actual world (which for purposes of easy reference I shall name "Charley"). Taking the term 'property' in a broad sense, we shall be obliged to concede that there must be some property that Socrates has in Charley but lacks in $W$. (At the very least, if we let '$\pi$' name the book on Charley, then one property Socrates has in Charley but lacks in $W$ is that of being such that every member of $\pi$ is true.) So let us suppose that there is some property— snubnosedness, let us say—that Socrates has in Charley but lacks in $W$. That is, the Socrates of Charley, Socrates-in-Charley, has snubnosedness, while the Socrates of $W$ does not. But surely this is inconsistent with the Indiscernibility of Identicals, a principle than which none sounder can be conceived. For according to this principle, if Socrates-in-Charley has snubnosedness but Socrates-in-$W$ does not, then Socrates-in-Charley is distinct from Socrates-in-$W$. We must conclude, therefore, that Socrates does not exist both in Charley and in $W$. There may be some person in $W$ that much resembles our Socrates, Socrates-in-Charley; that person is nonetheless distinct from him. And of course this argument can be generalized to show that nothing exists in more than one world.

Such an argument, however, is less than impeccable. We are asked to infer

(3)  Socrates-in-Charley is snubnosed and Socrates-in-$W$ is not

from

(4)  Socrates is snubnosed in Charley but not in $W$

We need not quarrel with this request; but the Indiscernibility of Identicals in no way licenses the inference that Socrates-in-Charley and Socrates-in-$W$ are distinct. For, contrary, perhaps, to appearances, there is no property that (3) predicates of Socrates-in-Charley and withholds from Socrates-in-$W$. According to (3) [so taken that it follows from (4)], Socrates-in-Charley (that is, Socrates) has the property of being snubnosed, all right, but *in Charley*. Socrates-in-$W$, however, lacks that property *in W*. But this latter, of course, means only that Socrates-in-$W$ has the property of being such that, if $W$ had obtained, he would not have been snubnosed. And, of course, this property— the property an object $x$ has iff $x$ would not have been snubnosed, had $W$ obtained—is not the complement of snubnosedness. Indeed, this property is not even incompatible with snubnosedness; Socrates himself is snubnosed, but would not have been had *W* been actual. So the Indiscernibility of Identicals does not apply here; there is no property *P* which (3) asserts that Socrates-in-Charley has but Socrates-in-*W* lacks. To suppose that Socrates has *P* in the actual world but lacks it in *W* is to suppose only that Socrates does in fact have *P* but would not have had it, had *W* been actual. The Indiscernibility of Identicals casts not even a hint of suspicion upon this supposition. This objection, therefore, is a snare and a delusion.

A more popular and more promising argument for TWI is the dreaded *Problem of Transworld Identity* said to confront anyone who rashly supposes the same object to exist in more than one world. Here the claim is that there are deep conceptual difficulties in *identifying* the same object from world to world—difficulties that threaten the very idea of Transworld Identity with incoherence. These difficulties, furthermore, presumbaly do not arise on TWI.[9]

But what, exactly, *is* the problem of Transworld Identity? What difficulties does it present for the notion that the same object exists in various possible worlds? Just how does this problem go? Although published statements of it are scarce,[10] the problem may perhaps be put as follows. Let us suppose again that Socrates exists in some world *W* distinct from this one—a world in which let us say, he did not fight in the battle of Marathon. In *W*, of course, he may also lack other properties he has in this world—perhaps in *W* he eschewed philosophy, corrupted no youth, and thus escaped the wrath of the Athenians. Perhaps in *W* he lived in Corinth, was six feet tall, and remained a bachelor all his life. But then we must ask ourselves how we could possibly *identify* Socrates in that world. How could we *pick him out?* How could we *locate* him there? How could we possibly tell which of the many things contained in *W* is *Socrates?* If we try to employ the properties we use to identify him in *this* world, our efforts may well end in dismal failure—perhaps in that world it is Xenophon or maybe even Thrasymachus that is Plato's mentor and exhibits the splendidly single-minded passion for truth and justice that characterizes Socrates in this. But if we cannot identify him in *W*, so the argument continues, then we really do not understand the assertion that he exists there. If we cannot even identify him, we would not know whom we were talking about, in saying that Socrates exists in that world or has this or that property therein. In order to make sense of such talk, we must have a *criterion* or *principle* that enables us to identify Socrates from world to world. This criterion must include some property that Socrates has in each world in which he exists—and if it is sufficient to enable us to *pick him out* in a given world, distinguish him from other things, it must be a property he alone has in these worlds. Further, if the property (or properties) in question is to enable us to pick him out, it must in some broad sense be "empirically manifest"—it must resemble such properties as having such-and-such a name, address, Social Security number, height, weight, and general appearance in that we can tell by broadly empirical means whether a given object has or lacks it. How, otherwise, could we use it to *pick out* or *identify* him? So, if it is intelligible to suppose that Socrates exists in more than one world, there must be some empirically manifest property that he and he alone has in each of the worlds in which he exists. Now obviously we do not know of any such property, or even that there is such a property. Indeed, it is hard to see how there *could* be such a property. But then the very idea of Transworld Identity is not really intelligible—in which case we must suppose that no object exists in more than one world.

The first thing to note about the objection outlined above is that it seems to arise out of a certain *picture* or *image*. We imagine ourselves somehow peering into another world; we ask ourselves whether Socrates exists in it. We observe the behavior and characteristics of its denizens and then wonder about which of these, if any, is Socrates. Of course, we realize that he might look quite different in W, if he exists there at all. He might also live at a different place, have different friends and different fingerprints, if, indeed, he has fingers. But how then can we tell which one he *is*? And does it so much as make sense to say that he exists in that world, if there is no way in principle of identifying him, of telling which thing there *is* Socrates?

Now perhaps this picture is useful in certain respects; in the present context, however, it breeds nothing but confusion. For it is this picture that slyly insinuates that the proposition *Socrates exists in other possible worlds* is intelligible to us only if we know of some empirically manifest property that he and he alone has in each world in which he exists. But suppose we consider an analogous temporal situation. In Herbert Spiegelberg's book *The Phenomenological Movement* there are pictures of Franz Brentano at ages 20 and 70 respectively. The youthful Brentano looks much like Apollo; the elderly Brentano resembles nothing so much as Jerome Hines in his portrayal of the dying Czar in Boris Godounov. Most of us will concede that the same object exists at several different times; but do we know of some empirically manifest property $P$ such that a thing is Brentano at a given time $t$ if and only if it has $P$? Surely not; and this casts no shadow whatever on the intelligibility of the claim that Brentano existed at many different times.

Still, isn't the argument made above available here? No doubt there was a time, some fifty years ago, when Spiro Agnew was a precocious baby. But if I understand that assertion, must I not be able to *pick him out, locate* him, at that time? If I cannot identify him, if I cannot tell which of the things that existed at that time was Agnew, then (so goes the argument) I cannot make sense of the claim that he existed at that time. And I could identify him, at $t$, only if I know of some empirically manifest property that he and he alone has at $t$.

But here the argument is manifestly confused. To suppose that Agnew was a precocious baby at $t$ it is not necessary that I be able to pick his picture out of a gallery of babies at $t$. Of course I must know *who he is* to understand this assertion; and perhaps to know that I must know of some property that he and he alone has. Indeed, we might go so far as to concede that this property must be 'empirically manifest' in some sense. But surely it is asking too much to require that I know of such a property that he and he only has *at every time at which he exists*. Of course I must be able to answer the question "Which of the things existing at $t$ is Agnew?" But the answer is trivial; it's that man sitting right over there—the Vice President of the United States.

If this is correct, however, why suppose otherwise in the Transworld case? I understand the proposition that there is a possible world in which Socrates did not teach Plato. Now let $W$ be any such world. Why suppose that a condition of my understanding this is my knowing something about what he would have looked like or where he would have lived, had $W$ been actual? To understand this proposition I must know who Socrates is. Perhaps this involves my knowing of some property that is empirically manifest (whatever exactly that comes to) and unique to Socrates. But what earthly (or otherwise) reason is there for supposing that I must know of some empirically manifest property he has *in that world $W$*? The picture suggests that I must be able to look into $W$ and sift through its inhabitants until I run across one I recognize as Socrates—otherwise I cannot identify him, and hence I do not know whom I am talking about. But here the picture is not doing right by us. For, taken literally, of course, this notion makes no sense. All I know about this world $W$ is that Socrates would not have taught Plato had $W$ obtained. I do not know anything about which other persons would have existed, or—except for his essential properties—which other properties Socrates has in that world. How could I know more, since all I have been told about $W$ is that it is one of the many worlds in which Socrates exists but does not teach Plato?

Accordingly, the claim that I must be able somehow to identify Socrates in $W$—pick him out—is either trivial or based on a confusion. Of course, I must know which of the persons existing in $W$—the persons who would have existed, had $W$ been actual—I am talking about. But the answer, obviously, and trivially, is Socrates. To be able thus to answer, however, I need know nothing further about what Socrates would have been like had $W$ been actual.

But let us imagine the objector regrouping. "If Socrates exists in several worlds," he says, "then even if there need be no *empirically manifest* property he and he alone has in each of them, there must at any rate be some property or other that he and only he has in each world in which he exists. Let us say that such a property is an essence of Socrates. Such an essence meets two conditions: (1) Socrates has it in every world he graces, and (2) nothing distinct from him has it in any world. (By contrast, a property need meet only the first condition to be *essential* to Socrates.) Now a property $P$ entails a property $Q$ if there is no world in which there exists an object that has $P$ but lacks $Q$. So any essence of Socrates entails each of his essential properties—each property that Socrates has in every world in which he exists. Furthermore, if $E$ is an essence of Socrates, then the class $C$ of his essential properties—the properties he has in each world in which he exists—will obviously entail $E$ in the sense that there is no world in which something exemplifies all of these properties but does not exemplify $E$. (What makes this particularly obvious is that any essence of Socrates is essential to him and hence is a member of $C$.) An essence of Socrates, therefore, is, in this sense, equivalent to the class of his essential properties; and Socrates exists in more than one possible world only if he has at least one essence in the explained sense. But at best it is far from clear which (if any) of Socrates' properties are essential to him and even less clear that he has an essence. Nor does there seem to be any way of determining whether he has such a property or, if he does, which properties are entailed by it. So is not the suggestion that he has an essence both gratuitous and problematic? We can and should avoid this whole problem by accepting TWI." Thus far the objector.

What can be said by way of reply? First, that if we follow this counsel, we gain all the advantages of theft over honest toil, as Russell says in another connection. The question is whether Socrates has an essence and whether objects do or do not exist in more than one world—not whether we would be saved some work or perplexity if we said they did not. But more fundamentally, TWI does not avoid the question which of Socrates' properties are essential to him. Obviously it gives an answer to that question, and an unsatisfactory one at that; for it says that *all* of his properties are essential to him and that any property he alone has—that of being married to Xantippe, for example—is one of his essences.

These caveats entered, however (and I shall return below to the second), let us consider the objector's main complaint. Is it really so difficult, on The Theory of Transworld Identity, to determine whether Socrates has an essence? In fact, in the actual world, Socrates has the property of being snubnosed. But now consider a world $W$ in which he is not snubnosed. Had $W$ obtained, Socrates would not have been snubnosed; we may say, therefore, that Socrates is non-snubnosed-in-$W$. In general, where $P$ is a property and $W$ a world, to say that $x$ has $P$-in-$W$ is simply to say that $x$ would have had $P$ if $W$ had been actual. So Socrates has the property of *being-non-snubnosed-in-W*; that is, he has this property in Charley, the actual world. In *W*, on the other hand, Socrates has the property of *being-snubnosed-in-Charley*. Indeed, in *any* world in which Socrates exists, he has the property of being snubnosed-in-Charley.[11] This property, therefore, is essential to him. And of course we can generalize the claim: Where *P* is any property Socrates has, the property of having-*P*-in-Charley is essential to him. But now consider some property *P* that Socrates has in fact and that he alone has—*being married to Xantippe*, perhaps, or *being born at such and such a place and time*, or *being A. E. Taylor's favorite philosopher*. The property *having-P-in-Charley* will, of course, be essential to Socrates. Furthermore, each thing distinct from Socrates has its complement essentially, for everything distinct from Socrates has the complement $\bar{P}$ of *P*; hence each such thing has $\bar{P}$-*in-Charley*, and has it essentially, that is, in every world in which it exists. But then everything distinct from Socrates has the complement of *having-P-in-Charley* and has that property essentially. So there is no possible world in which some object distinct from Socrates has the property of having *P*-in-Charley. Not only, then, is this property essential to him; it is also one of his essences. And obviously we can find as many essences of Socrates as you like. Take any property *P* and world *W* such that Socrates alone has *P* in *W*; the property of having *P* in *W* is an essence of Socrates.[12]

Now you may think the very idea of a property like *being-snubnosed-in-Charley* is muddled, perverse, ungainly, or in some other way deserving of abuse and contempt. But where, exactly (or even approximately), is the muddle? We must not let this terminology mislead us into thinking that if there is such a property, then Charley must be a geographical unit or place—like Wyoming, for example—so that this property would be like *being mugged in New Jersey*. Socrates elected to remain in Athens and drink the hemlock, instead of fleeing to Thebes. He had the opportunity to take the latter course, however, and it was certainly possible that he do so. So there are possible worlds in which Socrates flees to Thebes and does not drink the hemlock. Now let *W* be any such world. Certainly it is true of Socrates that if *W* had been actual, he would have fled to Thebes; but that is all that is meant by saying that Socrates had the property of fleeing-to-Thebes-in-*W*. It is certainly not easy to see that this property is mysterious, underhanded, inelegant, or that it merits much by way of scorn and obloquy.

The objector, therefore, is right in claiming that if Socrates exists in several worlds, he must have an essence. His objection to the latter idea, however, is not impressive. Is there really something problematic or untoward in the idea of Transworld Identity? Is there really a problem of Transworld Identification? If there is, I am at a loss to see what it might be.

Of course there are legitimate problems in the neighborhood— problems that often are exposed when the subject ostensibly under discussion is Transworld Identity. For we might ask such questions as these: Is there a world *W* and an object *x* existing in *W* such that *x* is identical with Socrates, and *x*, let us say, was born in 1500 B.C. or was an eighteenth-century Irish washerwoman? These questions advertise themselves as questions about Transworld Identity; in fact they are questions concerning which of Socrates' properties are essential to him. Could he have had the property of being disembodied-at-some-time-or-other? Or the property of having-an-alligator-body-at-some-time-or-other? These are legitimate questions to which there are no easy answers. (Socrates himself suggests that everyone actually has the former property, while some of his more snappish acquaintances may have the latter.) These are real questions; but they need not shake our confidence that some of Socrates' properties are ones he could have lacked, so that Charley is not the only possible world in which he exists. The fact that we are not confident about their answers means only that Socrates has *some* properties such that we cannot easily tell whether or not they are essential to him; it does not so much as suggest that *all* his properties are thus inscrutable. And further, of course, the Theory of Worldbound Individuals, as so far explained, does not avoid these questions; it simply answers them by fiat in insisting that each of Socrates' properties is essential to Socrates.

## II

The arguments for the Theory of Worldbound Individuals, then, are based upon error and confusion. But are there positive reasons for rejecting it? I think there are. The basic thrust of the theory is the contention that no object exists in more than one possible world; this implies the outrageous view that—taking property in the broadest possible sense—no object could have lacked any property that in fact it has. Had the world been different in even the tiniest, most Socrates-irrelevant fashion, Socrates would not have existed. Suppose God created *n* electrons. The theory in question entails the absolute impossibility of His having created both Socrates and *n* + 1 electrons. It thereby fails to distinguish the relation in which he stands to inconsistent attributes—being both married and unmarried, for example—from his relation to such attributes as *fleeing to Thebes*. It is as impossible, according to this theory, that Socrates should have had the latter as the former. Consider furthermore, a proposition like

(5) Socrates is foolish

a proposition which predicates of Socrates some property he lacks. Now presumably (5) is true, in a given possible world, only if Socrates exists in that world and has the property of being foolish therein. But on TWI, there is no such world, and (5) accordingly, is necessarily false, as will be any proposition predicating of Socrates a property he does not in fact have. In the same vein, consider any proposition *P* that is false but contingent. Since *Socrates exists* is true only in Charley, where *P* is false, there is no world in which *P* and *Socrates exists* are both true. The latter, therefore, entails the denial of the former. Accordingly, *Socrates exists* entails every true proposition. And all of this is entirely too extravagant to be believed. If we know anything at all about modality, we know that some of Socrates' properties are accidental, that *Socrates is foolish* is not necessarily false, and that *Socrates exists* does not entail every true proposition.

But here we must consider an exciting new wrinkle to this old theory. Embracing the Theory of Worldbound Individuals, David Lewis adds to it the suggestion that a worldbound individual typically has *counterparts* in other possible worlds:

> *The counterpart relation is our substitute for identity between* things in different worlds. Where some would say that you are in several worlds, in which you have somewhat different properties and somewhat different things happen to you, I prefer to say that you are in the actual world and no other, but you have counterparts in several other worlds. Your counterparts resemble you closely in content and context in important respects. They resemble you more closely than do the other things in their worlds. But they are not really you. For each of them is in his own world, and only you are here in the actual world. Indeed we might say, speaking casually, that your counterparts are you in other worlds, that they and you are the same; but this sameness is no more a literal identity than the sameness between you today and you tomorrow. It would be better to say that your counterparts are men you *would have been*, had the world been otherwise.[13]

Fortified with Counterpart Theory, TWI is no longer obliged to hold that each of Socrates' properties is essential to him; instead, a property is essential to him if and only if each of his counterparts (among whom is Socrates himself) has it. Accordingly, while indeed there is no world in which Socrates, *our* Socrates—the object that in our world is Socrates—lacks the property of being snubnosed, there are no doubt worlds containing *counterparts* of Socrates—counterparts which are not snubnosed. So the property of being snubnosed is not essential to him.

And let us now return to

(5) Socrates is foolish.

TWI seems to imply, paradoxically enough, that this statement is necessarily false. Can Counterpart Theory be of help here? Indeed it can, for, no doubt, Socrates has foolish counterparts in other worlds; and this is sufficient, according to TWI fortified with Counterpart Theory, for the contingency of (5). This proposition is contingently false if there is another world in which it is true; but its truth in a given world does not require the existence, in that world, of what is denoted by 'Socrates' in this. Like 'the first man to climb Mt. Rainier', 'Socrates', according to the present view, denotes different persons in different worlds. Or, as we may also put it, in different worlds different things have the property of being Socrates—just as, in different worlds, different things have the property of being the first man to climb Rainier.

Socrateity, then, or the property of being Socrates, is not the property of being identical with the person who in Charley, the actual world, is Socrates; it is not the property of being that person. It is, instead, a property that could have been had by someone else; roughly, it is the property that is unique to Socrates and his counterparts. You may think it difficult to see just what property that is; and indeed that *is* difficult. In the present context, however, what is important to see is that Socrateity is had by different objects in different worlds. Indeed, on Counterpart Theory an object may have more than one property in a given world; so no doubt there are worlds in which several distinct things exemplify Socrateity. And the point is that (5) is true, in a world *W*, just in case *W* contains an object that is both Socratic and foolish—that is, just in case Socrates has a foolish counterpart and Socrateity a foolish instance in *W*. So what (5) says is or is equivalent to

(6) Something exemplifies both Socrateity and foolishness.

And, of course, this proposition will be true in some but not all worlds.

But what about

(7) Socrates exists?

If nothing exists in more than one world, then presumably Socrates does not, in which case on TWI (fortified with Counterpart Theory though it be), (7) still seems to be true in just one world and still seems paradoxically to entail every true proposition. But here perhaps appearances are deceiving. Counterpart Theory affords the means of denying that (7) is true in only one world. For this proposition, we may say, is true in any world where Socrateity has an instance; since there are many such, there are many worlds in which it is true; hence there are many worlds in which both (7) and some false propositions are true. So the former does not entail every true proposition. But if (7) is true in many worlds, how does the central claim of TWI—that nothing exists in more than one—fit in? If Socrates, along with everything else, exists in only one world, that is, if

(8)  Socrates exists in more than one world

is false, how can (7) be true in more than one world?

But perhaps the partisan of TWI can go so far as to deny that his theory commits him to the falsity of (8). Perhaps he can construe it as the entirely accurate claim that *Socrates exists* is true in more than one world. But how, then, does (8) comport with the central claim of TWI? According to the latter, nothing has the property of existing in more than one world. How, then, can TWI sensibly hold that (8) is true? As follows, perhaps. Suppose the predicate "exists in more than one world" expresses a property that, according to TWI, no object has. Then (8), if true, must not, of course, be seen as predicating that property of Socrates—if it did, it would be false. Perhaps it *looks* as if it predicates that property of Socrates; in fact, however, it does not. What it does instead is to predicate *truth in more than one world of Socrates exists.* There is an instructive parallel between (8) so construed and

(9)  The number of planets is possibly greater than nine.

Read *de dicto*, (9) quite properly predicates possibility of

(10)  The number of planets is greater than nine.

It is plausible to add, furthermore, that the words "is possibly greater than nine" express a property—the property a thing has just in case it is possibly greater than nine. Every number greater than nine enjoys this property; that is to say, each number greater than nine is *possibly* greater than nine. The number of planets, however, being nine, does not have the property in question. (9), therefore, can be read as a true *de dicto* assertion; but, thus read, it does not predicate of the object named by "the number of planets" the property expressed by "is possibly greater than seven."

Similarly, then, for (8); the words "exists in more than one world" express a property that (if TWI is true) nothing has; the proposition in question, however, does not predicate that property of anything and hence need not (at any rate on that account) be false. Furthermore, the argument from

(11)  Nothing exists in more than one world

to the falsehood of (8) is to be rejected. We may compare this argument with another:

(12)  Every number greater than seven is necessarily greater than seven.
(13)  The number of planets is greater than seven.

Hence

(14)  The number of planets is necessarily greater than seven.

If we construe (14) as the *de dicto* claim that

(15)  The number of planets is greater than seven

is necessarily true, then it obviously fails to follow from (12) and (13). (12) says that every number meeting a certain condition has a certain property—that of being necessarily greater than seven. According to (13), the number of planets meets that condition. (14), however, is not the consequent *de re* assertion that the number of planets has that property; it is instead the false (and inconsequent) *de dicto* assertion that (15) is necessarily true. But now the same can be said for (8). This is not the *de re* assertion that some specific object has the property that (11) says nothing has. *That* assertion, indeed, is precluded by (11) and thus is false on TWI. Instead, we must look upon (8) as the *de dicto* allegation that *Socrates exists* is true in more than one world—an allegation quite consistent with (11). What we have here, then, as in the inference of (14) from (12) and (13), is another *de re-de dicto* ambiguity.

So the partisan of TWI need not hold that Socrates has all his properties essentially, or that *Socrates exists* entails every true proposition. Indeed, he can go so far as to join the upholder of Transworld Identity in affirming the truth of sentence (8). You may think this course on his part less ingenuous than ingenious; and so, perhaps it is. Indeed, as we shall see, a certain disingenuousness is perhaps a salient feature of TWI. But so far the addition of Counterpart Theory seems to provide TWI with a solution for difficulties it could not otherwise cope with.

Despite its fortification with Counterpart Theory, however, the Theory of Worldbound Individuals is open to a pair of decisive objections. Perhaps we can approach the first of these as follows. Consider the following eccentric proposition:

(16)  Everyone is at least as tall as he is.

It is plausible to consider that this proposition predicates a certain property of each person—a property that is universally shared. It predicates of Lew Alcindor, for example, the property of being at least as tall as he himself is, a property that in no way distinguishes him from anyone else. But the proposition also predicates of each person a property he need not share with others. For what it also says of Lew Alcindor is that he has the property of being at least as tall as Lew Alcindor—a property he shares with nearly no one. The same things hold for

(17)  Everything is identical with itself.

This proposition predicates of each object the property of being self-identical—a property it shares with everything else. But it also says of any given object $x$ that it has the property of being identical with $x$—a property unique to *x*. Socrates, for example, has the property of being essentially identical with Socrates, as well as that of being essentially self-identical. It is natural to say that these two properties *coincide* on Socrates in the sense that it is impossible that he have one but not the other.

But in TWI (henceforth understood to include Counterpart Theory) these two properties come apart. For while Socrates, of course, has no counterparts that lack self-identity, he does have counterparts that lack identity-with-Socrates. He alone of all of his counterparts, in fact, has the property of being identical with Socrates—the property, that is, of being identical with the object that in fact instantiates Socrateity. It is true, no doubt, that each of Socrates' counterparts has Socrateity, so that a counterpart (Socrates$_w$, say) of Socrates in a world *W* has the property of being identical with the thing that *in W* is Socrates or has Socrateity. But, of course, Socrates$_w$ is *distinct from* Socrates—the person who *in fact* is Socrates. Accordingly, some of Socrates' counterparts have the property of being distinct from Socrates. This means that (according to Counterpart Theory) the two properties predicated of Socrates by (17) do not coincide on Socrates. Indeed he has the property of being essentially self-identical, but he does not have the property of being essentially identical with Socrates. And this is the first of the two objections I promised. According to Counterpart Theory, the property of being identical with myself, unlike the property of self-identity, is not essential to me. Hence I could have been someone else. And this, I take it, is genuinely paradoxical. I could have been different in many ways, no doubt; but it makes no sense to suppose that I could have been someone else—someone, who, had he existed, would have been distinct from me. And yet Counterpart Theory, thus explained, implies not merely that I *could* have been distinct from myself, but that I *would* have been distinct from myself had things gone differently in even the most miniscule detail.

We can approach the same matter a bit differently. According to Counterpart Theory,

(18) I could have been taller than I am

is no doubt true. For what (18) requires is that there be a world in which I have a counterpart whose height exceeds the height I actually enjoy. But then similarly

(19) I could have been a different person from the one I am

will be true just in case there is a world in which I have a counterpart who is a different person from the one I actually am. And of course the Counterpart Theorist will hold that I do have such counterparts; so he must hold that (19) is true. Indeed, he must put up with something even worse; Counterpart Theory implies, not merely that I *could* have been a different person from the one I am, but that I *would* have been a different person, had things gone differently in even the most miniscule detail. More exactly, what Counterpart Theory implies is the truth of

(20) If *S*, then either I would not have existed or I would have been a different person from the one I am

where '*S*' is replaced by any false sentence. For such an instance of (20) will be true if every world in which *S* holds is one in which I lack a counterpart or have one that is a different person from the one I am. And, of course, if *S* is false, then every world in which it holds *is* one in which I either lack a counterpart or have one who is a different person from the one I am. If a leaf deep in the mountain fastness of the North Cascades had fallen in October 31, 1876, the day before it actually fell, then (according to Counterpart Theory) I should have been either nonexistent or else a different person from the one I am. And surely this is false.

According to TWI-Counterpart Theory, therefore, I have self-identity essentially but identity with myself accidentally. Although I could not have had self-diversity, I could have been diverse from myself, I could have been someone else. But there is a related and perhaps more important objection. The characteristic feature of TWI is that each of us (and everything else) would not so much as have existed had things been different in even the most insignificant fashion. This is itself not at all easy to believe. Asked to think of possible but non-actual states of affairs, we come up with such items as *Paul's being a good tennis player*; we suppose that there is a possible state of affairs such that, had it obtained, Paul himself—the very person we know and love so well—would have existed and had some property that, lamentably enough, he lacks. Perhaps this point becomes even more poignant if we take it personally. According to TWI, I would not have existed had things been in even the slightest way different. Had I had an extra cornflake for breakfast, I should not now exist. A narrow escape if there ever was one! The very idea fills one with existential Angst; the merest misstep has dramatic consequences indeed.

But of course the Angst is misplaced. For, according to TWI, there is no world in which I have that extra cornflake; it is not logically or metaphysically possible that I should have done so. And this holds whether or not TWI is fortified with Counterpart Theory; the latter's promise to relieve the former of this embarrassing consequence is not fulfilled. I am now confronted with what seems to me to be a choice; I can load my pipe with Dunhill's Standard Mixture or with Balkan Sobranie, both being available and congenial. I believe that it is possible for me to do either of these things and that which I do is up to me. According to TWI, however, one of these events will take place and the other has not so much as a ghost of a chance. For one of these takes place in the actual world and the other occurs in no possible world whatever. If I shall, in fact, smoke Sobranie, then smoking Dunhill is as far out of the question as smoking the number 7. No doubt the partisan of TWI will protest that it is possible for me to take an action *A* if there is a world in which I have a counterpart who takes that action. But is not this just to redefine, change, the meaning of the locution 'it is possible for me'? Of what relevance to my being able to take an action *A* is the fact, if it is a fact, that there is a possible state of affairs such that, had it obtained, someone very like but distinct from me would have taken *A*? Surely this gives me no reason at all for supposing it possible that *I* take this action. Of course we can give a new sense to the terms involved; but to do so is just to change the subject.

The difficulty with TWI in its original Leibnizian forms, I said, was that it implied that each object has each of its properties essentially; and the original attractiveness of Counterpart Theory was its promise to overcome that difficulty. This promise, I think, is illusory. Of course we can define the locution 'has *P* essentially' in the way suggested by Counterpart Theory; and then we will be in verbal agreement with the truth that objects have some of their properties accidentally. But the agreement, I suggest, is *only* verbal. For according to TWI, if in fact I have a property *P*, then there is no possible world in which I lack it. It is not possible that I should have lacked it. Of course there may be a state of affairs *S* such that had it obtained, there would have existed someone similar to me that would have lacked *P*; but how is this even relevant to the question where *I* could have lacked *P*—whether it is possible that *I* should not have had *P*? This seems no more to the point than the possibility that there be someone with my *name* who lacks *P*. And hence I do not think Counterpart Theory succeeds in overcoming the main objection to TWI; that difficulty remains.

By way of summary and conclusion, then: our initial insight into these matters is that objects have only some of their properties essentially; and an object *x* has a property *P* contingently only if there is a possible state of affairs *S* such that *x* would not have had *P* had *S* obtained. This joint affirmation obviously implies that the same object exists in more than one possible world—an idea that some find difficult or incoherent. The objections to this idea, however, do not withstand careful scrutiny. To reject it, furthermore, is to hold that an object exists in exactly one possible world, and this alternative entails—with or without the fortification of Counterpart Theory—that each object has each of its properties essentially.

NOTES

1. See chapters 1 and 2 of this volume.

2. As has been argued by Benson Mates, "Leibniz on Possible Worlds," *Logic, Methodology, and Philosophy of Science*, 3rd ed. (Amsterdam: Van Rootsclaar and Staal, 1968).

3. "Transworld Identification," read at an APA Symposium, Chicago, 1967.

4. "Identity through Possible Worlds: Some Questions," *Nous*, I (1967), 1.

5. "Counterpart Theory and Quantified Modal Logic," *Journal of Philosophy*, LXV (March, 1968), 113.

6. "External and Internal Relations," *Philosophical Studies* (London: Routledge and Kegan Paul, 1922), p. 287.

7. Ibid., p. 289.

8. Letter from Leibniz to Arnauld, July 14, 1686. Leibniz makes very nearly the same statement in a letter to Count von Hessen-Rheinfels, May 1686 (p. 111), *Discourse on Metaphysics* (LaSalle, Ill.: Open Court, 1962), pp. 127–28. Published in the *Discourse* as well.

9. So David Lewis: "$P_2$ [the postulate according to which nothing exists in more than one world] serves only to rule out avoidable problems of individuation" ("Counterpart Theory").

10. But see Chisholm, "Identity through Possible Worlds," pp. 1–8.

11. If, as I do, we make the $S_2$-like sopposition that if a given state of affairs (or proposition) $S$ is possible, then $S$ is possible in every world. See chapter 2, this volume.

12. For more discussion of his essences (and for discussion of more of his essences) see chapter 2, this volume.

13. "Counterpart Theory," pp. 114–15. I said David Lewis embraces TWI; but this is not entirely accurate. Speaking of the Counterpart Relation, he says, "Yet with this substitute in use, it would not matter if some things *were* identical with some of their counterparts after all! $P_2$ [the postulate according to which objects are worldbound] serves only to rule out avoidable problems of individuation." One may offer and study means of formalizing modal discourse for a variety of reasons, and TWI is not really essential to Lewis's program. What I shall be quarreling with in ensuing pages is not that program, but the view which takes TWI as the sober, metaphysical truth of the matter.

# 4

## The Nature of Necessity, Chapter VIII

*Possible but Unactual Objects: On What There Isn't*

### 1. Predicative and Impredicative Singular Propositions

Our subject has been the venerable contention that there are or could be objects that do not exist—more specifically, the Classical Argument for that claim. This argument, you recall, had three essential premises:

(1) There are some singular negative existential propositions,
(2) Some singular negative existentials are possibly true,

and

(3) Any world in which a singular proposition is true, is one in which *there is* such a thing as its subject, or in which its subject has being if not existence.

In chapter 7 we examined objections to (1); we have found them wanting. Among the things there are we do indeed find such singular existential propositions as

(23*) Socrates exists

i.e., Socrates has the property of existing; and such singular negative existentials as

(13*) Socrates does not have the property of existing.

Furthermore, some of these singular negative existentials are indeed possible. So if we accept the Ontological Principle we seem to find the original argument intact. We seem committed to the supposition that there are or could have been possible but nonexistent objects.

But now suppose we take a closer look at singular propositions and the Ontological Principle. The former, we recall, come in two varieties: those that *predicate* a property of their subject, and those that *deny* a property of it. We may call them respectively *predicative* and *impredicative* singular propositions.

(4)  Socrates was snubnosed

for example, is a predicative singular proposition. What would be an example of an impredicative singular proposition?

(5)  Socrates was not snubnosed,

we say, pleased with our alacrity. But sentence (5) is ambiguous; it may express either

(5')  Socrates was nonsnubnosed

which is really a predicative singular proposition, or

(5")  It is false that Socrates was snubnosed

which is properly impredicative. There is a *de re-de dicto* difference here; (5') predicates of Socrates the property of being nonsnubnosed, while (5") predicates of (4) the property of being false.

Now the Ontological Principle does have a certain attractiveness and plausibility. But (as presently stated, anyway) it exploits our tendency to overlook the difference between (5') and (5"). Its plausibility, I suggest, has to do with *predicative* rather than impredicative singular propositions; with propositions like (5') rather than ones like (5"). It *is* plausible to say that

(6)  Any world in which a *predicative* singular proposition is true, is one in which the subject of that proposition has being or existence.

Call this the *Restricted Ontological Principle*. Not only is it plausible; I think it is true. For any world in which there is a true predicative singular proposition whose subject is Socrates, let us say, is a world in which Socrates has some property or other. If such a world had been actual, Socrates would have had some property. And how could he have had a property if there simply were no such thing as Socrates at all? So (6) is true. But if we fail to note the distinction between

(5')  Socrates was nonsnubnosed

and

(5")  It is false that Socrates was snubnosed

we may inadvertently credit the Ontological Principle with a plausibility that property belongs to the Restricted Ontological Principle alone. For if we fail to note that a proposition *denying* a property $P$ of Socrates need not predicate its complement of him, we easily fall into the error of supposing that the contradictories of predicative propositions are themselves predicative. And in the presence of this error, the Restricted and unrestricted Ontological Principles are equivalent. Feeling the legitimate tug of the former, we seem obliged to assert the latter, which together with the truths (1) and (2), entails that there are or could have been things that do not exist.

But once we recognize the distinction between predicative and impredicative singular propositions, we can give the Restricted Ontological Principle its due without endorsing the Classical Argument. For this distinction applies, of course, to singular existentials as well as to other singular propositions. We must distinguish the impredicative

(13*)  Socrates does not have the property of existing

better put, perhaps, as

(13*)  It is false that Socrates has the property of existing

from the predicative

(13**)  Socrates has the property of nonexistence.

(13*) is the contradictory of (23*) and is true in just those worlds where the latter is false. We need not conclude, however, that (13**) is true in those or any other worlds; and in fact, I suggest, this proposition is true in no possible worlds whatever. If there *were* a world in which (13**) *is* true, then certainly in that world Socrates would be but not exist. But the fact is there are no such worlds. (13**) is necessarily false; and Socrates is essentially existent.

## 2. The Classical Argument Fails

The sentence 'Socrates does not exist', therefore, can be used to express three quite different propositions: (13), the proposition, whatever exactly it is, that a historian might claim to discover; (13*), the impredicative singular proposition; and (13**), a necessarily false proposition predicating of Socrates the property of nonexistence. Accordingly, the proper response to the Classical Argument is this. Indeed some singular negative existentials are possibly true: those that are impredicative. But once we have the distinction between predicative and impredicative singular propositions clear, we see that it is the Restricted Ontological Principle, not its unrestricted colleague, that is intuitively plausible. Given this principle and the possible truth of impredicative singular negative existentials, however, it does not follow that there are or could have been things that do not exist.

A firm grasp on the distinction between predicative and impredicative singular propositions enables us to clear up a residual anomaly attaching to (6). That principle affirms that a world in which a singular predicative proposition is true, is one in which its subject either exists or *has being*; but now we see that this second disjunct is as pointless as it is puzzling. The truth of the matter is

(7) Any world in which a singular predicative proposition is true, is one in which its subject *exists*.

Failing to note the distinction between predicative and impredicative singular propositions (and consequently assuming them all predicative) we may reason that (7) must be false as follows: clearly there are worlds where singular negative existentials are true; but by hypothesis their subjects do not *exist* in those worlds; so (7) must be false. But now we see the error of our ways: although some singular negative existentials are possibly true, none of these are predicative. So this implausible notion of being or thereisness is uncalled for; and there remains no obstacle to accepting (7)—which, after all, is both the source of the attractiveness of the Ontological Principle and the truth in it.

Accordingly, singular propositions like

(8) Socrates is wise

and

(9) Socrates is unwise

are true only in worlds where their subject exists. (8) and (9) are not true where Socrates does not exist, where Socrateity is not exemplified. If *W* is a world where Socrates does not exist, both (8) and (9) are false in *W* and their impredicative denials are both true. In worlds where he does not exist, Socrates has no properties at all, not even that of nonexistence.[1]

## 3. CREATURES OF FICTION

But now we must recognize a consideration that has been clamoring for attention all along. Statements like

(10) Hamlet was unmarried

and

(11) Lear had three daughters

are obviously, we shall be told, true singular statements about Hamlet and Lear. Hence Hamlet and Lear must be objects of some kind or other and must have being of some kind or other. Now Hamlet and Lear do not in fact exist; but clearly they could have. So there must be possible worlds in which Lear and Hamlet exist; hence they are possible but unactual objects; hence there are some.

Essential to this argument is the idea that when we say 'Hamlet was unmarried' we are talking about an object named 'Hamlet' and describing it by predicating of it a property it actually has—the idea that such statements as (10) and (11) are indeed singular statements about objects named 'Hamlet' and 'Lear'. Call this 'the Descriptivist Premise; and suppose we examine it. Stories (taken broadly) are to be thought of as descriptions of something or other; they consist in true assertions about objects of a certain sort. Ophelia was indeed Hamlet's girl friend, just as the play has it; and when we make this assertion we are predicating that property of an object that does not exist but could have.

There are initially at least three objections to this account—three peculiar and interesting facts about fiction that the view in question does not easily accommodate. First of all, both 'Lear exists' and 'Lear does not exist' express true propositions. Although Lear does not *really* exist, he does exist *in the play*—just as certainly as he has three daughters in the play. In this regard, his status differs from that of the Grand Inquisitor in the *Brothers Karamazov*; the latter is only a character in Ivan's parable and exists neither in reality nor in the novel. On the Descriptivist Account it is easy to see that Lear does not exist; after all he is a nonexistent possible object. But how then shall we contrast his status with that of the Grand Inquisitor? Shall we say that the latter is a merely possible possible object?

Second, sentences such as

(12)  Santa Claus wears a size ten shoe

seem to have a peculiar status. The myths and legends say nothing about the size of Santa's feet. It seems wrong, however, to say that we just do not happen to *know* whether (12) is true or false; there seems nothing *to* know here. But on the descriptivist view presumably Santa Claus (who clearly has feet) does have either a size ten foot or else a foot of some other size.

Thirdly, such statements as (10) and (11) are presumably *contingent* on the Descriptivist View. In fact Lear had just three daughters, but no doubt in other possible worlds he has maybe one son and three daughters. Now how did Shakespeare know just how many children to give him? If it is only a contingent truth that he has just three daughters, then is it not quite possible that Shakespeare made a mistake? Perhaps he had only two daughters, Goneril being the fruit of an illicit liaison between Lear's wife and Gloucester. Perhaps Shakespeare, in ignorance of this, made a simple factual mistake. Or perhaps Shakespeare was unaware of the fact that Lear once took a trip through the Low Countries, was enamored of a Frisian milkmaid, and became the progenitor of a long line of Calvinist clergymen.

But of course these suppositions are absurd. *You and I* can get Lear's properties wrong; not having read the play recently I may perhaps think that he had just one daughter; but Shakespeare could not have made that sort of mistake in creating the play. Still, does the Descriptivist View not imply that he could? If Shakespeare, in writing his play, *is describing* something, it would certainly seem plausible to suppose that he could *misdescribe* it, get its properties wrong. And how can the Descriptivist View accommodate this fact?

Another difficulty has been emphasized by David Kaplan. According to Descriptivism, (10) and (11) express singular predicative propositions about Hamlet and Lear. If so, then 'Lear' in (11) must be functioning as a proper name—a name of a possible but unactual object. But how could it be? On the Searlean view of proper names, one who thus uses 'Lear' must be able to produce an *identifying description* of what he uses it to name. And how could he do that? He starts as follows: Lear is the possible individual who has the properties $P_1, P_2, \ldots, P_n$. But why does he suppose that there is just *one* possible individual with the $P_i$? If there are *any* possible objects that have the $P_i$ there will be as many as you please. For take any property $P_n + 1$ such that $P_n + 1$ and its complement are both consistent with the $P_i$; there will be a possible object that has the $P_i$ and also $P_n + 1$, and another with the $P_i$ and the complement of $P_n + 1$. So how can he single out any one possible but unactual object? A similar fate awaits this view on the historical chain account of names. For the latter requires that a name originate in some kind of dubbing or baptism, broadly conceived. But this means that some person or persons were able to specify or identify the dubbee—perhaps ostensively, perhaps by description. And how could this be done? Clearly no possible but nonexistent individual was dubbed 'Lear' by someone who had it in full view and solemnly (or frivolously) intoned "I dub thee 'Lear.' " So it must have been by description. But then we are back to the previous problem: what was the description and what reason is there for thinking there is just *one* possible individual meeting it? As Kaplan says,

> I fear that those who would so speak have adopted a form of dubbing which corresponds to the logician's existential instantiation: There is at least one cow in yonder barn. Let's call one of them 'Bossie'. Now, how much do you think she weighs? I am skeptical of such dubbings. The logician is very careful in *his* use of such names.[2]

Still the Descriptivist is perhaps not entirely without reply. Suppose we try to develop his reply, as much, perhaps, in the spirit of playful exercise as in that of sober inquiry. No doubt we cannot name just *one* possible object, just as it is not possible (without further ado) to name just one of the cows in Kaplan's barn. But perhaps we need not name things one at a time. Perhaps we can name *all* the cows in the barn at one fell swoop—we could name them all 'Bossie'. If we felt so inclined, we could name every lion in Africa 'Frazier'. No doubt this would be a pointless procedure; still, it could be done. Now why cannot the friend of possibles do the same? He thinks there are many possible objects with the properties Shakespeare attributes to Lear. Why not suppose that when Shakespeare writes his play, he engages in a peculiar kind of dubbing? Perhaps in telling this story Shakespeare is naming every possible object that fits the specifications of the play; he is naming them all 'Lear'.

But here we meet a couple of complications. First, consider these possible objects he is naming 'Lear'. *Where* do they have the relevant properties? According to Descriptivism, the answer is in α, the actual world. But there are reasons for doubt; a wiser answer would be that these are the things that have those properties *in some world or other.* For first, a story may imply that one of its characters is unique. Suppose Frederick Manfred (formerly Feike Feikema) writes a story about someone described as the meanest man in North Dakota. Presumably the friend of possibles will not wish to commit himself to the claim that there is a possible man in North Dakota that has the property of being meaner than any other man—actual or possible—in North Dakota. He may prefer to hold that for any degree of meanness you pick, there is a possible North Dakotan meaner than that. And even if there is a maximal degree of North Dakotan meanness—one such that it is not possible to be both meaner and in North Dakota—it is at best extremely unlikely that Manfred's hero displays it. On the other hand, there are (on this view) any number of possible objects and worlds such that the former have in the latter the property of being the meanest man in North Dakota. Second, a story may detail certain relationships between its characters and actual objects. In H. G. Wells's *War of the Worlds* the Martians destroy New York City sometime during the first half of the twentieth century. But the fact is New York was not destroyed during that period. Not in α, that is; but in plenty of other possible worlds. So Wells's story must be about creatures that destroy New York City in some world distinct from α. Third, we have already seen that some fictional characters are presented as really existing—Ivan, for example, as opposed to the Grand Inquisitor. But Ivan does not exist in α; so the story describes him as he is in some other possible world.

A second complication: Hamlet is not the only character in *Hamlet*; there are also Ophelia, Rosencrantz, Polonius, and all the rest. So in writing the play Shakespeare is not confined to naming things 'Hamlet'. He also dubs things 'Rosencrantz,' 'Guildenstern,' 'Polonius', and the like. (Indeed, perhaps he is naming some object both 'Rosencrantz' and 'Guildenstern'; for perhaps there is a possible object $x$ and worlds $W$ and $W^*$ such that $x$ has the properties the play ascribes to Rosencrantz in $W$ and those of Guildenstern in $W^*$.) The play determines a complex n-place relation ($n$ fixed by the number of its characters); and where $R$ is this relation, the playwright gives the name 'Hamlet' to each possible object $x_1$ for which there are n—1 possible objects $x_2, \ldots, x_n$ such that there is a possible world in which $x_1, x_2, \ldots, x_n$ stand in $R$.

So on this neo-Descriptivist view sentences like

(10) Hamlet was unmarried

and

(11) Lear had three daughters

express singular propositions. Indeed, each expresses an enormous multitude of such propositions: (10), for example, expresses a different singular proposition for each possible object named 'Hamlet'—one for each object that is the first member of some appropriate n-tuple. Now none of these propositions is true in $\alpha$; but where, then, *are* they true? Consider the possible worlds in which R is exemplified by an *n*-tuple of objects that do not exist in $\alpha$: call these *Hamlet Worlds*. For each possible object $x$ dubbed 'Hamlet' by the play, there is a class of Hamlet Worlds in which $x$ exists and has the appropriate properties. Furthermore, for each such class there will be some state of affairs $S$ such that $S$ but no state of affairs including but distinct from $S$, obtains in each member of the class; these are *Hamlet Situations*. For each object named 'Hamlet' there is a distinct Hamlet Situation. And a sentence like (10) expresses a multitude of propositions, each true in at least one Hamlet situation.[3] So propositions from fiction are not in *fact* true; when we say of such propositions as (10) that they *are* true, we are to be understood as pointing out that they are true in some Hamlet Situation.

Thus (10) expresses indefinitely many singular propositions; this embarrassment of riches is no real embarrassment, however, since each is true—that is, each is true in a Hamlet Situation. Hence for most purposes we can ignore their plurality and pretend that (10) expresses but one proposition. And now note how neatly we thus elude the three difficulties that initially beset descriptivism. First, there was the objection that both 'Hamlet exists' and 'Hamlet never really existed' seem to express true propositions. Now we see that the second expresses a bevy of propositions each true in fact, in the actual world, while the first expresses a host of propositions true in the fashion appropriate to fiction—that is, each is true in a Hamlet Situation. Second, there was the fact that a sentence like

(13)  Hamlet wore size ten shoes

seems to have a peculiarly indeterminate status: we feel uncomfortable ascribing either truth or falsity to it. Now we see that our hesitation is justified; for while this sentence expresses a vast company of propositions, none is true or false in any Hamlet Situation. Third, we asked how the Descriptivist can handle Shakespeare's apparent immunity from error in asserting what appear to be contingent propositions. But now we see that in writing the play he concurrently names objects 'Hamlet' and selects states of affairs—the very states of affairs in which the named objects have the properties with which he credits them. So it is no wonder that he cannot easily go wrong here.

Thus does neo-Descriptivism retain the descriptivist posture. But perhaps we must concede that it has about it an air of the arcane and epicyclic. And anyway a descriptivism without the claim that stories give us the sober literal truth—truth in the actual world—about possible objects is like a Platonism without the forms: emasculated, at best. More important, however, is the following point. The Descriptivist position as initially presented contained an *argument* for the claim that there are nonexistent possibles. This argument loses whatever force it may have had once the descriptivist concedes that stories do not apprise us of properties their subjects have in the actual world. For if descriptivist intuitions are satisfied by the suggestion that a story describes its characters as they are *in other possible worlds*, why not hold instead that a piece of fiction is about n-tuples of *actual* objects, ascribing to them properties *they* have in other worlds? If we think stories must be *about* something, why not think of them as about existent objects? No doubt there are possible worlds in which Ronald Reagan, for example, is named 'Rip van Winkle' and has the properties depicted in Irving's story. If we are bent upon a descriptivist account we may suppose that Irving is describing Reagan as he is in these worlds (and the rest of us as we are in our Rip van Winkle worlds). For any fictional character there will be real objects and worlds such that the former have in the latter the properties credited to the fictional character. And hence we have no reason for supposing that stories about Pegasus, Lear, and the rest are about possible but unactualized objects—even if we accept the dubious supposition that they must be about objects of some kind or other.

## 4. NAMES: THEIR FUNCTION IN FICTION

The fact, however (or so it seems to me), is that names such as 'Lear', 'Hamlet', 'Superman', and the like do not (as they normally function in fiction) serve to denote any objects at all. How then *do* they function? Perhaps as follows. Someone writes a story entitled "George's

Adventures": "Once upon a time", he begins, "there was a boy named George who lived in Jamestown, North Dakota. George had many splendid adventures. For example, once he was attacked by an aroused prairie dog when he inadvertently stepped on its burrow. . . ." No doubt "George's Adventures" will not win many prizes; but what, fundamentally, is the author doing in telling this story? Fundamentally, I suggest, he presents and calls our attention to a certain proposition or state of affairs. He brings it to mind for us, helps us focus our attention upon it, enables us to entertain, explore, and contemplate it, a procedure we find amusing and titillating or edifying and instructive as the case may be.

But what sort of proposition does the author present? In the simplest typical case—where, let us say, the story has only one character—a general proposition, one that could be expressed by an existentially quantified sentence whose conjuncts correspond roughly to the results of replacing 'George' in the story's sentences by the quantifier's variable. Let us call the proposition thus related to a story the story's *Story Line* and such an existentially quantified sentence expressing it a *Stylized Sentence*. The initial segment of a Stylized Sentence expressing the Story Line of "George's Adventures" will look like this:

(14)  $(Ex)x$ was named 'George' and $x$ had many splendid adventures and. . . .

where the succeeding conjuncts result from the story's succeeding sentences by replacing occurrences of 'George' therein by the variable '$x$'. Of course the correspondence is *rough*. For example, "George's Adventures" could have begun thus: "George lived in Jamestown, North Dakota. Many interesting things happened to him there; for example, one day. . . ." Here the Story Line is the same as in the previous case even though the author does not explicitly say that someone was named George. But for each fictional name in a story, I suggest, a stylized sentence expressing its Story Line will contain a quantifier and a conjunct introducing that name.

Now of course only an author wooden *in excelsis* could present the Story Line by means of a Stylized Sentence such as (14). A more accomplished storyteller employs an artful mode of presentation complete with all the cunning and pleasing embellishments of stylistic technique. So naturally he replaces subsequent occurrences of the variable by the name introduced in the first conjunct; and he will probably omit that conjunct altogether. Then (unless he is writing in German) he breaks up the result into a lot of shorter sentences and adds his other embellishments.

The essential feature of this account (tentative and incomplete as it is) is that names such as 'George' in "George's Adventures" do not denote anything at all; they function substantially as stylistic variants of variables appearing in a Stylized Sentence. To ask, "Who or what does 'George' denote in 'George's Adventures'?"—is to misunderstand. This name denotes nothing at all in that story. To illustrate a point or give a counterexample I might speak of a pair of philosophers, McX and Wyman[4] who hold peculiar views on some topic or other. Here it would be the sheerest confusion to ask for the denotation of 'McX' and 'Wyman'. It is the same in the case of serious fiction.

Of course this account requires much by way of supplementation and qualification before it can be so much as called an account; many questions remain. For example, real persons and places often turn up in fiction, as do Jamestown in "George's Adventures" and Denmark in *Hamlet*; then the Story Line entails the existence of these persons or objects. Sometimes real people and places are given fictitious names, as is Grand Rapids, Michigan, in Frederick Manfred's *The Primitive*. Sometimes the author pauses to express his own views on some appropriate subject, as Tolstoy does in *War and Peace*; he then briefly deserts fiction for sober assertion. Sometimes it is difficult to discern the Story Line; we may be unable to tell whether it includes the existence of a real person—Henry Kissinger, let us say—detailing his adventures in a state of affairs quite different from the actual world, or whether it only includes the existence of someone similar to Kissinger. Sometimes a story appears to be inconsistent or incoherent as in some time-travel fiction and fairy stories about people who turn into teacups or pumpkins. But then what goes into the Story Line of such a story?

There are plenty of other questions about what to include in the Story Line. Whatever is entailed by what the author explicitly says? Shall we therefore suppose that all of mathematics and necessary truth generally is included in every Story Line, and that *everything* is included in the Story Line of an inconsistent story? Does the Story Line include causal laws if the author seems to be taking them for granted but explicitly mentions none? Does it include trivial and obvious truths known to the author and his intended audience—e.g., that most people are under nine feet tall? Does it include items of misinformation—e.g., that a bilious person suffers from an excess of bile—the author shares with his audience or thinks shared by his audience? These questions all await resolution; I shall say nothing about them here.

So the peculiar talent and virtue of an author of fiction is his wide-ranging and fertile imagination; he helps us explore states of affairs we should never have thought of, left to our own devices. Of course he does not *assert* the propositions that form his stock in trade; as Sir Philip Sydney puts it:

> Now for the poet, he nothing affirms, and therefore never lieth. For, as I take it, to lie is to affirm that to be true which is false . . . But

the poet (as I said before) never affirmeth. . . . And therefore, though he recount things not true, yet because he telleth them not for true, he lieth not—without we will say that Nathan lied in his speech before-alleged to David; which as a wicked man durst scarce say, so think I none so simple would say that Aesop lied in the tales of his beasts; for who thinks that Aesop writ it for actually true were well worthy to have his name chronicled among the beasts he writeth of.[5]

The author does not assert these propositions; he exhibits them, calls them to our attention, invites us to consider and explore them. And hence his immunity from error noted earlier on.

Of course *we* are not thus immune. A critic who insists that Othello was an Eskimo has fallen into egregious error, whether through excess of carelessness or sophistication. For

(15)  Othello was a Moor

is true and

(16)  Othello was an Eskimo

is false. The first is true (again, roughly and subject to qualification and amendment) because the appropriate Story Line entails the existence of a Moor named Othello. (16), however, is false, because the Story Line entails the existence of someone named Othello who was not an Eskimo and it does not entail the existence of anyone else named Othello. (Here I venture no necessary and sufficient conditions for truth and falsehood in fiction; I mean only to indicate a promising line of approach.) But surely there will be sentences such as

(17)  Hamlet wore size 13 shoes

that are neither true nor false. The appropriate Story Line does not entail the existence of someone named Hamlet who wore size 13 shoes; but neither does it entail the existence of someone named Hamlet who did not wear size 13 shoes. So (17) is neither true nor false. Of course a careless critic writing a book on literary characters with large feet might write "Hamlet, furthermore, wore size 13 shoes, as did . . . ." Such a critic would probably be saying what is false; for very likely he would be asserting something that entails that (17) is true; and *that* is false.

As I said, this account requires much by way of development and supplementation and qualification. Here I am less interested in filling out the account than in simply sketching its basic features, thus pointing to an understanding of fiction according to which stories are about nothing at all and the names they contain denote neither actual nor possible objects.

NOTES

    1. And this redeems a promissory note issued in chapter 4, section 8, of *The Nature of Necessity*.

    2. "Bob and Carol and Ted and Alice," in *Approaches to Natural Language*, ed. J. Hintikka, Moravesic, and Suppes (Dordrecht: D. Reidel, 1973).

    3. Recall that a proposition $P$ is true in a state of affairs $S$ if and only if it is impossible that $S$ obtain and $P$ be false; similarly $P$ is false in $S$ if and only if it is impossible that $S$ obtain and $P$ be true.

    4. See W. V. Quine, "On What There Is," in *From a Logical Point of View* (New York: Harper & Row, 1963), p. 2.

    5. *Apology for Poetry*. Quoted in N. Wolterstorff, "A Theory of Fiction," unpublished.

# 5

# Actualism and Possible Worlds

The idea of possible worlds has both promised and, I believe, delivered understanding and insight in a wide range of topics. Pre-eminent here, I think, is the topic of broadly logical possibility, both *de dicto* and *de re*. But there are others: the nature of propositions, properties, and sets; the function of proper names and definite descriptions; the nature of counterfactuals; time and temporal relations; casual determinism; in philosophical theology, the ontological argument, theological determinism, and the problem of evil (see Plantinga 1974, chs. 4 & 9). In one respect, however, the idea of possible worlds may seem to have contributed less to clarity than to confusion; for if we take this idea seriously, we may find ourselves committed to the dubious notion that there are or could have been things that do not exist. Let me explain.

## I. THE CANONICAL CONCEPTION OF POSSIBLE WORLDS

The last quarter-century has seen a series of increasingly impressive and successful attempts to provide a semantical understanding for modal logic and for interesting modal fragments of natural language (see, for example, Kripke [1963] 1974; Lewis 1972, p. 169; and Montague 1974). These efforts suggest the following conception of possible worlds: call it 'the Canonical Conception.' Possible worlds themselves are typically 'taken as primitive,' as the saying goes: but by way of informal explanation it may be said that a possible world is a *way things could have been*—a *total* way. Among these ways things could have been there is one—call it 'α'—that has the distinction of being actual; this is the way things actually are. α is the one possible world that obtains or is actual; the rest are merely possible. Associated with each possible world $W$, furthermore, is a set of individuals or objects: the *domain* of $W$, which we may call $\psi(W)$.' The members of $\psi(W)$ are the objects that *exist in* $W$; and of course different objects may exist in different worlds. As Kripke put it ([1963] 1974, p. 65).

> Intuitively, $\psi(W)$ is the set of all individuals existing in $W$. Notice, of course, that $\psi(W)$ need not be the same set for different arguments $W$, just as, intuitively, in worlds other than the real one, some actually existing individuals may be absent, while new individuals . . . may appear.[1]

Each possible world $W$, then, has its domain $\psi(W)$; but there is also the union—call it $U$—of the domains of all the worlds. This set contains the objects that exist in α, the actual world, together with those, if any, that do not exist in α but do exist in other possible worlds.

On the Canonical Conception, furthermore, *propositions* are thought of as set-theoretical entities—sets of possible worlds, perhaps, or functions from sets of worlds to truth and falsehood. If we think of propositions as sets of worlds, then a proposition is true in a given world $W$ if $W$ is a member of it. *Necessary* propositions are then the propositions true in every world; possible propositions are true in at least one world; impossible propositions are not true in any. Still further, the members of $U$ are thought of as *having properties* and *standing in relations* in possible worlds. Properties and relations, like propositions, are set-theoretic entities: functions, perhaps, from possible worlds to sets of $n$-tuples of members of $U$. If, for simplicity, we ignore relations and stick with properties, we may ignore the $n$-tuples and say that a property is a function from worlds to sets of members of $U$. A property $P$, then, has an *extension* at a given world $W$: the set of objects that is the value of $P$ for that world $W$. An object has a property $P$ in a world $W$ if it is in the extension of $P$ for $W$; and of course an object may have different properties in different worlds. In the actual world, W. V. Quine is a distinguished philosopher; but in some other world he lacks that property and is instead, let us say, a distinguished politician. Modal properties of objects may now be explained as much like modal properties of propositions: an object $x$ has a property $P$ *accidentally* or *contingently* if it has $P$, but does not have $P$ in every possible world; thus the property of being a philosopher is accidental to Quine. $X$ has $P$ *essentially* or *necessarily*, on the other hand, if $x$ has $P$ in every possible world. While *being a philosopher* is accidental to Quine, *being a person*, perhaps, is essential to him; perhaps there is no possible world in which he does not have that property.

Quantification with respect to a given possible world, furthermore, is over the domain of that world; such a proposition as

(1)  (∃x)  x is a purple cow

is true in a given world W only if ψ(W), the domain of W, contains an object that has, in W, the property of being a purple cow. To put it a bit differently, (1) is true, in a world W, only if there is a member of U that is contained in the extension of *being a purple cow* for W and is also contained in ψ(W); the fact, if it is a fact, that some member of U not contained in ψ(W) has the property of being a purple cow in W is irrelevant. And now we can see how such propositions as

(2)  ◊ (∃x)  x is a purple cow

and

(3)  (∃x)  ◊  x is a purple cow

are to be understood. (2) is true if there is a possible world in which (1) is true; it is therefore true if there is a member of U that is also a member of ψ(W) for some world W in which it has the property of being a purple cow. (3), on the other hand, is true if and only if ψ(α), the domain of α, the actual world, contains an object that in some world W has the property of being a purple cow. (2), therefore, would be true and (3) false if no member of ψ(α) is a purple cow in any world, but some member of U exists in a world in which it is a purple cow; (3) would be true and (2) false if some member of ψ(α) is a purple cow in some world, but no member of U is a purple cow in any world in which it exists.

Now here we should pause to celebrate the sheer ingenuity of this scheme. Life is short, however; let us note simply that the Canonical Conception is indeed ingenious and that it has certainly contributed to our understanding of matters modal. In one regard, however, I think it yields confusion rather than clarity: for it suggests that there are things that do not exist. How, exactly, does the question of non-existent objects rear its ugly head? Of course the Canonical Scheme does not as such tell us that there are some objects that do not exist, for perhaps ψ(α), the domain of the actual world, coincides with U. That is, the Canonical Conception does not rule out the idea that among the possible worlds there are some in which exists everything that exists in any world; and for all the scheme tells us, α may be just such a world. There is, however, a very plausible proposition whose conjunction with the Canonical Conception entails that ψ(α) ≠ U. It is certainly plausible to suppose that there could have been an object distinct from each object that does in fact exist; i.e.,

(4)  Possibly, there is an object distinct from each object that exists in α.

If (4) is true, then (on the Canonical Scheme) there is a possible world W in which there exists an object distinct from each of the things that exists in $\alpha$. $\psi(W)$, therefore, contains an object that is not a member of $\psi(\alpha)$; hence the same can be said for $U$. Accordingly, $U$ contains an object that does not exist in $\alpha$; this object, then, does not exist in the actual world and hence does not exist. We are committed to the view that there are some things that don't exist, therefore, if we accept the Canonical Conception and consider that there could have been a thing distinct from each thing that does in fact exist.

And even if we reject (4), we shall still be committed, on the canonical scheme, to the idea that there *could have been* some non-existent objects. For surely there are possible worlds in which you and I do not exist. These worlds are impoverished, no doubt, but not on that account impossible. There is, therefore, a possible world $W$ in which you and I do not exist; but then $\psi(W) \neq U$. So if $W$ had been actual, $U$, the set of possible objects, would have had some members that do not exist; there would have been some nonexistent objects. You and I, in fact, would have been just such objects. The canonical conception of possible worlds, therefore, is committed to the idea that there are or could have been nonexistent objects.

## II. THE ACTUALIST CONCEPTION OF POSSIBLE WORLDS

I said that the canonical conception of possible worlds produces confusion with respect to the notion of nonexistent objects. I said this because I believe there neither are nor could have been things that do not exist; the very idea of a nonexistent object is a confusion, or at best a notion, like that of a square circle, whose exemplification is impossible. In the present context, however, this remark may beg some interesting questions. Let us say instead that the Canonical Conception of possible worlds exacts a substantial ontological toll. If the insight and understanding it undeniably provides can be achieved only at this price, then we have a reason for swallowing hard, and paying it—or perhaps a reason for rejecting the whole idea of possible worlds. What I shall argue, however, is that we can have the insight without paying the price. (Perhaps you will think that this procedure has, in the famous phrase, all the advantages of theft over honest toil; if so, I hope you are mistaken.) Suppose we follow Robert Adams (1974, p. 211) in using the name 'Actualism' to designate the view that there neither are nor could be any nonexistent objects. Possible worlds have sometimes been stigmatized as "illegitimate totalities of undefined objects"; from an actualist point of view this stigmatization has real point. But suppose we try to remove the stigmata; our project is to remain actualists while appropriating what the possible worlds scheme has to offer. I shall try to develop an actualist conception of possible worlds under the following five headings:

(1)  worlds and books;
(2)  properties;
(3)  essence and the α-transform;
(4)  domains and propositions; and
(5)  essences and truth conditions.


## 1. Worlds and Books

We begin with the notion of *states of affairs*. It is obvious, I think, that there are such things as states of affairs: for example, *Quine's being a distinguished philosopher*. Other examples are *Quine's being a distinguished politician, 9's being a prime number*, and the state of affairs consisting in all men's being mortal. Some states of affairs—*Quine's being a philosopher* and *7 + 5's being 12*, for example—obtain or are actual. *Quine's being a politician*, however is a state of affairs that is not actual and does not obtain. Of course it isn't my claim that this state of affairs *does not exist*, or that there simply is no such state of affairs; indeed there is such a state of affairs and it exists just as serenely as your most solidly actual state of affairs. But it does not obtain; it isn't actual. It *could have been* actual, however, and had things been appropriately different, it *would* have been actual; it is a *possible* state of affairs. *9's being prime*, on the other hand, is an impossible state of affairs that neither does nor could have obtained.

Now a possible world is a possible state of affairs. But not just any possible state of affairs is a possible world; to achieve this distinction, a state of affairs must be *complete* or *maximal*. We may explain this as follows. Let us say that a state of affairs $S$ *includes* a state of affairs $S^*$ if it is not possible that $S$ obtain and $S^*$ fail to obtain; and let us say that $S$ *precludes* $S^*$ if it is not possible that both obtain. A maximal state of affairs, then, is one that for every state of affairs $S$, either includes or precludes $S$. And a possible world is a state of affairs that is both possible and maximal. As on the Canonical Conception, just one of these possible worlds, α, has the distinction of being such that every state of affairs it includes is actual; so α is the actual world. Each of the other *could have been* actual but in fact is not. A possible world, therefore, is a state of affairs and is hence an abstract object. So α, the actual world, is an abstract object. It has no center of mass; it is neither a concrete object nor a mereological sum of concrete objects; indeed α, like *Ford's being ingenious*, has no spatial parts at all. Note also that we begin with the notions of possibility and actuality for states of affairs. Given this explanation of possible worlds, we couldn't sensibly go on to explain possibility as inclusion in some possible world, or actuality as inclusion in the actual world; the explanation must go the other way around.

It is also obvious, I believe, that there are such things as *propositions*—the things that are true or false, believed, asserted, denied, entertained, and the like. That there are such things is, I believe, undeniable; but questions may arise as to their nature. We might ask, for example, whether propositions are sentences, or utterances of sentences, or equivalence classes of sentences, or things of quite another sort. We might also ask whether they are *states of affairs*: are there really *two* sorts of things, propositions and states of affairs, or only one? I am inclined to the former view on the ground that propositions have a property, truth or falsehood, not had by states of affairs. But in any event there are propositions and there are states of affairs; and what I say will be true, I hope, even if propositions just are states of affairs.

We may concur with the Canonical Conception in holding that propositions are true or false *in* possible worlds. A proposition $p$ is true in a state of affairs $S$ if it is not possible that $S$ be actual and $p$ be false; thus

(5) Quine is a philosopher

is true in the state of affairs *Quine's being a distinguished philosopher*. A proposition $p$ is true in a world $W$, then, if it is impossible that $W$ obtain and $p$ be false; and the propositions true-in-$\alpha$, evidently, are just the true propositions. Here, of course, it is *truth* that is the basic notion. Truth is not to be explained in terms of truth-in-the-actual-world or truth-in-$\alpha$; the explanation goes the other way around. Truth-in-$\alpha$, for example, is to be defined in terms of truth plus modal notions. The set of propositions true in a given world $W$ is the *book* on $W$. Books, like worlds, have a maximality property: for any proposition $p$ and book $B$, either $B$ contains $p$ or $B$ contains $\bar{p}$, the denial of $p$. The book on $\alpha$, the actual world, is the set of true propositions. It is clear that some propositions are true in exactly one world;

(6) $\alpha$ is actual,

for example, is true in $\alpha$ and $\alpha$ alone. If we wish, therefore, we can take a book to be, not a set of propositions, but a proposition true in just one world.

## 2. Properties

On the canonical conception, objects have properties in worlds. As actualists we may endorse this sentiment: an object $x$ has a property $P$ in a world $W$ if and only if it is not possible that $W$ be actual and $x$ have the complement of $P$. We *are* obliged, however, to reject the Canonical Conception of properties. On that conception a property is a set-theoretical entity of some sort: perhaps a function from worlds to sets of individuals. This conception suffers from two deficiencies. In the first place, it entails that there are no distinct but necessarily coextensive properties—i.e., no distinct properties $P$ and $P^*$ such that there is no world $W$ in which some object has $P$ but no $P^*$. But surely there are. The property of being the square of 3 is necessarily coextensive with the property of being $\int_0^3 x^2 dx$; but surely these are not the very same properties. If the ontological argument is correct, the property of knowing that God does not exist is necessarily coextensive with that of being a square circle; but surely these are not the *same* property, even if that argument is correct.

The second deficiency is more important from the actualist point of view. Clearly enough the property of being a philosopher, for example would have existed even if one of the things that *is* a philosopher—Quine, let's say—had not. But now consider the Canonical Conception: on this view, *being a philosopher* is a function from possible worlds to sets of individuals; it is a set of ordered pairs whose first members are worlds and whose second members are sets of individuals. And this is in conflict with the truth just mentioned. For if Quine had not existed, neither would any set that contains him. Quine's singleton, for example, could not have existed if Quine had not. For from the actualist point of view, if Quine had not existed, there would have been no such thing as Quine at all, in which case there would have been nothing for Quine's singleton to contain; so if Quine had not existed, Quine's singleton, had it existed, would have been empty. But surely the set whose only member is Quine could not have existed but been empty; in those worlds where Quine does not exist, neither does his singleton. And of course the same holds for sets that contain Quine together with other objects. The set $S$ of philosophers, for example—the set whose members are all the philosophers there are—would not have existed if Quine had not. Of course, if Quine had not existed, there would have been a set containing all the philosophers and nothing else; but $S$, the set that does in *fact* contain just the philosophers, would not have existed.

And here we come upon a crucial difference between sets and properties. No distinct sets have the same members; and no set could have lacked any member it has or had any it lacks. But a pair of distinct properties—*being cordate* and *being renate*, for example, or *being Plato's teacher* and *being the shortest Greek philosopher*—can have the same extension; and a property such as *being snubnosed* could have been exemplified by something that does not in fact exemplify it. We might put the difference this way: all sets but not all properties have their extensions essentially. If this is so, however, the actualist must not follow the Canonical Scheme in taking properties to be functions from worlds to sets of individuals. If no set containing Quine exists in any world where Quine does not, the same must be said for any set whose transitive closure contains him. So properties cannot be functions from worlds to sets of individuals; for if they were, then if Quine had not existed, neither would any of his properties; which is absurd.

As actualists, then, we must reject the Canonical Conception of properties; a property is not a function or indeed any set whose transitive closure contains contingent objects. We must agree with the canonical conception, however, in holding that properties are the sorts of things exemplified by objects, and exemplified by objects in possible worlds. An object $x$ has a property $P$ in a world $W$ if $W$ includes $x$'s *having P*. Quine, for example, has that property of being a distinguished philosopher; since that is so, he has that property in $\alpha$, the actual world. No doubt he has it in many other worlds as well. Abstract objects as well as concrete objects have properties in worlds. The number 9 has the property of numbering the planets in $\alpha$; but in some other worlds 9 lacks that property, having its complement instead. The proposition

(7)  Quine is a distinguished philosopher

has the property *truth* in the actual world; in some other worlds it is false. A property $P$ is *essential* to an object $x$ if $x$ has $P$ in every world in which $x$ exists; $x$ has $P$ *accidentally*, on the other hand, if it has $P$ but does not have it essentially. Thus Quine has the property of being a philosopher accidentally; but no doubt the property of being a person is essential to him. (7) has *truth* accidentally; but

(8)  All distinguished philosophers are philosophers

has truth essentially. Indeed, a necessary proposition is just a proposition that has truth essentially; we may therefore see modality *de dicto* as a special case of modality *de re*. Some properties—truth, for example—are essential to some of the things that have them, but accidental to others. Some, like *self-identity*, are essential to all objects and indeed *necessarily* essential to all objects; that is, the proposition

(9)  Everything has self-identity essentially

is necessarily true. Others are essential to those objects that have them, but are had by only some objects; *being a number*, for example, or *being a person*.

Among the properties essential to all objects is *existence*. Some philosophers have argued that existence is not a property; these arguments, however, even when they are coherent, seem to show at most that existence is a special kind of property. And indeed it is special; like self-identity, existence is essential to each object, and necessarily so. For clearly enough, every object has existence in each world in which it exists. That is not to say, however, that every object is a *necessary being*. A necessary being is one that exists in every possible world; and only some objects—numbers, properties, pure sets, propositions, states of affairs, God—have this distinction. Many philosophers have thought there couldn't be a necessary being, that in no possible world is there a being that exists in every possible world.

But from the present point of view this is a whopping error; surely there are as many necessary as contingent beings.

Among the necessary beings, furthermore, are states of affairs and hence possible worlds themselves. Now an object $x$ exists in a world $W$ if and only if it is not possible that $W$ be actual and $x$ fail to exist. It follows that every possible world exists in every possible world and hence in itself; $\alpha$, for example, exists in $\alpha$. This notion has engendered a certain amount of resistance, but not, so far as I can see, for anything like cogent reasons. A possible world $W$ is a state of affairs; since it is not possible that $W$ fail to exist, it is not possible that $W$ be actual and $W$ fail to exist. But that is just what it means to say that $W$ exists in $W$. That $\alpha$ exists in $\alpha$ is thus, so far as I can see, totally unproblematic.


## 3. Essences and the $\alpha$-Transform

Among the properties essential to an object, there is one (or some) of particular significance; these are its *essences*, or individual natures, or, to use Scotus' word, it's haecceities. I'll use 'essence'; it's easier. Scotus did not discover essences; they were recognized by Boethius, who put the matter thus:

> For were it permitted to fabricate a name, I would call that certain quality, singular and incommunicable to any other subsistent, by its fabricated name, so that the form of what is proposed would become clearer. For let the incommunicable property of Plato be called 'Platonity'. For we can call this quality 'Platonity' by a fabricated word, in the way in which we call the quality of man 'humanity'. Therefore, this Platonity is one man's alone, and this not just anyone's, but Plato's. For 'Plato' points out a one and definite substance, and property, that cannot come together in another.[2]

So far as I know, this is the earliest explicit recognition of individual essences; accordingly we might let "Boethianism" name the view that there are such things. On the Boethian conception, an essence of Plato is a property he has essentially; it is, furthermore, "incommunicable to any other" in that there is no possible world in which there exists something distinct from him that has it. It is, we might say, essential to him and essentially unique to him. One such property, says Boethius, is the property of being Plato, or the property of being identical with Plato. Some people have displayed a certain reluctance to recognise such properties as this, but for reasons that are at best obscure. In any event it is trivially easy to state the conditions under which an object has Platonity; an object has it, clearly enough, if and only if that object is Plato.

But this is not the only essence of Plato. To see the others we must note that Plato has *world-indexed* properties. For any property $P$

and world *W*, there is the world-indexed property *P-in-W*; and an object *x* exemplifies *P*-in-*W* if *W* includes *x*'s having *P*. We have already encountered one world-indexed property: truth-in-$\alpha$. Truth-in-$\alpha$ characterizes all the propositions that are in fact true. Furthermore, it characterizes them in every possible world; there are worlds in which

(7)  Quine is a distinguished philosopher

lacks truth, but none in which it lacks truth-in-$\alpha$. (7) could have been false; but even if it *had* been, $\alpha$ would have included the truth of (7), so that (7) would have been true-in-$\alpha$. Truth-in-$\alpha$ is *non-contingent*; every object has it, or its complement, essentially. But the same goes for every world-indexed property; if *P* is a world-indexed property, then no object has *P*, or its complement, accidentally.

Where *P* is a property, let's say that the world indexed property *P*-in-$\alpha$ (call it '$P_\alpha$') is the $\alpha$-transform of *P*; and if *P* is a predicate expressing a property *P*, its $\alpha$-transform $\mathfrak{p}_\alpha$ expresses $P_\alpha$. And now consider any property *Q* that Quine alone has: *being the author of* Word and Object, for example, or *being born at P, T*, where *P* is the place and *T* the time at which he was born. *Q* is accidental to Quine; but its $\alpha$-transform $Q_\alpha$ is essential to him. Indeed, $Q_\alpha$ is one of Quine's essences. To be an essence of Quine, we recall, a property *E* must be essential to him and such that there is no possible world in which there exists an object distinct from him that has *E*. Since $Q_\alpha$ is world-indexed, it satisfies the first condition. But it also satisfies the second. To see this, we must observe first that the property of being identical with Quine is essential to anything that has it; i.e.,

(10)  Necessarily, anything identical with Quine has *being identical with Quine* essentially.

But then it follows that anything that has the complement of *identity-with-Quine*—that is, *diversity from Quine*—has that property essentially:

(11)  Necessarily, anything diverse from Quine has diversity from Quine essentially.

We must also observe that

(12)  Necessarily, an essence of an object *x* entails each property essential to *x*

where a property *P* entails a property *Q* if it is not possible that *P* be exemplified by an object that lacks *Q*. And now suppose there is a world *W* in which there exists an object *x* that is distinct from Quine but has $Q_\alpha$. Then there must be an essence *E* that is exemplified in *W* and entails (11) and (12), both *being distinct from Quine and $Q_\alpha$*. Since *E* entails $Q_\alpha$, *E* is exemplified in $\alpha$—and exemplified by some object that is distinct from Quine and has *Q*. But by hypothesis there is nothing in α that is distinct from Quine and has $Q$; accordingly, $Q\alpha$ is an essence of Quine.

For any property $P$ unique to Quine, therefore, $P\alpha$, its α-transform, is one of his essences. So for any definite description $(ix)$ $Fx$ that denotes Quine, there is a description $(ix)$ $F_\alpha x$ that *essentially* denotes him—singles him out by expressing one of his essences. Here we see an explanation of a phenomenon noted by Keith Donnellan (1974). A sentence containing a description, he says, can sometimes be used to express a proposition equivalent to that expressed by the result of supplanting the description by a proper name of what it denotes. Thus the sentence

(13)  the author of *Word and Object* is ingenious

can be used to express a proposition equivalent to

(14)  Quine is ingenious.

The proposition expressed by (13) is true in a world $W$ where not Quine but someone else—Gerald R. Ford, let's say—writes *Word and Object* if and only if it is *Quine* who is ingenious in $W$; Ford's ingenuity or lack thereof in $W$ is irrelevant. We may see this phenomenon as an implicit application of the α-transform to 'the author of *Word and Object*'; what (13) thus expresses can be put more explicitly as

(15)  the (author of *Word and Object*)$_\alpha$ is ingenious,

a proposition true in the very same worlds as (14).

Now what Donnellan noted is that sentences containing *descriptions* display this phenomenon. For any predicate $\mathfrak{P}$, however, there is its α-transform $\mathfrak{P}_\alpha$. We should therefore expect to find Donnellan's phenomenon displayed in other contexts as well—by universal sentences, for example. These expectations are not disappointed. Rising to address the Alpine Club, I say

(16)  every member of the Alpine Club is a splendid climber!

Here, but for an untoward bit of prolixity, I might as well have gone through the membership roll, uttering a long conjunctive sentence of the form

(17)  $N_1$ is a splendid climber & $N_2$ is a splendid climber & . . . & $N_n$ is a splendid climber

where for each member of the club there is a conjunct attaching 'is a splendid climber' to his name. If $M_1$ . . . $M_n$ are the members of the Club, the proposition expressed by (16) is true, in a given world $W$ only if each of $M_1$ . . . $M_n$ is a splendid climber in $W$; the fact, if it is a fact, that in $W$ the Club contains some non-climbers, or some unsplendid ones, is irrelevant. But then (16) can be put more explicitly as

(18) every (member of the Alpine Club)$_\alpha$ is a splendid climber

We may state the point a bit differently. Suppose '*S*' is a name of the set of members of the Alpine Club; then (16), (17) and (18) express a proposition equivalent to

(19) every member of *S* is a splendid climber.

If we use (16) without implicitly applying the $\alpha$-transform, of course what we assert is not equivalent to (19); for what we then assert is true in a world *W* only if *in W* the Alpine Club contains none but splendid climbers.[3]

## 4. Domains and Propositions

But now back to our main concern. As actualists we reject the canonical conception of properties while agreeing that objects have properties in worlds and that some of their properties are essential to them; and among the properties essential to an object, we have noted, in particular, its essences. But what about domains? On the Canonical Conception, each possible world has its domain: the set of objects that exist in it. Here I have two *caveats*. First, what are domains *for*? For quantifiers to range over, naturally enough. But now we must be careful. On the usual domain-and-variables account, quantification is understood as follows. Consider a universally quantified sentence such as

(20) All spotted dogs are friendly

or

(20) (*x*) (if *x* is a spotted dog, then *x* is friendly).

Here the quantifier is said to range over a set *D* of objects; and what (20) says is true if and only if every spotted dog in *D* is also friendly. But this seems fair enough; why must we be careful? Because it suggests that (20) expresses a proposition equivalent if not identical to

(21) every member of *D* is friendly, if a spotted dog

where *D* is the domain of the quantifier in (20). And this suggestion is clearly false. For consider a possible world where *D* and its members exist, the latter being, if spotted dogs, then friendly, but where there are other spotted dogs—dogs not in *D*—of a nasty and churlish disposition. What (21) expresses is true in that world; what (20) expresses, however, is flatly false therein. (20) and (21) are materially but not logically equivalent—both true or both false, but not true in the same worlds. We may say, if we wish, that in a sentence of the form '(*x*)*Fx*' the quantifier has a domain *D*; but propositions expressed by such a sentence will not in general be equivalent to the claim that every member of $D$ has $F$.

And now for the second, and, in the present context, more relevant *caveat*. On the Canonical scheme, each world $W$ has a domain: the set of objects that exist in $W$. And though it is seldom stated, it is always taken for granted that a possible world $W$ with domain $\psi(W)$ has *essentially* the property of having $\psi(W)$ as its domain. Having $\psi(\alpha)$ as domain is essential to $\alpha$; had another world $\beta$ been actual, other individuals might have existed, but $\psi(\alpha)$ would have been the domain of $\alpha$. From an actualist point of view, however, this pair of claims, i.e.,

(22) for any world $W$ there is a set $\psi(W)$ that contains just those objects that exist in $W$

and

(23) if $D$ is the domain of $W$, then $W$ has essentially the property of having $D$ as its domain

leads to trouble. For a set, as we have already seen, can exist only in those worlds where all of its members exist. Hence $\psi(\alpha)$ would not have existed if any of its members had not. $\psi(\alpha)$, therefore, would not have existed had Socrates, let's say, failed to exist. But if, as (23) affirms, $\alpha$ has essentially the property of being such that $\psi(\alpha)$ is its domain, then $\alpha$ can exist only if $\psi(\alpha)$ does. Hence if Socrates had not existed, the same would have held for $\psi(\alpha)$ and $\alpha$ itself. If we accept both (22) and (23), we are burdened with the alarming consequence that possible worlds are not necessary beings; even the most insignificant pebble on the beach has the distinction of being such that if it had failed to exist, there would have been no such things as $\alpha$ (or any other world whose domain includes that pebble) at all.

This difficulty induces another with respect to the Canonical Conception of propositions as set theoretical entities—sets of possible worlds, let's say. That conception must be rejected in any event; for it entails that there are no distinct but logically equivalent propositions. But clearly this is false.

(24) All bachelors are unmarried

and

(25) $\int_0^3 x^2 dx > 7$

are equivalent. There are those, however, who believe the first without believing or even grasping the second. The first, therefore, has a property not had by the second and is, accordingly, distinct from it. But the principal difficulty with the Canonical Conception is due to the deplorable fragility of sets and domains—their deplorable liability to nonexistence in the worlds where some of their members do not exist.

For consider any true proposition $p$; on the Canonical Conception $p$ will be a set of worlds containing $\alpha$. But now suppose some object—the Taj Mahal, let's say—had not existed; then neither would $\psi(\alpha)$, $\alpha$, or $p$. So if the Taj Mahal had not existed, the same would have held for the truths that $7 + 5 = 12$ and that Socrates was wise; and this is absurd. On the Canonical Conception, only necessarily false propositions together with such items as

(26)  there are no contingent beings

turn out to be necessary beings. This is a distinction, surely, that they do not deserve.

How, then, shall we as actualists think of the domains of possible worlds? We may, if we wish, concur with the Canonical Conception that for each world $W$ there is indeed the set $\psi(W)$ that contains just those objects that exist in $W$. On the actualist view, however, domains lose much of their significance; and they also display some anomalous properties. First of all, domains, as we have seen, are typically contingent beings. If Socrates had not existed, no set that includes him would have, so that $\psi(\alpha)$ would not have existed. Possible worlds, however, are necessary beings; hence worlds do not in general have their domains essentially. If Socrates had not existed, there would have been a set distinct from $\psi(\alpha)$ that would have been the domain of $\alpha$; and if *no* contingent beings had existed, the domain of $\alpha$ would have contained only necessary beings. Second, the domain of any possible world $W$, from the actualist perspective, is a subset of $\psi(\alpha)$. Since there are no objects distinct from those that exists in $\alpha$, $\psi(W)$ cannot contain an object distinct from each that exists in $\alpha$. Of course the actualist will happily concede that there *could have been* an object distinct from any that exists in $\alpha$. Hence there is a possible world $W$ in which there exists an object distinct from any that actually exists. The actualist must hold, therefore, that $\psi(W)$ is a subset of $\psi(\alpha)$— despite the fact that $W$ includes the existence of an object that does not exist in $\alpha$. How can this be managed? How can the actualist understand

(27)  there could have been an object distinct from each object
      that actually exists

if he holds that $\psi(W)$, for any $W$, is a subset of $\psi(\alpha)$?

## 5. Essences and Truth Conditions

Easily enough; he must appeal to essences. Socrates is a contingent being; his essence, however, is not. Properties, like propositions and possible worlds, are necessary beings. If Socrates had not existed, his essence would have been unexemplified, but not non-existent. In worlds where Socrates exists, Socrateity is his essence; *exemplifying Socrateity* is essential to him. Socrateity, however, does not have essentially the property of being exemplified by Socrates; it is not exemplified by him in worlds where he does not exist. In those worlds, of course, it is not exemplified at all; so *being exemplified by Socrates if at all* is essential to Socrateity, while *being exemplified by Socrates* is accidental to it.

Associated with each possible world $W$, furthermore, is the set $\psi_E(W)$, the set of essences exemplified in $W$. $\psi_E(W)$ is the *essential domain* of $W$; and $U_E$, the union of $\psi_E(W)$ for all worlds $W$ is the set of essences. Essential domains have virtues where domains have vices. Properties exist in every world; so, therefore, do sets of them; and hence essential domains are necessary beings. Furthermore, if $\psi_E(W)$ is the essential domain of a world $W$, then $W$ has essentially the property of having $\psi_E(W)$ as its essential domain. And just as properties of other sorts are sometimes unexemplified, so there may be unexemplified essences. If Socrates had not existed, then Socrateity would have been an unexemplified essence. Very likely there are in fact some unexemplified essences; probably there is a world $W$ whose essential domain $\psi_E(W)$ contains an essence that is not in fact exemplified. $U_E$, therefore, no doubt contains some unexemplified essences.

We are now prepared to deal with (27). Before we do so, however, let us see how some simpler types of propositions are to be understood from the actualist perspective. Consider first

(1) $(\exists x)$ $x$ is a purple cow.

(1) is true if and only if some member of $U_E$ is coexemplified with the property of being a purple cow; and (1) is true in a world $W$ if $\psi_E(W)$ contains an essence that is coexemplified with that property in $W$.

(2) Possibly $(\exists x)$ $x$ is a purple cow

is true if there is a world in which (1) is true—if, that is, there is an essence that in some world is coexemplified with *being a purple cow*. (2) is therefore non-contingent—either necessarily true or necessarily false.

(3) $(\exists x)$ possibly $x$ is a purple cow,

on the other hand, is true if some member of $U_E$ is coexemplified with the property of possibly being a purple cow. So (3) is true if some exemplified essence is coexemplified in some possible world with the property *being a purple cow*. More generally, (3) is true in a possible world $W$ if some member of $\psi_E(W)$ is coexemplified in some world $W^*$ with *being a purple cow*. (3) entails (2); but if, as seems likely, it is possible that there be purple cows but also possible that there be no things that could have been purple cows, then (2) does not entail (3).

When we turn to singular propositions, it is evident that one like

(28)  Ford is ingenuous

is true in a world *W* if and only if an essence of Ford is coexemplified with ingenuousness in *W*.

But what about

(29)  Ford is not ingenuous?

The sentence (29) is in fact ambiguous, expressing two quite different propositions. On the one hand it expresses a proposition predicating lack of ingenuousness of Ford, a proposition true in just those worlds where an essence of Ford is coexemplified with lack of ingenuousness. This proposition could be put more explicitly as

(29)*  Ford is disingenuous;

i.e., Ford has the complement of ingenuousness. But (29) also expresses the denial of (28):

(29**)  it is not the case that Ford is ingenuous.

(28) is clearly false in worlds where Ford does not exist; (29**), therefore, is true in those worlds. Indeed, a crucial difference between (29*) and (29**) is that the former but not the latter entails that Ford exists; (29**), unlike (29*), is true in worlds where Ford does not exist.

We may see the distinction between (29*) and (29**) as a *de re—de dicto* difference. (29*) predicates a property of Ford: disingenuousness. (29**), on the other hand, predicates falsehood of (28) but nothing of Ford. (29*) is true in those worlds where an essence of Ford is coexemplified with disingenuousness. Since there neither are nor could have been non-existent objects, there neither are nor could have been non-existent exemplifications of disingenuousness. (29*), therefore, entails that Ford exists. (29**), however, does not. It is true where (28) is false, and true in those worlds in which Ford neither exists nor has any properties.

We may see the ambivalence of the sentence (29) as due to scope ambiguity. In (29**) the sign for negation applies to a sentence and contains the name 'Ford' within its scope. In (29*), however, the sign for negation applies, not to a sentence, but to a predicate, yielding another predicate; and 'Ford' is not within its scope. Where 'Ford' has widest scope, as in (29*), the resulting sentence expresses a proposition that predicates a property of Ford and entails his existence; where the name has less than widest scope the proposition expressed may fail to predicate a property of Ford and may be true in worlds where he does not exist. This interplay between *de re-de dicto* distinctions and scope ambiguity is to be seen elsewhere. A sentence like

(30)  if Socrates is wise, someone is wise

is ambiguous in the same way as (29). It can be read as predicating a property of Socrates: the property of being such that if he is wise then someone is. What it expresses, so read, is put more explicitly as

(30\*)  Socrates is such that if he is wise, then someone is wise,

a proposition true in just those worlds where Socrates exists. But (30) can also express a proposition that predicates a relation of the propositions *Socrates is wise* and *someone is wise*. Since these propositions stand in that relation in every possible world, this proposition is necessarily true. Unlike (30\*), therefore, it is true in worlds where Socrates does not exist. Similarly for

(31)  If anything is identical with Socrates, then something is a person

If we give 'Socrates' widest scope in (31), then what it expresses is a contingent proposition that predicates a property of Socrates and is true only in those worlds where he exists. If we give it narrow scope, however, (31) expresses a necessary proposition—provided, of course that *being a person* is essential to Socrates.

What about singular existential propositions?

(32)  Ford exists

is true in just those worlds where an essence of Ford is coexemplified with existence—the worlds where Ford exists.

(33)  Ford does not exist,

however, is ambiguous in the very same way as (29); it may express either

(33\*)  Ford has nonexistence (the complement of existence)

or

(33\*\*)  it is not the case that Ford exists.

(33\*\*) is the negation of (32) and is true in just those worlds where (32) is false. (33\*), however, is true in just those worlds where an essence of Ford is coexemplified with nonexistence. As actualists we insist that there neither are nor could have been things that don't exist; accordingly there is no world in which an essence is coexemplified with nonexistence; so (33\*) is a necessary falsehood.

We may now return to

(27) there could have been an object distinct from each object
that actually exists.

On the Canonical Conception, (27) is true only if there is a member
x of U such that x does not exist in fact but does exist in some possible
world distinct from α; (27), therefore, is true, on that conception, if
and only if there are some things that don't exist but could have. On
the actualist conception, however, there are no things that don't exist.
How then shall we understand (27)? Easily enough; (27) is true if and
only if there is a world where

(34) there is an object that does not exist in α

is true. But (34) is true in a world W if and only if there is an essence
that is exemplified in W but not in α. (27) is true, therefore, if and
only if there is at least one essence that is exemplified in some world
but not exemplified in fact—if and only if, that is, there is an unexemplified essence. Hence (27) is very likely true. As actualists,
therefore, we may state the matter thus:

(35) although there could have been some things that don't *in
fact* exist, there are no things that don't exist but could have.

These, then, are the essentials of the actualist conception of possible
worlds. It has the virtues but not the vices of the Canonical Conception; we may thus achieve the insights provided by the idea of possible
worlds without supposing that there are or could have been things
that do not exist.[4]

## NOTES

1. For the sake of definiteness, I substantially follow the semantics developed in
this piece. The essentials of the canonical conception, however, are to be found not
just here but in very many recent efforts to provide a semantics for modal logic or
modal portions of natural language.

2. In *Librium de interpretatione editio secunda*, PL 64, 462d–464c. Quoted in Castañeda 1975, pp. 135–36.

3. The α-transform can also help us fathom the behavior of proper names; in
particular it can help us bridge the gap between a broadly Fregean view and the anti-
Fregean claims of Donnellan, Kaplan, Kripke and others. See chapter 6, this volume.

4. In "An actualist semantics for modal logic," Thomas Jager has developed and
axiomatized a semantics for quantified modal logic that presupposes neither that
things have properties in worlds in which they don't exist, nor that there are or could
have been objects that do not exist. In the intended applied semantics, the domain
of a model is taken to be a set of essences; and a proposition expressed by a sentence
of the form $(\exists x)Fx$ is true in a world if and only if some essence is coexemplified, in
that world, with the property expressed by $F$. Copies may be obtained from Professor
Thomas Jager, Department of Mathematics, Calvin College, Grand Rapids, Mich.
49506, U.S.A.

# REFERENCES

Adams, Robert. "Theories of Actuality." *Noûs* 8 (1974), pp. 211–31.

Castañeda, Hector-Neri. "Individuation and Non-identity: A New Look." *American Philosophical Quarterly* 12 (1975), pp. 131–40.

Donnellan, Keith. "Speaking of Nothing." *Philosophical Review* 83 (1974), pp. 3–31.

Kripke, Saul. "Semantical Considerations on Modal Logic." *Acta Philosophica Fennica* 16 (1963), pp. 83–94. Reprinted in *Reference and Modality*, ed. Linsky, pp. 62–72 (Oxford, 1974).

Lewis, David. "General Semantics." In *Semantics of Natural Language*, ed. D. Davidson and G. Harman, pp. 169–218 (Dordrecht, 1972).

Montague, R. *Formal Philosophy*, ed. R. M. Thomason (New Haven, 1974).

Plantinga, Alvin. *The Nature of Necessity* (Oxford, 1974).

Plantinga, Alvin. "The Boethian Compromise." *American Philosophical Quarterly*. Reprinted as ch. 6 of the present volume.

# 6

## The Boethian Compromise

Russell held that ordinary proper names—such names as "Socrates," "Aristotle" and "Muhammad Ali"—are really truncated definite descriptions; "Socrates" for example, may be short (in a given person's use) for something like, say, "the snubnosed Greek philosopher who taught Plato."[1] If so, the result of replacing a name in a sentence by the right description will ordinarily express the same proposition; descriptions can be substituted for names *salva propositione*. On this view, proper names are *semantically equivalent* to descriptions. Frege's view is both more subtle and less clear; but he too held that in many contexts a proper name such as "Aristotle" has the same sense as such a definite description as "the pupil of Plato and teacher of Alexander the Great," so that the sentence "Aristotle was born in Stagira" expresses the same thought as the result of replacing "Aristotle" therein by that description.[2] Let us call such views of proper names *Fregean* views.

According to John Stuart Mill, on the other hand, "Proper Names are not connotative; they denote the individuals who are called by them, but they do not indicate or imply an attribute as belonging to these individuals."[3] More recently, Keith Donnellan,[4] Saul Kripke,[5] David Kaplan[6] and others have joined Mill against Frege and Russell. As they quite properly point out, no description of the sort Russell and Frege had in mind is semantically equivalent to a name like "Socrates." Clearly "the snubnosed teacher of Plato," for example, will not fill the bill, since

(1)  the snubnosed teacher of Plato never taught Plato

or better

(2) the subnosed teacher of Plato was a non-teacher

expresses an impossible proposition, unlike

(3) Socrates was a non-teacher.

But the heart and soul of Fregean views is not that proper names are semantically equivalent to descriptions (after all, the right sort of description might not be available), but that they *have sense*, or *descriptive content*, or that they *"indicate or imply an attribute"*: more briefly, that they *express properties*. And the denial of this claim is the heart and soul of the anti-Fregean views. How then, on these views, *do* proper names function? Mill says proper names have denotation but no connotation; a proper name denotes without expressing a property. He seems to mean that the sole semantic function performed by a proper name is that of denoting its referent; its semantic function is *exhausted* in denoting its referent. The crucial contrast, then, between Fregean and anti-Fregean views is that on the former proper names express properties; on the latter they do not. In what follows I shall first argue that the anti-Fregeans are mistaken; I shall then suggest an alternative in the Fregean spirit.


I

Russell instructs us to test a logical and semantical theory by "its capacity for dealing with puzzles."[7] His own theory of ordinary proper names nicely passes muster with respect to three such puzzles: those presented by empty proper names, by negative existentials containing proper names, and by propositional identity in the context of propositional attitudes. On the other hand the anti-Fregean view, as I shall argue, founders on these rocks.

(i) If, as the anti-Fregeans claim, proper names do not express properties and do no more than denote their referents, then how shall we understand such sentences as

(4) Romulus founded Rome

as used by someone who believes the legend and is intending to assert part of what he believes? In his use "Romulus" denotes nothing at all. But then what proposition, on the anti-Fregean view, does (4) express? It is hard to see, on this view, how such a sentence could express any proposition at all. If a proper name does not express a property but serves merely to denote its referent, then when it fails to have a referent it presumably performs no semantic function at all—in which case (4) would express no proposition at all. Faced with these considerations, Donnellan suggests that sentences like (4) (under the envisaged conditions) do indeed fail to express propositions:

> [A] true negative existence statement expressed by using a name involves a name with no referent and the corresponding positive existence statement, if false, will also. But in other contexts, when a name is used and there is a failure of reference, then no proposition has been expressed—certainly no true proposition. If a child says, 'Santa Claus will come tonight,' he cannot have spoken the truth, although, for various reasons, I think it better to say that he has not even expressed a proposition.[8]

He adds, via a footnote, "Given that this is a statement about reality and that proper names have no descriptive content, then how are we to represent the proposition expressed?"

But surely this is wrong. Someone who utters (4), intending to tell the sober truth, has surely asserted *something*. What he asserts entails, for example, that Rome has not always existed but had a founder. If so, however, (4) does express a proposition, under these conditions, and the semantic function of "Romulus," therein, can't be that of denoting its referent, since it has no referent to denote. But then there will be no adequate anti-Fregean account of an empty proper name as used by someone who mistakenly believes it nonempty and intends to predicate a property of what it denotes.

(ii) A second difficulty for the anti-Fregean is presented by negative existentials. How, on this view, are we to understand such a sentence as

(5)  Romulus did not exist?

Here, of course, we cannot sensibly say that the sentence expresses no proposition; clearly it expresses a truth. But *what* truth? And how does the name "Romulus" there function? Obviously it does not denote an *existent* object; so if it denotes anything at all, it denotes a *non-existent* object. Accordingly, one can give an anti-Fregean account of (5) only by holding that "Romulus" denotes a non-existent object therein, the rest of the sentence quite properly predicating nonexistence of that object. In addition to the things that exist, there are, on this view, some more that do not. The above-mentioned anti-Fregeans show little inclination toward this view, and for (as I see it) good reason: the view is clearly false.[9] So "Romulus" denotes nothing at all in (5). Clearly enough, however, (5) expresses a proposition (since it expresses a truth); hence "Romulus" plays a semantical role of *some* sort therein, though not that of denoting its referent. But how then *does* it function? Is it semantically equivalent in this special existential case to a description? No, says Donnellan:

> . . . [O]n any view we must, I think, accept the following:

(E) That Socrates did not exist entails that it is not true that Socrates was snub-nosed.

Our theory tells us that the second occurrence of 'Socrates' in
(E) is not a concealed definite description. But then neither can
the first occurrence be one. For if we take some definite description
such as the one suggested as what the first occurrence of 'Socrates'
stands for, rejection of the principle of identifying descriptions for
the second occurrence means that it *could* be true that Socrates was
snub-nosed even though no unique individual existed who satisfied
that description. That is to say, if "Socrates" in "Socrates did not
exist" is a concealed definite description, but is not in "Socrates was
snub-nosed," then the antecedent of (E) could be true while the
consequent is false. Since we want to accept the entailment expressed by (E) our theory cannot treat "Socrates" as a concealed
description in existential statements. (p. 22)

How then *are* we to understand (5) and the function of "Romulus"
therein? Donnellan's "Speaking of Nothing" (1976) is the most explicit published treatment of existentials by an anti-Fregean; but he
tells us little, there, about the function of empty proper names in
sentences like (5), and less about the propositions expressed by such
sentences. What he gives is a "rule for negative existential statements
. . . that purports to give the truth conditions for negative existential
statements containing a name. . . . :

(R) if *N* is a proper name that has been used in predicative statements with the intent to refer to some individual, then "*N*
does not exist" is true if and only if the history of those uses
ends in a block. (p. 25)

I refer you to Donnellan's piece for the idea of a block. What is important to see in the present context is that a rule like (R) could
function in more than one way. On the one hand it could give logically necessary and sufficient conditions for the truth of the *proposition*
ordinarily expressed by "*N* does not exist," in which case it would
identify that proposition up to logical equivalence. But (R) does not
function in that way. If it did, the proposition

(6) Socrates does not exist

would be equivalent to

(7) The history of (some specific use of) "Socrates" ends in a
block.

But clearly (6) is not equivalent to (7): clearly Socrates could have
existed no matter what the history of anyone's use of "Socrates"; he
could have had another name or no name at all. Hence (7) is true
but (6) is false in those worlds where, let us say, Socrates exists but is
named "Muhammad Ali," and the history of the appropriate uses of

"Socrates" ends in a block. (6) is logically independent of such propositions as (7) that detail the history of "Socrates."

If so, however, (R) does not give necessary and sufficient conditions for such propositions as (5) and (6). What then does it do?
Presumably it tells us, not under what conditions the *propositions* (5)
and (6) are true, but under what conditions the *sentences* (5) and (6)
express true propositions. These, of course, are quite different enter-
prises. The sentence (6) expresses a truth in just those situations in
which the history of certain uses of the name "Socrates" ends in a
block; and, as we have seen, these are not the same situations as those
in which Socrates does not exist—that is, they are not the same situations as those in which the proposition in fact expressed by (6) is
true. So Donnellan's (R) does not give truth conditions for the *propositions* expressed by (5) and (6); nor does he tell us what those propositions *are*. The question therefore becomes acute: how, from the
anti-Fregean vantage point, shall we understand sentences like (5)
and (6) when they contain empty proper names? What proposition
is expressed by such a sentence? The answer is unclear. What is clear,
however, is that the anti-Fregean cannot properly stick to his anti-
Fregean principles for proper names in existential sentences.

(iii) The third difficulty is presented by propositional identity. If
we think, with the anti-Fregeans, that a proper name typically ex-
hausts its semantic role in denoting its referent, then presumably the
result of replacing it in a sentence like

(8)  Mark Twain was a pessimist

or

(9)  Mark Twain is the same person as Samuel Clemens

by another name of the same object will express the same proposition.
In other words, the anti-Fregean seems committed to the principle
that codesignative proper names in such contexts are intersubstitutable *salva propositione*. Donnellan,[10] indeed, explicitly endorses this
principle; and it certainly seems to follow from the views of Mill sec-
onded by Kripke. But surely it is wrong. Clearly a person could know
the proposition expressed by (8) without knowing that expressed by

(9.5)  Samuel Langhorne Clemens was a pessimist,

just as Lois Lane knows, of course, that Superman is faster than a
speeding bullet but does not know that the same goes for Clark Kent.
There are various expedients that might tempt anti-Fregeans here;
none, I believe, is satisfactory. I don't have the space to pursue the
matter here; some of these problems are clearly brought out in Diana
Ackerman's "Recent Work in the Theory of Reference."[11]

In what follows I shall suggest a view that (dare I say it?) displays
the virtues of both Fregean and anti-Fregean views, but the vices of

neither. The first principle of this view is that proper names do indeed express properties. But what is it, exactly, for a singular term to express a property? The anti-Fregeans deny that proper names express properties; precisely what is it they are anti? We might make a beginning as follows. Suppose we agree that such a singular term as "the shortest spy" expresses at least one property: that of being the shortest spy. It is because that term expresses this property that the sentence.

(10) The shortest spy is a non-(shortest spy)

expresses an impossible proposition, as does

(11) The shortest spy is a non-spy.

This suggests the following initial attempt to capture the notion of property expression. Let's suppose we know what it is for a predicate, such as "is a spy" to express a property, such as *being a spy*. Then we might say that

(12) A singular term *t* expresses a property *P* (with respect to a given context of use) if the sentence ⌜*t* is $\mathscr{P}$⌝ expresses a necessary falsehood (with respect to that context of use)

where $\mathscr{P}$ is a predicate that expresses *P* and ⌜$\overline{\mathscr{P}}$⌝ is its complement. It is then clear that "the shortest spy" expresses the properties *being a spy* and *being a shortest spy*, while "Paul J. Zwier" does not, despite the fact that Paul J. Zwier *is* the shortest spy. On the other hand, it is obvious, given (12), that proper names do express *some* properties—those, for example, like *self-identity* or *being unmarried, if a bachelor*, that are trivially essential to everything. Clearly the sentence

(13) Quine is self-diverse

(where "is self-diverse" expresses the complement of *self-identity*) expresses a necessarily false proposition; hence "Quine" expresses self-identity. It also expresses a more interesting property: (13) is impossible; but so is

(14) Quine is diverse from Quine.

But then "Quine" expresses identity-with-Quine as well as self-identity. The former, of course, is distinct from the latter; *everything*, naturally enough, has self-identity, but Quine alone has identity-with-Quine. Some philosophers find this property somehow objectionable; but the fact (as it seems to me) is that identity-with-Quine is a perfectly intelligible property. In any event it is gratifyingly easy to state the conditions under which an object has it: *x* has identity-with-Quine if and only if *x* is Quine.

Identity-with-Quine is an *individual essence*[12] (individual concept, haecceity) of Quine. Let's say that a property *P* is *essential* to an object *x* iff it is not possible that *x* have its complement—equivalently, iff there is no possible world in which $x$ exists but lacks $P$.[13] Then an essence of Quine is a property that he has essentially and is such that it is not possible that there be an object distinct from him that has it. In terms of possible worlds, an essence of Quine is a property he has in every world in which he exists, and one such that in no possible world is there an object distinct from him that has it. The view that proper names express individual essences has impressive historical credentials: it goes back to Scotus and, before him, to Boethius, who put the matter thus:

> For were it permitted to fabricate a name, I would call that certain quality, singular and incommunicable to any other subsistent, by its fabricated name, so that the form of what is proposed would become clearer. For let the incommunicable property of Plato be called 'Platonity'. For we can call this quality 'Platonity' by a fabricated word, in the way in which we call the quality of man 'humanity'. Therefore, this Platonity is one man's alone, and this not just anyone's but Plato's. For 'Plato' points out a one and definite substance, and property, that cannot come together in another.[14]

So far as I know, this is the first explicit recognition that proper names express essence; let us therefore call this view "Boethianism." On the Boethian conception, an essence of Plato is a property he has essentially; it is, furthermore, "incommunicable to any other" in that it is impossible that something distinct from him should have had it.

The second principle of the present view, then, is that proper names express essences. It is crucially important to see, furthermore, that an object typically has *several* essences. This is evident as follows. Suppose we say that Plato has the *world-indexed* property $P$-*in-W* if and only if $W$ includes Plato's having $P$ (if and only if, that is, it is not possible that $W$ be actual and Plato not have $P$). Now consider any property $P$ that Plato has—*being erudite* for example—and note that the world-indexed property *being-erudite-in-α* (where 'α' is a proper name of the actual world) is essential to him. For while indeed there may be worlds in which Plato is not erudite, there are none in which it is not the case that α includes Plato's being erudite. World-indexed properties are *non-contingent*: for any object $x$ and world-indexed property $P$-*in-W*, $x$ has $P$-*in-W* essentially, or $x$ has its complement essentially.[15] Where $P$ is a property, let's say that the α-transform of $P$ (call it "Pα") is the world-indexed property $P$-*in-α*; and if $\mathcal{P}$ is a predicate expressing $P$, its α-transform $\mathcal{P}α$ expresses $Pα$. And now consider a property Plato alone has—*being Socrates' best student,* for example, or *being born at P,T* where 'P' names the place and 'T' the time at which he was born. The α-transforms of these properties are *essences* of Plato. All of Plato's world-indexed properties are essential to him; hence these two are. There is no possible world, furthermore, in which there is an object distinct from Plato that has either of these properties[16];

they are therefore among his essences. But (*being Socrates' best student*)$\alpha$ is certainly not the same property as (*being born at P, T*)$\alpha$; for clearly a person could know of the first that Plato has it without knowing of the second that he has it. They are therefore (by Leibniz's Law) distinct properties; hence Plato has several distinct essences.

The several essences of Plato, furthermore, are logically but not epistemically equivalent. They are logically equivalent: for any such essences $E$ and $E^*$ there is obviously no possible world in which $E$ is exemplified by an object that does not exemplify $E^*$. On the other hand, they are epistemically inequivalent: it is clearly possible to know or believe that an object has $E$ without knowing or believing that it has $E^*$. I might know, for example, that Plato has the $\alpha$-transform of *being Socrates' best student* without knowing that he has the $\alpha$-transform of *being Aristotle's teacher*. This multiplicity of essences, furthermore, is crucially important to the Boethian view I want to suggest. For if Plato has several distinct essences, then distinct proper names of Plato can express distinct essences. But then (just as Frege and Russell thought) the result of replacing an ordinary proper name in a simple sentence $S$ by a codesignative proper name need not express the same proposition as $S$. The Boethian view is an improvement on Frege and Russell, however, in that on the former but not the latter proper names express only *essential* properties of the objects they denote. Boethius therefore deserves credit for making an important improvement on the Frege-Russell view and for offering a more subtle, adequate, and up-to-date version of it.

But if we are to hold that different proper names of an object express different essences, we shall need a more discriminating account of property expression than that provided by (12). According to (12) a term expresses any property entailed[17] by any property it expresses; but then if a proper name expresses an essence of an object, it will express every property essential to that object and hence all of its essences.[18] How can we achieve a more discriminating notion?

We must begin by noting that the sentence

(15)  $3^2$ is odd

expresses a different proposition from that expressed by

(16)  $\frac{27}{8} \int_0^2 x^2$ is odd;

clearly one might know the one without knowing the other. Indeed, those of us with an imperfect grasp of the calculus may know the first proposition but not even possess the concepts necessary to apprehend the second, thus being unable to *believe* it, let alone know it. (15) and (16), therefore, express different propositions; and this is due to the fact that their singular terms express different properties. "$3^2$ and "$\frac{27}{8} \int_0^2 x^2$" both express essences of *9*, but epistemically inequivalent and hence *different* essences. But if these singular terms can express epistemically inequivalent and hence *different* essences, why can't the same be said for proper names? Perhaps, for example, "Phosphorus" expresses something like the α-transform of being *the last heavenly body to disappear in the morning,* while "Hesperus" expresses the α-transform of *being the first heavenly body to appear in the evening.* And perhaps we can state the relevant notion of property expression as follows. Let us suppose, once more, that we know what it is for a predicate to express a property. The predicate "is the square of 3" expresses the property *being the square of three*; it does not express the properties *being* $\sqrt[3]{729}$ or being $\frac{27}{8} \int_0^2 x^2$, despite the fact that anything having one of these properties is obliged to have the others. A definite description ⌜the $\mathcal{P}$⌝ then expresses the same property as ⌜is the sole $\mathcal{P}$⌝; and a proper name $N$ expresses (in English) a property $P$ if there is a definite description $D$ (in English or some extension of English) such that D expresses $P$ and $N$ and $D$ are intersubstitutable *salva propositione* in sentences of the form "$t$ is $\mathcal{P}$".

The third principle, then, of the Boethian view I advocate is this: different proper names of an object can express logically equivalent but epistemically inequivalent essences of that object. This view, I believe, displays at least three important virtues. First, it enables us to accommodate the insights of the anti-Fregeans within a Fregean context. Second, the Boethian view succeeds where the anti-Fregean view fails: (a) it enables us to see how such sentences as

(17)  Hesperus is the evening star

and

(18)  Phophorus is the evening star

can express epistemically inequivalent propositions, and how

(19)  Hesperus is identical with Phosphorus

can express an informative proposition; (b) it enables us to see what propositions are expressed by sentences containing empty proper names; and (c) it enables us to see what propositions are expressed by existential sentences containing proper names. Finally, as a sort of bonus, the Boethian view enables us to see that proper names in existential sentences function in just the way they do in singular sentences generally.

(i) One of the insights of the anti-Fregeans, of course, is that proper names do not express the sorts of properties Frege, Russell, and their followers take them to. More specifically, in criticizing Frege and Russell, what they really point out (although they don't always put it this way themselves) is that proper names do not express properties *inessential* to their bearers.[19] With this, of course, the Boethian enthusiastically concurs; a use of a proper name of Socrates expresses an essence of Socrates and hence does not express any property in-essential to him. But the anti-Fregeans have other insights. Kripke states one as follows:

> A rough statement of a theory might be the following: an initial baptism takes place. Here the object may be named by ostension, or the reference may be fixed by description. When the name is 'passed from link to link' the receiver of the name must, I think, intend when he learns it to use it with the same reference as the man from whom he heard it.[20]

and according to Donnellan:

> The main idea is that when a speaker uses a name intending to refer to an individual and predicate something of it, successful reference will occur when there is an individual that enters into the historically correct explanation of who it is that the speaker intended to pred-icate something of. That individual will then be the referent and the statement made will be true or false depending upon whether it has the property designated by the predicate.[21]

Donnellan and, less explicitly, Kripke hold that proper names do not express properties; and we might suppose that this is a conse-quence of their view as to how the reference of a proper name is determined. But it isn't. It is entirely possible both that the reference of a proper name is determined in the way they say it is and that proper names express essences. For consider that complex historical relation *R*, whatever exactly it is, that on the Kripke-Donnellan view holds between an object and the names that name it. There is an initial complication: the same proper name may name different ob-jects. So what an objects stands in *R* to is not a name *simpliciter* but a name in a given use—in the case of "Socrates," perhaps its use in Plato's *Dialogues* and in history books and philosophy classes. But sup-pose we ignore this complication, or deal with it by pretending that such names are homonymous: for each person named "Socrates" there is a different name spelled "S o c r a t e s." Now of course

(20) The person that stands in *R* to "Socrates" was wise

does not express the same proposition as

(21) Socrates was wise

(21) but not (20) is true in a world where Socrates is wise but no one is named "Socrates." So "Socrates" does not express the property *being the person that stands in R to "Socrates."* But perhaps it can express the α-transform of that property. If the fact is Socrates alone *does* stand in *R* to "Socrates" then (*being the person that stands in R to "Socrates"*) α is an essence of Socrates, so that the proposition expressed by

(22) the (person that stands in *R* to "Socrates") α was wise

is at least equivalent to (23). And if "Socrates" does express this property, then the reference of "Socrates" is determined in the way Kripke and Donnellan say it is; for then "Socrates" refers to an object $x$ if and only if $x$ stands in $R$ to "Socrates." Thus from our Boethian vantage point we see how it could be both that proper names express essences and that their reference is determined in the way the anti-Fregeans say it is.

And now consider John Searle's Fregean view. Searle holds, roughly, that the name "Socrates" expresses the property *being the person who had enough of the $S_i$*, where the $S_i$ are the identity criteria associated with that name.[22] "Socrates", however, does not express *that* property:

(23)  Socrates had scarcely any of the $S_i$

and

(24)  the person who had enough of the $S_i$ had scarcely any of the $S_i$

do not express equivalent propositions; the proposition expressed by (24) is necessarily false, while that expressed by (23) is true in those possible worlds where, let's say, Socrates meets with a fatal accident at the age of 6 months, thus having scarcely any of the properties that constitute the identity criteria we associate with "Socrates." But the fact is Socrates alone did have enough of the $S_i$, so that the $\alpha$-transform of *being the person that had enough of the $S_i$* is an essence of Socrates. Hence

(25)  the (person who had enough of the $S_i$) $\alpha$ had scarcely any of the $S_i$

expresses a contingent proposition equivalent to (23). "Socrates" can't express the property Searle says it does; but there's no reason why it can't express the $\alpha$-transform of that property.

According to Frege, a proper name of a person may express different properties in the mouths of different persons or in the mouth of the same person on different occasions; perhaps the truth, then, is that "Socrates" serves on some occasions to express the $\alpha$-transform of *being the person who stands in R to "Socrates"* and on others to express the $\alpha$-transform of *being the person who had enough of the $S_i$*. In this way we can bring about a *rapprochement* between the Fregeans and the anti-Fregeans—a sort of group marriage, California style, among Donnellan, Frege, Kaplan, Kripke, Russell, Searle, and anyone else who is interested, with Boethius as presiding clergyman. On the Boethian compromise, proper names express properties, just as the Fregeans hold; but their references, in at least some cases, are determined in the way the anti-Fregeans suppose. We can then see the Fregean–anti-Fregean dispute as a relatively minor domestic quarrel as to just which

essence of an object its name expresses. Perhaps the truth is: sometimes one, sometimes another.

(ii) Secondly, let us note how the Boethian view copes with the
difficulties besetting the anti-Fregeans.

(a) In *The Nature of Necessity* I unwisely conceded that if proper
names express essences, then it is plausible to suppose that different
proper names of the same object express the same essence—in which
case

(19) Hesperus = Phosphorus

expresses the same proposition as

(26) Hesperus = Hesperus.

If so, however, we shall have to say that the ancient Babylonians, despite their sincere protestations to the contrary, knew all along that
Hesperus is identical with Phosphorus. After all, they knew the truth
expressed by (26); but that is the very truth expressed by (19). They
knew the truth expressed by (19) and (26); what they didn't know
was that (19) and (26) express the same truth. They were thus de-
ceived about the *sentence* (19) (or its counterpart in Ancient Babylonian) thinking it expressed a proposition distinct from that expressed
by (26).

Now perhaps this is not wholly implausible; it does have about it,
however, a certain air of the arcane.[23] In any event, a better explanation is available, once we recognize that different names of the
same object may express different essences. For then we can say simply and straightforwardly that the Babylonians knew (26) but did not
know (19). This, after all, coincides with their own claims and seems
to be no more than the simple truth. On our Boethian account the
sentence (19) expresses something like

(19*) the (morning star) $\alpha$ = the (evening star) $\alpha$

or perhaps

(19**) the (heavenly body last visible in the morning) $\alpha$ = the
(heavenly body first visible in the evening) $\alpha$;

and we can see how the Babylonians could have gone wrong with
respect to such items as (19*) and (19**). Here their situation is like
that of one who knows, of course, that

(27) $3^2=3^2$

but doesn't believe that

(28) $3^2=\frac{27}{8}\int_0^2$

"$3^2$" and "$\frac{27}{8}\int_0^2$" both express essences of 9, but *different* essences; and
it is easy enough to fail to realize that these essences are exemplified

by the same object. (27) and (28) thus express epistemically inequivalent propositions. But the same goes for (19) and (26); since "Hesperus" and "Phosphorus" express epistemically inequivalent essences of Venus, (19) and (26) express epistemically inequivalent propositions, so that (19) can be informative. And of course exactly similar considerations apply to

(29)  Hesperus is visible in the morning

and

(30)  Phosphorus is visible in the morning;

these also express epistemically inequivalent propositions. Surely this is the natural and intuitively plausible position; surely a person could believe (26) and (29) without believing either (19) or (30).[24]

The second and third difficulty for the anti-Fregean, you recall, are presented by empty proper names and by proper names in existential sentences. It is extremely difficult, on anti-Fregean principles, to see what propositions are expressed by sentences containing empty proper names; it is equally hard to see what propositions are expressed by simple existential sentences containing proper names—in particular, true negative existentials or false affirmative existentials. The Boethian view encounters no difficulty at all here; its felicitous account of these matters, indeed, is one of its strengths. As we have seen, in the typical case where a proper name occurs in such a sentence as

(31)  Leigh Ortenburger is the author of *The Climber's Guide to the Grand Tetons*

the name expresses an essence. (31) expresses a truth, furthermore, if and only if Leigh Ortenburger has the property of being the author of *The Climber's Guide to the Grand Tetons*—if and only if, that is, the essence expressed by that name is coexemplified with that property. More generally, where $N$ is a non-empty proper name and $F$ a predicate that expresses a property, a singular sentence of the form "$N$ is $F$" expresses a proposition that is true in just those possible worlds where the essence expressed by $N$ is coexemplified with the property expressed by $F$.

But the case of the existential sentence is just a special case.

(32)  Leigh Ortenburger exists

expresses a proposition true in just those possible worlds where the essence expressed by "Leigh Ortenburger" is coexemplified with existence; these, of course, are the worlds where that essence is exemplified. If "Leigh Ortenburger" expresses *being the (author of The Climber's Guide to the Tetons) α*, then (32) expresses the same proposition as

(33) the (author of The Climber's Guide to the Tetons) α exists

which is equivalent to

(34) There exists just one (*author of The Climber's Guide to the Tetons*) α

And of course the denial of (32), namely

(35) Leigh Ortenburger does not exist

is true in those worlds where (32) is false.

But now suppose $N$ is empty. Suppose you come to doubt the existence of Ortenburger. How, you say, could any one man know as much about the Tetons as the *Climber's Guide* contains? You come to believe that the Stanford mathematics department collaborated on the *Guide*—and that, inspired by the example of Bourbaki, they invented Ortenburger out of whole cloth, playfully ascribing the *Climber's Guide* to him. And now let's add that you are right. When you assert (35) and I assert (32), do I predicate a property of some object? And is there an essence $E$ such that what I say is true if and only if $E$ is exemplified? How shall we understand a negative existential sentence like

(5) Romulus did not exist

where the proper name is empty?

Here we must recognize, as Boethians, that proper names display a certain subtlety of function. The name "Romulus," on the Boethian view, expresses the α-transform of such a property as *being the thing that stands in R to "Romulus."* But this property is unexemplified; so its α-transform is unexemplified in α. But if a world-indexed property *having-P-in-W* is not exemplified in $W$, then it is not exemplified in any possible world at all. We saw earlier that the α-transform of an exemplified singular[25] property is an essence; we now see that the α-transform of an unexemplified singular property is incapable of exemplification. But then "Romulus" in (5) expresses an impossible property. The proposition expressed by (5), however, is true if and only if the property expressed by "Romulus" is not coexemplified with existence—if and only if, that is, it is not exemplified. (5), therefore, expresses a necessary truth and its negation,

(36) Romulus existed

a necessary falsehood.[26]

Take another example: suppose Socrates had never existed—suppose he'd been frivolously invented by Plato, Xenophon, and Aristophanes, the rest of us having been quite unaware of the hoax. What property would have been expressed by "Socrates"? In fact, that name expresses an essence—perhaps the α-transform of some such property as *standing in R to "Socrates."* But if Socrates had not existed, some world β distinct from α would have been actual; our name "Socrates" would have expressed a property not exemplified in any possible world; and the sentence

(37)  Socrates existed

would have expressed a necessarily false proposition. It follows, of course, that (37) would not have expressed the proposition it does *in fact* express; for *that* proposition is contingently true and hence not necessarily false in any possible world. So if Socrates had not existed, (37) would not have expressed the proposition it *does* express, but a necessary falsehood instead. On the Boethian account, therefore, a proper name $N$ in an existential sentence ⌜$N$ exists⌝ expresses the α-transform $P\alpha$ of a singular property. If $N$ is non-empty, $P\alpha$ is an essence and ⌜$N$ exists⌝ expresses a proposition true in just those worlds where $P\alpha$ is exemplified. If $N$ is empty, $P\alpha$ will be an impossible property and ⌜$N$ exists⌝ will express an impossible proposition.

I said empty proper names display a certain subtlety of function in existential sentences; but this subtlety does not distinguish existentials from other sentences. For consider, again,

(4)  Romulus founded Rome

This sentence expresses a proposition true in just those worlds where the property expressed by "Romulus" is coexemplified with the property expressed by "founded Rome." But here, as in (36), "Romulus" expresses the α-transform of an unexemplified property such as *standing in R to "Romulus"* or *having enough of the $R_i$.* Hence (4) expresses a necessarily false proposition and

(38)  it is not the case that Romulus founded Rome

a necessary truth. We thus see what propositions are expressed by simple sentences containing empty proper names. Such a name expresses the α-transform of an unexemplified singular property and therefore expresses an impossible property; as a consequence, a sentence like (4) expresses a necessary falsehood and one like (38) a necessary truth. And it is thus clear that proper names function in existential sentences in just the way they do in predicative sentences generally.

By way of summary: on the Boethian view I mean to suggest, a sentence of the form "$N$ is $F$" (where $N$ is a proper name and $F$ expresses a property) typically expresses a proposition true in the worlds where the property expressed by $N$ is coexemplified with the property expressed by $F$. If $N$ is non-empty, then it expresses an essence, and ⌜$N$ is $F$⌝ expresses a proposition true in the worlds where that essence is coexemplified with the property expressed by $F$. If $N$ is empty, then it expresses not an essence but an impossible property, so that $\ulcorner N$ is $F\urcorner$ expresses a necessary falsehood. Singular existential sentences of the form $\ulcorner N$ exists$\urcorner$ present the special case where $F$ is "exists." If $N$ is non-empty, then $\ulcorner N$ exists$\urcorner$ expresses a proposition true in just those worlds where the essence expressed by $N$ is coexemplified with existence: the worlds, that is where this essence is exemplified. If $N$ is empty, then it expresses an impossible property, so that $\ulcorner N$ exists$\urcorner$ expresses a necessary falsehood and its denial a necessary truth.

These, then, are the essentials of the Boethian view: proper names express essences, and different proper names of the same object (or the same name on different occasions of use) can express different and epistemically inequivalent essences. In an effort to promote amity, I have suggested that proper names sometimes express the α-transforms of such properties as *stands in R to "Socrates"* and *has enough of the $S_i$*. But they can also express other essences. According to Frege[27] and Chisholm[28] each of us has a property that he alone can grasp or apprehend. Perhaps they are right; perhaps for each person there is an essence he alone grasps, an essence expressed by his own use of his name but not by anyone else's. Perhaps in dubbings by description, as Kaplan calls them, [29] the name in question expresses the α-transform of the description; if I say "Let's name the shortest spy 'Shorty,' " perhaps "Shorty" expresses the α-transform of *being the shortest spy*. If, furthermore, I name someone in full view "Sam," it may be that "Sam" expresses (in my idiolect) a property such that my only alternative means of expressing it then is by way of some such description as 'that person right there', where this latter is accompanied by an appropriate pointing. (There are further subtleties here, but I don't have the space to explore them here.) By way of conclusion, then, I repeat the essential points of the Boethian account: proper names express essences, and different names of the same object may express epistemically inequivalent essences.

## NOTES

1. Bertrand Russell, "The Philosophy of Logical Atomism," in *Logic and Knowledge*, ed. Robert Marsh (London 1956), p. 200.
2. Gottlob Frege, "On Sense and Reference," in *Translations from the Philosophical Writings of Gottlob Frege*, ed. P. T. Geach and M. Black (Oxford, 1952), p. 58.
3. *A System of Logic* (New York, 1846), p. 21.
4. "Speaking of Nothing," *The Philosophical Review*, vol. 85 (1976): 11–12.
5. "Naming and Necessity," in *Semantics of Natural Language*, ed. D. Davidson and G. Harman (Dordrecht, 1972), pp. 320, 327; "Identity and Necessity," in *Identity and Individualion*, ed. M. Munitz (New York, 1971), p. 140.
6. "Demonstratives," his hitherto unpublished address to the Pacific Division of the American Philosophical Association (March, 1976).
7. "On Denoting" (Marsh, op. cit.), p. 47.
8. "Speaking of Nothing," p. 22.

9. See my *The Nature of Necessity* (Oxford, 1974), chs. 7 and 8 (the latter chapter is reprinted as ch. 4 of this volume).

10. "Speaking of Nothing," p. 28.

11. *American Philosophical Quarterly*, forthcoming.

12. See *The Nature of Necessity*, ch. 5.

13. Ibid, p. 55.

14. *In Librum de Interprelatione editio secunda*, PL 64, 462d–464c. Quoted in H. N Casteñeda, "Individuation and Non-Identity: A New Look," *American Philosophical Quarterly*, vol. 12 (1975), pp. 135–36.

15. See *The Nature of Necessity*, pp. 62–63.

16. For argument, see ibid., p. 72.

17. Where a property *P* entails a property *Q* iff it is not possible that there be an object that exemplifies *P* but not *Q*.

18. See *The Nature of Necessity*, pp. 72–73.

19. See, e.g., Kripe, *loc. cit.*

20. "Naming and Necessity," p. 302.

21. Ibid., p. 302.

22. See his "Proper Names," *Mind*, vol. 67 (1958): 171, and *Speech Acts* (Cambridge, 1969), p. 169.

23. See Diana Ackerman's "Plantinga, Proper Names and Propositions," *Philosophical Studies*, vol. 28 (1976); pp. 409–12.

24. This corrects the account of the Babylonian intellectual economy given in *The Nature of Necessity*, pp. 83–87.

25. A property that is possibly exemplified, but not possibly exemplified by more than one object.

26. But can't we easily imagine possible circumstances under which (36) would have been true? Isn't it possible that there should have been someone who was named "Romulus," collaborated with his brother in the founding of Rome, and so on for all the rest of the properties depicted in the story? That is indeed possible; those circumstances, however, are ones under which the *sentence* (36) would have expressed a truth; they are not ones under which the proposition (36) *does* express would have been true.

27. See "The Thought: A Logical Inquiry," trans. A. M. and Marcelle Quinton, *Mind*, vol. 65 (1956); 298.

28. Roderick Chisholm, *Person and Object* (London, 1976), p. 37.

29. "Bob and Carol and Ted and Alice" in *Approaches to Natural Language*, ed. Hintikka, Moravesic, and Suppes (Dordrecht, 1973), p. 499.

# 7

# De Essentia

Roderick Chisholm has a happy penchant for applying contemporary techniques to traditional issues and ideas, sometimes rescuing them from the Cimmerian gloom to which more positivistically inclined philosophers had consigned them. I want to raise some questions about Chisholm's account of the idea of an *individual essence*—an idea which goes back at least as far as Boethius and may perhaps be found in Plotinus and Aristotle. Chisholm defines this notion as follows:

> (1) $G$ is an *individual essence* (or *haecceity*) = def. $G$ is a property which is such that, for every $x$, $x$ has $G$ if and only if $x$ is necessarily such that it has $G$, and it is impossible that there is a $y$ other than $x$ such that $y$ has G.[1]

This definition, I think, requires two emendations. The *definiens* is of the form

> (2) for every $x$, $x$ has $G$ if and only if ($x$ has $G$ necessarily and . . . ).

Clearly any impossible property—any property not exemplified in any possible world—meets this condition; we must therefore appropriately insert the clause 'G is possibly exemplified'. Secondly, (1) so amended still awards essencehood to any property that is possibly but not in fact exemplified—the property of being a flying horse, for example. The simplest repair is to insert 'necessarily' between 'its' and 'such' in the *definiens*. This gives us

> (3) G is an *individual essence* (or *haecceity*) if and only if G is a property that (a) is possibly exemplified, and (b) is necessar-

ily such that for every $x$, $x$ has $G$ if and only if $x$ is necessarily such that it has $G$, and it is impossible that there is a $y$ other than $x$ such that $y$ has G.

So thought of, an essence of an object is a property it has necessarily and that is necessarily unique to it: (3) is equivalent to

(4)  $G$ is an essence if and only if it is possible that $G$ is exemplified by an object $x$ that (a) has $G$ necessarily and (b) is such that it's not possible that something distinct from $x$ have $G$.

An essence of Plato, then, is a property that Plato has in every possible world in which he exists, and which is such that there is no possible world in which it is exemplified by an object distinct from Plato. (Boethius speaks in this regard of what he calls "Platonity"—a property, he says, that "is singular and incommunicable to any other subsistent"; it is "one man's alone, and this not just anyone's, but Plato's.")[2]

I wish to ask three questions about Chisholm's account of individual essences.

## I

Chisholm suggests that "according to the traditional account of individual essence, each thing has only one individual essence and it includes all the characteristics that the thing has necessarily" (29); and he goes on to endorse this account. My first question, therefore:

(A)  Is it true that each thing has but one essence?

The answer, I think, is that it isn't true. Of course, if an object has more than one essence, these essences will be *necessarily coextensive* in the sense that there is no possible world in which there exists an object that has one but not the other; but might they not be distinct properties for all of that? Where $P$ and $Q$ are *propositions*, Chisholm holds, $P$ and $Q$ are distinct if it is possible that there be a person who believes $P$ but fails to believe $Q$ (p. 118). Presumably, then, Chisholm will be prepared to agree that *properties* $P$ and $Q$ are distinct if it is possible that there be a person that believes that $P$ is exemplified but does not believe that $Q$ is. But then objects will typically have several distinct (but equivalent) essences. Consider, for example, the properties *being the square root of 4* and *being the least prime*; clearly a person could believe that the first is exemplified without believing that the second is: he might never have considered whether there is a least prime, or might never have so much as acquired the concept of being prime. But *being the least prime* and *being the square root of 4* are both essences, in Chisholm's sense, of 2; hence they are *distinct* essences.

It isn't only abstract objects, furthermore, that have essences. An easy way to see this is by way of the notion of world-indexed properties. Suppose we name the actual world '$\alpha$'. '$\alpha$' is not an abbreviation for the description 'the actual world'; it is a proper name of the actual world. So the sentence '$\alpha$ is actual', unlike the sentence 'the actual world is actual,' expresses a contingent proposition—a proposition, indeed, that is contingent in *excelsis* because true in only one possible world. And now consider the world-indexed property *being-wise-in-$\alpha$*, a property Socrates has just in case *a* includes *Socrates' being wise*. Wisdom, of course, is a contingent property of Socrates, but *being wise in $\alpha$* is essential to him. While there are possible worlds in which Socrates exists but lacks wisdom, there are none in which he exists and lacks *being wise in* $\alpha$. For (presuming that what is possible or necessary does not vary form world to world) there are no possible worlds in which $\alpha$ does not include *Socrates' being wise*; hence there are no possible worlds in which Socrates exists but lacks the property *being wise in* $\alpha$. More generally, world-indexed properties are non-contingent: for any object *x* and world-indexed property *P*, either *x* has *P* essentially or *x* has the complement of *P* essentially.[3]

But now take any property *Q* that Socrates alone has—*being the shortest Greek philosopher*, perhaps, or *being born at P, t*, where 'P' names the place and 't' the time at which he was born: the world-indexed property *having Q in* $\alpha$ will be an essence of Socrates. First, it is one he has necessarily, for Socrates has all his world-indexed properties necessarily; second, it is such that in no possible world is there an object distinct from him that has it[4]; it therefore follows that this property is an essence of Socrates. So for any property *P* uniquely exemplified by Socrates, there is an essence of Socrates: *having P in W*. But clearly there are many pairs of properties of this sort such that a person could believe that one but not the other was exemplified; one might believe, for example, that the property *being the shortest Greek philosopher in* $\alpha$ is exemplified, but fail to believe that the same holds for *being born at P, t in* $\alpha$; hence these are distinct properties. Accordingly, Socrates has several distinct essences.

At least if we characterize 'essence' in the way Chisholm does. Of course this characterization can easily be amended to secure the result that each object has just one essence. We could, for example, take Socrates' essence to be the set of properties he has necessarily, or the intersection of those properties; either way Socrates will have just one essence. But the only reason I can see for taking this course is ancestral piety—and that is not a weightly reason since, so far as I know, the tradition never really raised the question whether there might be distinct but necessarily coextensive properties. Furthermore, there is a good reason *not* to take this course; noting that objects have distinct and epistemically inequivalent essences can help make sense of the behavior of proper names.[5]

## II

Now suppose we concede, for purposes of argument, that a person has just one essence. Professor Chisholm also holds that a person's essence is in a certain way *inaccessible* to anyone else:

> Each person who uses the first person pronoun uses it to refer to himself in such a way that, in that use, its *Bedeutung* or reference is himself and its *Sinn* or intention is his own individual essence. A corollary would be that, whereas each person knows directly and immediately certain propositions implying his own individual essence, no one knows any proposition implying the individual essence of anyone else. (36)

Chisholm speaks here of a proposition's *implying* an essence. This, I think, is a slip; he nowhere explains what it is for a proposition to imply a property but *does* say what it is for a proposition to *entail* a property:

> D.1.3. *p* entails the property of being F = def. *p* is necessarily such that (i) if it obtains [i.e., is true], then something has the property of being F and (ii) whoever accepts *p* believes that something is F (28).

And Chisholm's claim is that each of us knows some proposition entailing his own essence, but no one knows any proposition entailing someone else's essence. Suppose we say that a person *grasps* a property if he knows some proposition entailing it. Then Chisholm's claim is that each of us grasps only his own essence. My second question, then, is

(B) Is there reason to think no one grasps anyone else's essence?

We should note first that the "corollary" Chisholm mentions does not obviously follow from the alleged theorem. Perhaps it is true that when I use 'I' that pronoun expresses my essence; how does it follow that I can't gasp anyone else's essence? Chisholm considers the following suggestion as to how I could grasp an essence other than my own:

> We would have to say that these demonstrative expressions are like the word 'I' in that they may be used to intend certain individual essences or haecceities. This seems to have been the view of St. Thomas and Duns Scotus. According to this way of looking at the matter, if I pick you out as being *that* person or *that* thing, then I pick you out *per se.* For I pick you out as being something that has uniquely a certain property—the property of being that person or that thing. And this property, like the property of being identical with me, will be an individual essence or haecceity. In support of this latter point, one may urge: 'If you *are* that thing, then you are

*necessarily* that thing. After all, that thing *has* to be that thing and it couldn't be anything *other* than that thing. (34)

Suppose I refer to Paul M. Zwier in using the sentence

(5) That person is elegantly attired.

Scotus would say that the phrase 'that person' on that occasion intends (or expresses) an essence of Zwier. And isn't this plausible? Suppose that phrase does, on that occasion, express a property. What property does it express? It expresses the property denoted by the phrase 'the property of being that person' on an occasion of use where the phrase 'that person' denotes Zwier. But how could Zwier have lacked *that* property? Surely, there is no possible world in which he lacks it. But equally clearly it's not possible that someone distinct from Zwier should have had the property expressed, on that occasion, by 'that person.' Accordingly, that property is Zwier's essence. But on the occasion in question I know the proposition expressed by (5); and that proposition, presumably, entails the property expressed by 'that person' on that occasion. Accordingly, I grasp Zwier's essence.

Chisholm, surprisingly, rejects this conclusion:

> But if today I individuate something *per se* as being *that thing* and if tomorrow I individuate something *per se* as being *that thing*, I may well have picked out two different things; whereas if today I individuate something *per se* as being identical with me and if tomorrow I individuate something *per se* as being identical with me, then I will have picked out one and the same thing.

How, exactly, are we to construe this objection? Perhaps as follows. The phrase 'that person' can be used by the same person on different occasions to pick out different objects; that is, that phrase, as I use it, may denote an object $x$ at time $t$ and a different object $y$ at time $t^*$. But what it denotes on a given occasion, must have the property it expresses. The property expressed by 'that person' then, cannot be an essence, since (unlike any essence) it is exemplified by distinct objects at distinct times.

But here we must demur. In the passage just quoted Chisholm seems to assume that the phrase 'that person', as I use it, expresses the *same* property today and tomorrow. And why should we suppose that is so? Chisholm holds that 'I' expresses a different property when used to denote different persons; when 'I' denotes me (when *I* use it), it expresses *my* essence; when it denotes *you* (when *you* use it) it expresses *your* essence. But if 'I' can do that sort of thing, why can't 'that person'? Why can't it express different properties when used to denote different persons? Perhaps when I use it to refer to Zwier, it expresses an essence of Zwier; when I use it to refer to Quine, it expresses an essence of Quine. It is true that today I may use 'that person' to individuate an object $x$, and tomorrow use it to individuate a different object *y*; but it does not follow that the phrase expresses, on these occasions, a property had today by *x* and tomorrow by *y*.

These considerations, therefore, do nothing to show that the phrases 'that person' and 'that thing' don't typically express or intend essences. And isn't that the natural account to give of those phrases? Suppose I refer to Zwier as 'that person': surely he couldn't have existed but lacked the property of being that person—i.e., the property expressed on that occasion by 'that person'; and surely no one distinct from him could have been *that* person. So when I use the phrase to refer to Zwier, it expresses an essence; and when I use it to refer to someone else it expresses a *different* essence—just as the word 'I', when you use it expresses an essence, and a different essence from the one it expresses when I use it.

Chisholm, however, suggests another account of such demonstrative phrases:

> But 'that thing' could also be taken in a relational sense—as relating the thing in question to the one who is using the expression. So interpreted, it might be put as I have suggested, in some such phrase as 'the thing I'm now looking at' or 'the thing I'm concentrating on', And when it is taken in this way, then, of course, it doesn't intend the individual essence or haecceity ot the thing referred to (35).

I think this requires reconsideration. Presumably the suggestion is that some such phrase as 'the thing I'm now concentrating on' or 'the thing I'm now looking at' can typically be substituted for 'that thing' (with respect to a given occasion of use) *salva propositione*. But this is not so. Consider the sentences

(6) I'm not looking at that thing

and

(7) I'm not looking at the thing I'm now looking at,

or their less idiomatic but less ambiguous equivalents:

(6\*) that thing is such that I'm not looking at it

and

(7\*) the thing I'm now looking at is such that I'm not looking at it.

(7\*) (and (7)) express necessary falsehoods; (6) and (6\*), however, do not. For suppose on a given occasion I'm looking at the Grand Teton. What proposition do (6) and (6\*) express with respect to such an occasion of use? A proposition clearly, that is true in those possible worlds in which I am not then looking at the Grand Teton. (6) and (6\*), therefore, express a contingent falsehood (with respect to that occasion of use); (7) and (7*), however, express (with respect to that occasion) a necessary falsehood. Accordingly, I do not think Chisholm's suggestion here is satisfactory; phrases like 'that person' do indeed express essences, so that if I know such a proposition as *that person is elegantly attired*, I know a proposition entailing someone else's essence.

## III

Now we must turn to some existential questions. Chisholm's definition D.1.6 runs as follows:

> *p* implies *x* to have the property of being *F* = def. there is a property *G* such that (1) *G* is an individual concept, (ii) *p* entails the conjunction of *G* and the property of being *F*, and (iii) *x* has *G* [where an individual concept is a property that is possibly exemplified but not possibly exemplified by more than one object at a time].

Both

(8) The teacher of Plato is wise

and

(9) Socrates is wise,

then, imply Socrates to have the property of being wise. That (8) does so is a *contingent* feature of that proposition; if not Socrates but Xenophon had been the teacher of Plato, (8) would have implied Xenophon but not Socrates to have the property of being wise. But what about (9)? Could it have failed to imply Socrates to have the property of being wise? Suppose there had simply been no such thing as Socrates; would (9) have implied Socrates to have the property of being wise?

I should think not—not, at any rate, if what, following Robert Adams, we may call 'actualism' is true. Actualism, as I shall construe it, is the doctrine that there neither are nor could have been nonexistent objects. The actualist denies that there are, in addition to all the things that exist, some more things—merely possible objects, for example—that do not.[6] According to actualism, therefore,

(10) Necessarily, there are no objects that do not exist.

It is a corollary of actualism, however, that

(11) An object *x* has a property *P* in a world *W* only if *x* exists in *W*.

For suppose actualism is true; and suppose that there is an object—Socrates, let's say—that has a property *P* in a world *W* in which he does not exist. If (10) is true, then

(12)  There are no nonexistent objects

is true in every possible world and hence in *W*. Accordingly,

(13)  There are no nonexistent objects that have *P*

is also true in *W*, as is

(14)  Whatever has *P*, exists.

If Socrates has *P* in *W*, however, the proposition

(15)  Socrates has *P*

is true in *W*; it follows, therefore, that

(16)  Socrates exists

is true there, which contradicts our assumption that Socrates does not exist in *W*. (10), therefore, entails (11).

Suppose we call (11) *serious* actualism. According to serious actualism no object has properties in a world in which it does not exist. But then (9) does not imply Socrates to have the property of being wise in any world *W* in which Socrates does not exist. For (9) implies Socrates to have that property only if Socrates has the property of being Socrates; as we have just seen, however, Socrates has no properties at all in *W*, and hence does not have the property of being Socrates there. *Implying Socrates to have the property of being wise* is a contingent property of (9) just as it is of (8). (The difference is that (9) but not (8) could have implied *someone else* to have the property. Someone distinct from Socrates—Xenophon, let's say—could have had the property of being Plato's teacher; but it is impossible that anyone else should have had the property of being Socrates.)

But what about (9) itself? Could *it* exist, if Socrates didn't? (9), we might think, involves Socrates in a much more intimate way than does (8). The latter refers to Socrates, so-to-say, only indirectly—only by virtue of the fact that Socrates happens to be the teacher of Plato. (9), on the other hand, makes a direct reference to him, or, to use Arthur Prior's term, is "directly about" him.[7] Let's say that a proposition directly about some object (or objects) is a *singular* proposition. Perhaps a singular proposition directly about an individual exists only in those possible worlds in which that individual exists. This idea has a certain attractiveness; it is accepted by Prior,[8] John Pollock,[9] Kit Fine,[10] and others. Russell,[11] David Kaplan,[12] probably Keith Donnellan,[13] and others hold that what a singular proposition is directly about is a *constituent* of it; singular propositions have among their constituents not just *abstracta*, such as Socrates' essence, but *concreta*, such as Socrates. It is plausible to suppose, furthermore, that if a proposition *p* contains an object *x* as constituent, then *p* could not have existed if *x* had not; it is therefore plausible to suppose, on their view, that (9) would not have existed if Socrates had not. The view in question, furthermore, is relevant to such theological concerns as the nature of God's foreknowledge; it also offers some attractive possibilities for the Free Will Defense. Furthermore, Chisholm has expressed sympathy for this view and has at any rate entertained it with considerable hospitality. He has never endorsed it in print, however, and in *Person and Object* (1976, p. 118) assumes that it is false. In what follows I want to explore the view and give some reasons for endorsing this assumption. My third question, therefore, is

(C) Does *Socrates is wise* exist in worlds in which Socrates does not?

We might be inclined to argue, initially, that (9) is an *abstract* object, and accordingly exists necessarily. But not all abstract objects are necessary beings; sets with contingent members, for example, are not[14]—not, at least, if serious actualism is correct. For if it is, then if Quine had not existed, Quine's singleton would not have contained him. But surely Quine's singleton could not have existed but been empty (in which case it would have been the null set); neither could it have contained something distinct from Quine. *Containing Quine* and *containing nothing distinct from Quine* are surely essential properties of Quine's singleton; hence there is no possible world in which it exists but he does not. Quine's singleton, then, is just as contingent as is Quine himself. And of course the same goes for other sets that contain him. If Quine had not existed, the set in fact denoted by the phrase 'the set of human beings' would not have existed. Of course that phrase would have denoted a set, even if Quine had not existed—but a *different* set.

So not all abstract objects are necessary beings. Still, what about (9)? Granted, the unit set of Socrates could not exist if Socrates did not; but why suppose (9) is thus dependent upon Socrates? Why suppose, for example, that Socrates himself is a constituent of (9)? Instead of taking *Socrates* to be a constituent of such singular propositions as (9), we could take Socrateity, the essence of Socrates; then the existence of (9) might be independent of that of Socrates. Pershaps (9) has as constituents wisdom and Socrateity, being true in those worlds where these properties are exemplified and existing in those worlds where these properties exist.

But what about Socrateity? No doubt anyone who believes that (9) is ontologically dependent upon Socrates will credit his essence with a similar dependence; he will hold that Socrateity could not have existed if Socrateity had not. Call this view *existentialism*; according to existentialism existence precedes (or at any rate is not preceded by) essence. The existentialist need not hold, of course, that *all* properties are like Socrateity in being ontologically dependent upon particulars; he can hold that such properties as *wisdom, being red*, and *being the first man to climb a mountain* are not thus dependent. Such properties, he might say, vaguely, "make no direct or essential reference to an individual." Call such properties *qualitative* properties, and contrast them with *quidditative* properties, which do make an essential reference to an individual. (Perhaps we need not presently press him for an account of this obscure notion of direct reference.) Not all quidditative properties are essences; *being more bloodthirsty than Nero*, though not an essence, is nonetheless quidditative in that it makes essential reference to Nero. Similarly for *being mugged in Chicago* and *being the shortest Greek philosopher*. Perhaps, furthermore, the existentialist will count as quidditative such properties as *being either Plato or Socrates* and *being either Plato or wise*. And now the existentialist claim is that qualitative properties may be necessary beings; but quidditative properties—in particular, those that directly refer to a contingently existing object—are not.

Now this claim will be false if essences can be constructed from qualitative properties. Suppose, first of all, that for any sets (finite or infinite) of properties, there is the property of having each property in *S*—the generalized conjunction of *S*—and the property of having at least one property in *S*—the generalized disjunction of *S*. (The generalized conjunction and disjunction of a set of properties will be *properties*, not sets.) Let's say, furthermore, that a set *S* is the *closure* of a set *S*\* if *S* contains all generalized disjunctions of all generalized conjunctions of each subset of *S*\*; and say that a property *P* can be *constructed from qualitative properties* if it is a member of the closure of some set of qualitative properties. It is plausible to suppose that if each member of a set *S* is a necessary being, then so is its generalized union and intersection. But then any essence that can be constructed from qualitative properties will be a necessary being.

But *are* essences thus constructible? Socrates has a maximal set of qualitative properties: i.e., for each qualitative property Q, Socrates has Q or its complement. Call the generalized conjunction of a maximal possible set of qualitative properties a *completedescription* (description, for short): Socrates exemplifies a description, and in other possible worlds exemplifies other descriptions. Accordingly, if his essence can be constructed from qualitative properties, it would presumably be the generalized disjunction of the set of descriptions each of which is exemplified by Socrates in some possible world: that is, if *S* is the set of descriptions *D* such that there is a possible world in which Socrates exemplifies *D*, then an essence of Socrates will be the generalized disjunction of *S*.

I think we can see that Socrates' essence is *not* thus constructible. First, an argument designed to appeal to those who see *similarity* as crucial in determining which properties are essential to Socrates. Presumably it is on the basis of qualitative properties that we make judgments of similarity. For any complete descriptions $D_1$, $D_2$, and $D_3$, therefore, suppose we say that $D_1$ resembles $D_2$ more than $D_3$ if a person who exemplified $D_1$ would be more similar to one who exemplified $D_2$ than to one who exemplified $D_3$. (For present purposes it doesn't matter whether this relation is connected in the set of descriptions.) Now those who see similarity as crucial here will find the following principle plausible:

> (17) For any object $x$ and descriptions $D_1$, $D_2$, and $D_3$, if $x$ exemplifies $D_1$, and it is possible that $x$ exemplify $D_3$, and $D_1$ resembles $D_2$ more than $D_3$, then it is possible that $x$ exemplify $D_2$.

That is, if an object $x$ exemplifies a description $D_1$, and there is a possible world in which it exemplifies $D_3$, then for any description $D_2$ 'between' $D_1$ and $D_3$—i.e., any description such that $D_1$ resembles it more than $D_1$ and $D_3$—there is a possible world in which $x$ exemplifies $D_2$.

But if (17) is true, an essence of Socrates will not be a construction of qualitative properties. For clearly Socrates could have been very different from the way he was in fact, in $a$, the actual world. Xenophon on the other hand, could have been even more similar to Socrates than he was. Indeed there are descriptions $D_1$, $D_2$, and $D_3$, such that (a) Socrates exemplifies $D_1$ in $a$, (b) Xenophon exemplifies $D_2$ in some possible world, (c) Socrates exemplifies $D_3$ in some possible world, and (d) $D_1$ resembles $D_2$ more than $D_1$ resembles $D_3$. Socrates, after all, could have died at the age of six months (or six minutes) thus exemplifying a description quite different from the one he *does* exemplify. Xenophon, on the other hand, did in fact substantially resemble Socrates: both were eminent Athenians who made significant contributions to the culture of the Western world; and he could have been even more like Socrates was. (The argument does not require, of course, that it be possible that Socrates and Xenophon *concurrently* exemplify $D_3$ and $D_2$; there need be no possible world $W$ such that Socrates could have exemplified $D_3$ and Xenophon $D_2$ in $W$.) But then it follows by (17) that Socrates could have exemplified $D_2$. And if so, his essence $E$ is not equivalent to any union of descriptions. For suppose it is; then $D_2$ is in the union; but of course Xenophon could have exemplified $D_2$; so Xenophon could have exemplified $E$; but then $E$ is not an essence of Socrates after all. So if we accept (17), we shall have to suppose that Socrates' essence is not constructible from qualitative properties.

Now for a slightly less fanciful argument for the same point. Socrates could have been much like he was except for an identical twin— that is, there is a possible world $W$ in which Socrates has an identical twin $S^*$ but is otherwise just like he is in $a$, the actual world. In $W$ Socrates exemplifies a certain description $D$ that substantially resembles the description he exemplifies in fact. Now if $W$ had been actual, it would have been possible, surely, that Socrates' twin rather than Socrates should have exemplified *D*. That is, suppose *W* had been actual: then surely it would have been possible that *S\** should have exemplified *D*. But then it is possible, in *W*, that someone not identical with Socrates exemplify *D*. Now what is possible does not vary from world to world; it is therefore possible in fact that *D* be exemplified by someone not identical with Socrates. It follows that no essence of Socrates' can be constructed from qualitative properties. For suppose there were an essence *E* thus constructible: *E* would be a union of descriptions, one of which was *D* (since in *W* Socrates exemplifies *D*); but *D* could be exemplified by someone not identical with Socrates; so the same goes for *E*; but then *E* is not an essence of Socrates after all. So if it is possible that Socrates should have had a twin who could have exemplified a description Socrates could have exemplified, then Socrates' essence is not a construction from qualitative properties.

I am inclined to think, therefore, that Socrates' essence is not thus constructible; it is an irreducible haecceity or thisness, not reducible to any suchness. So it is at best implausible to hold that Socrateity is a necessary being on the grounds that it can be constructed from purely qualitative properties.

But now suppose we drop the supposition that Socrates has just one essence. We noted earlier that for any property *P* unique to Socrates, the world-indexed property *having P in a* (call it the *a-transform* of P) is one of his essences. Consider, then, the *a*-transform *Pa* of a qualitative property *P* unique to Socrates: won't *Pa* be an essence of Socrates that exists necessarily?

Here the whole-hearted existentialist will not be convinced: for *a* itself, he will say, would not have existed if Socrates had not. If Socrates had not existed, there would have been no such thing as the proposition

(9) Socrates is wise

or the state of affairs

(18) Socrates' being wise.

But *a*, the actual world, includes (18); hence, he will say, if (18) had not existed, neither would *a*; and he might give as a reason

(19) If a contingent state of affairs *S* includes the existence of a contingent object *O*, then *S* is directly about *O*.

Of course (19) and the characteristic existentialist claim that a state of affairs *S* can exist only if its constituents exist together entail that no possible world including a state of affairs directly about Socrates would have existed if Socrates had not; hence if Socrates had not existed, there would have been no such thing as *a*. On this view, then, possible worlds are not, in general, necessary beings. Those worlds that contain only necessary beings—numbers, pure sets, God—are themselves necessarily existent; the others, however, suffer from the deplorable fragility characterizing their contingent constituents. But of course if *a* had not existed, there would have been no such thing as *Pa*: there would have been no *a*-transforms at all.

The whole-hearted existentialist view of these matters, therefore, will include at least the following elements:

(20) A proposition or state of affairs *P* directly about an object *x* is ontologically dependent upon *x* in that it is not possible that *P* exist and *x* fail to exist;

(21) Essences are similarly dependent upon their exemplifications, so that there neither are nor could have been any unexemplified essences:

and

(22) Possible worlds are ontologically dependent upon the objects whose existence they include.

According to the Existentialist, then, if Socrates had not existed, there would have been no such thing as (9), no such thing as Socrateity, and no such thing as *a* or any other possible world that includes the existence of Socrates.


IV

Suppose we explore existentialism a bit further. Crucial to it is the claim that such propositions as

(9) Socrates is wise

and such states of affairs as

(18) Socrates' being wise

(if, indeed, (9) and (18) are distinct) are not necessary beings; like Socrates himself, they could have failed to exist. This means that the existentialist will have to distinguish at least two kinds of possibility (and necessity) where on the classical view there is but one. As Arthur Prior suggests, following Buridan, we shall have to distinguish *the possible* from *the possibly-true*.[15] Buridan's example was

(23) No propositions are negative:

(23) is *possible*, says Buridan, because God could have destroyed all negative propositions.[16] in which case things would be as (23) states. On the other hand, (23) is not *possibly true*, he says, since it could be

true only if it existed, in which case there would be at least one negative proposition, making (23) false. Perhaps a less problematic example is presented by

(24)  Socrates does not exist.

This proposition, clearly enough, is possible; Socrates is not a necessary being. On the other hand, the existentialist is obliged to claim that (24) is not possibly *true*. (24) could be true only if existent; but it could not exist unless Socrates did, in which case it would not be true after all. So (24) is possible but not possibly true. Hence possible truth is stronger than possibility: whatever is possibly true is possible, but the converse does not hold. And of course there will be two corresponding grades of necessity: *weak* necessity, the dual of possible truth, and *strong* necessity, the dual of possibility *simpliciter*. Thus

(16)  Socrates exists

will be weakly necessary in that its denial isn't possibly true, while

(25)  7 + 5 = 12

will be strongly necessary; it's denial isn't so much as possible, let alone possibly true.

Indeed, the fact is the existentialist will have to distinguish *three* grades of possibility; for *truth in some possible world* will presumably be distinct from possibility and from possible truth. Consider, for example,

(26)  There is an object distinct from each object that exists in $\alpha$.

(26), presumably, is both possible and possibly true; on the existentialist view, however, there is no possible world in which it is true. For suppose $W$ is a world in which (26) is true. Then $W$ includes the state of affairs

(27)  There being an object distinct from each object that exists in $\alpha$.

Now presumably the existentialist will hold that a possible world includes an existential state of affairs only if it also includes a corresponding singular state of affairs; that is, he will endorse

(28)  Necessarily, every possible world that includes a state of affairs of the form *there existing an object that has P* will include a singular state of affairs that is directly about some object and predicates *P* of it.

Accordingly, $W$ must include some singular state of affairs $S$ that is directly about some object $x$ and predicates *being distinct from each object that exists in a* of it. $S$, furthermore, will have to be a *possible* state of affairs, since some possible world includes it. But of course the existentialist holds that there aren't any states of affairs directly about what does not exist; every singular state of affairs is directly about some object that exists. Since *a* is the actual world, every singular state of affairs is directly about some object that exists in *a*. But where *x* is an object that exists in *a*, a state of affairs directly about *x*, predicating *being distinct from each object that exists in a* of it, will be an impossible state of affairs. *Existing in a*, and hence *being identical with some object that exists in a*, are world-indexed properties of *x*. We might be inclined to conclude that these properties are therefore essential to *x*; from the existentialist point of view, however, this conclusion would be hasty. For *x* could have existed even if *a* had not; but if *a* had not existed, the properties *exists in a* and *being identical with some object that exists in a* would not have existed; hence *x* could have existed and lacked these properties. The existentialist will concede, however, that it isn't possible that *a* exist and *x* lack the properties in question; hence *x* could not have had the complement of either of these properties. Hence there is no possible state of affairs directly about an object of which it predicates *being distinct from each object that exists in a*; but then there is no possible world in which (26) is true. *Truth in some possible world* is thus distinct both from truth and from possible-truth, and presumably stronger than either.

No doubt this proliferation of grades of possibility is a bit embarrassing for the existentialist; but is it any more than that? That *truth in some possible world* should diverge from possible truth and possibility is no real problem; if possible worlds are, as the existentialist claims, *contingent* beings, *truth-in-a-possible-world* is no longer of fundamental significance and should not be expected to match the basic notion of possibility; that notion will be better matched by something like being *such that there could have been a possible world in which it is true.* But the contrast between possible truth and possibility is not so easily dealt with. What could it mean to say of a proposition that it is *possible* but not *possibly true?* Possibility and necessity, after all, are *alethic* modalities—modalities of *truth.* How then could a proposition be *possible* but not possibly *true?* What, besides possible truth, could possibility be for a proposition? What else is there in the neighborhood? How could a distinction like this make sense?

The only possibility I can see is suggested (though not wholly explicitly) by Prior: possibility, as opposed to possible truth, is *possible non-falsehood.* To understand this suggestion we must turn to the idea of essential attribution. An object *x* has a property *P* essentially if and only if it is impossible that *x* exists and lack *P*—alternatively (given serious actualism), if and only if it is impossible that *x* have the complement of *P.* Socrates, for example, has essentially the properties *being a person* and *being self-identical;* hence it is impossible that Socrates should have existed and lacked these properties, and impossible that he should have had either of their complements. On the other hand,

Socrates could have failed to exist, in which case no essence of Socrates would have been co-exemplified with any property and Socrates would not have had these or any other properties. Accordingly, it is possible that Socrates should not have had these properties. There are possible worlds in which Socrates lacks these properties: the worlds in which he does not exist.

Like Socrates, the number nine has some of its properties essentially—*being a number*, for example, and *being composite*. In distinction from Socrates, however, nine could not have failed to exist; and hence it is not possible that nine should have lacked these properties. We might mark this difference by saying that Socrates has the property of being a person essentially, but nine has the property of being a number *necessarily* (thus departing from Chisholm's use of that term). An object $x$ has a property $P$ necessarily if and only if $x$ has $P$ essentially and $x$ is a necessary being. So Socrates has the property of being a person essentially; God, if classical theists are right, has that property necessarily. Everything, trivially, has existence essentially—i.e., nothing could have existed but failed to exist, or had the complement of existence. Only such necessary beings as God, however, have existence necessarily.

But now we must note a similar distinction among propositions. If only some of them are necessary beings, we shall have to distinguish *having truth essentially* from *having truth necessarily*. A proposition $p$ has truth essentially if and only if it is not possible that $p$ should have existed and lacked truth—alternatively (given that no proposition can be neither true nor false) if and only if it is not possible that $p$ exist and be false, that is, if and only if it is not possible that $p$ be false. A proposition will have truth *necessarily* or be *necessarily true*, however, if and only if it has truth essentially and furthermore exists necessarily, could not have failed to exist. So $p$ is necessarily true if and only if it is not possible that $p$ fail to be true. Every necessary truth is an essential truth; but if existentialism is right, the converse does not hold. The proposition *Socrates exists*, for example, could not have been false. It could have failed to exist, however, and hence could have failed to be true; it is therefore essentially but not necessarily true.

Existentialism has a certain seductive plausibility and can seem quite compelling. The proposition *Socrates is wise is about* Socrates, *refers* to him; but it obviously couldn't have been about him if there had been no such thing as Socrates. And how could this proposition exist but not be about Socrates? This line of thought, however, rests heavily on the notion of *aboutness*, which is at best a frail reed. I think we can see, moreover, that Existentialism thus explained—*Priorian* Existentialism—cannot be right. The fundamental reason is that if it *were* right, propositions like

(24) Socrates does not exist

would not be possible after all; and if we know anything at all about these matters, we know that (24) is possible. Let me explain.

First, the existentialist will concede, of course, that (24) is not *possibly true*. (24) would be true only if it existed, which it could do only if Socrates also existed; but then of course it would not be true. Nor, furthermore, is (24) true in some possible world. If there were a possible world in which (24) is true, that would be a world in which Socrates does not exist. But (24) does not exist in any world in which Socrates does not; so if (24) is true in some world, it is true in a world in which it does not exist. As we have seen, however, serious actualism is a corollary of actualism; hence no object has any property in any world in which it does not exist. But then no proposition has truth in any world in which it does not exist.

According to Priorian Existentialism, then, (24) is neither possibly true nor true in some possible world. How, then, can it be thought of as *possible*? The existentialist will reply, of course, that (24) could have failed to be *false*. It could not have been true; but it could have failed to be false. There are possible worlds in which it is not false: the worlds in which Socrates does not exist. I said that if we know anything at all about modality, we know that (24) is possible; from the point of view of Priorian Existentialism this intuition does not require possible truth. Possible non-falsehood is possibility enough. But surely this is wrong; possible non-falsehood is *not* possibility enough. In the first place, entirely too many propositions are possibly non-false: for example,

(29) Socrates is self-diverse

and even such explicit contradictions as

(30) Socrates is wise and Socrates is not wise.

According to the existentialist (29) and (30) are possibly non-false; they would not have existed and hence would not have been false if there had been no such thing as Socrates. But surely there is no sensible conception of possibility at all in which (29) and (30) are possible. If the only conception of possibility in which (24) is possible is one in which contradictions are possible, then (24) is not really possible.

Second, (29) and (30) imply, respectively,

(31) there is at least one thing that is self-diverse

and

(32) there is at least one thing that is both wise and not wise

in first order logic. But (31) and (32) aren't even so much as possibly non-false. Possible non-falsehood is therefore not closed under logical implication—a crucially serious impairment for a candidate for possibility.

But the clinching point, I think, is the following. What was the alleged insight behind existentialism in the first place? That it is impossible that objects of which Socrates is a constituent—singular propositions directly about him, possible worlds containing him, his essence, and the like—should have existed if he had not. If *E* is any entity of that sort, the idea was that

(33)  *E* exists and Socrates does not

is impossible. This is the central existentialist insight. But note that (33), from the existentialist perspective, is possibly non-false; it would have failed to be false if Socrates had not existed. So if possible non-falsehood is possibility enough, (33) is possible after all. The existentialist is thus hoist on his own petard. His fundamental insight is that (33) is not possible; he therefore argues that propositions such as (24) are not necessary beings. This apparently conflicts with the obvious truth that such propositions are possible. The preferred resolution consists in claiming that possible non-falsehood is sufficient; but then (33) is possible after all.

The moral to be drawn, I think, is that possibility, for a proposition, is possible truth; there is nothing else for it to be. The alleged distinction between possible truth and possibility is a confusion. Perhaps, following Buridan, we can make this distinction for *sentences*, or more exactly, sentence *tokens*. A sentence token is true (or true in English) if it express (in English) a true proposition; it is possible if the proposition it express (in English) is possible, i.e., possibly true. The sentence token

(34)  there are no sentence tokens,

then, is possible. It could not have been true (in English), however; for to be true it would have had to exist: in which case it would not have been true. We could therefore say, if we wished, that (34) is possible but not possibly true. But there is no similar distinction in the case of propositions: possibility, for a proposition is possible truth. Truth and falsehood are the salient characteristics of propositions: it is therefore natural to use 'possible' to abbreviate 'possibly true' (rather than, say, 'possibly Paul's favorite proposition'). But to argue that (24) is possible on the grounds that it could have failed to be false, is like arguing that Socrates is possibly a number or possibly self-diverse on the grounds that he could have failed to have the properties of being a non-number and being self-identical. Indeed he could have failed to have these properties; had he not existed Socrates would not have had these or any other properties. It is sheer confusion, however, to conclude that he is possibly a number or possibly self-diverse. Similarly, then, for propositions: if some propositions—

e.g., (24)—are contingent objects, then those propositions could have failed to be false. It is sheer confusion, however, to conclude that they are possible.

We must therefore reject existentialism.

(9) Socrates is wise

and

(16) Socrates exists

would have existed even if Socrates had not; and the same goes for his essences.

## Notes

1. Roderick Chisholm, *Person and Object* (London: Allen and Unwin, 1976), p. 29. Subsequent references to Chisholm's work are to this book.

2. *Librum de Interpretatione editio secunda*, PL 64, 462–464C. Quoted in H. N. Castañeda, "Individuation and Identity: A New Look," *American Philosophical Quarterly*, vol. 12 (1975), p. 135.

3. I give an argument for this claim in *The Nature of Necessity* (Oxford: Clarendon Press, 1974), p. 63.

4. As I argue in "Actualism and Possible Worlds," in David Holdcroft, ed., *Papers on Logic and Language* (Warwick, University of Warwick Philosophy Dept., 1977), pp. 145–46.

5. See chapter 6, this volume.

6. See Plantinga 1974, chs. 7 and 8, the latter of which is reprinted as chapter 4, this volume.

7. A. N. Prior and Kit Fine, *Worlds, Times, and Selves* (Amherst: University of Massachusetts Press, 1977), p. 109.

8. See, e.g., *Past, Present and Future* (Oxford: Clarendon Press, 1976), pp. 150–51, and *Worlds, Times, and Selves*, p. 103.

9. See chapter 16 of *Language and Thought*, duplicated.

10. See A. N. Prior and Kit Fine, *Worlds, Times, and Selves* (Amherst: University of Massachusetts Press, 1977), p. 128.

11. "On Denoting," in *Logic and Knowledge*, ed. R. Marsh (New York: The Macmillan Co., 1956).

12. See "How to Russell a Frege-Church," *Journal of Philosophy*, vol. LXXII (1975), pp. 724–25.

13. See "Speaking of Nothing," *Philosophical Review*, 1974, p. 12.

14. See "Actualism and Possible Worlds," pp. 142–43.

15. "The Possibly-true and the Possible," in *Papers in Logic and Ethics* (Amherst: University of Massachusetts Press, 1976), p. 202.

16. Buridan apparently thought of propositions as *sentences*—indeed, as *sentence tokens*.

# 8

# On Existentialism

According to Jean Paul Sartre, existentialism is the view that existence precedes essence. As I shall use the term, existentialism is the thesis that existence, even if it does not precede essence, is at any rate not preceded by it. Let me explain.

## I. Existentialism Expounded

Suppose we begin by endorsing or at any rate not contesting the view that objects have individual essences. An individual essence $E$ of an object $x$ is a property that meets two conditions: (1) $E$ is essential to $x$, so that it is not possible that $x$ exists but lacks $E$, and (2) $E$ is essentially unique to $x$, so that it is not possible that there should have been an object distinct from $x$ that had $E$. I believe it is obvious that there are individual essences. Consider, for example, the property of being William F. Buckley or being identical with William F. Buckley. Surely that property is essential to Buckley; he couldn't have existed but lacked it. (Of course he could have lacked the *name* 'William F. Buckley'; no doubt his parents could have named him 'Pico della Mirandola' if they'd wished.) But the property in question is also essentially unique to him; it is not possible that someone distinct from Buckley should have had the property of being identical with William F. Buckley. One kind of essence, then, is the property of being identical with some object—i.e., the property, for some object $x$, of being identical with $x$. Following Robert Adams and Duns Scotus, suppose we call such a property a *thisness*; the thisness of an individual is the property of being that individual. It is not necessary that we use proper names to specify or refer to thisnesses; when I use the words "the property of being I" or "the property of being identical with me," the property they denote is a thisness. And consider the meanest man in North Dakota: the property of being identical with *him* is also a thisness.

So objects have thisnesses and thisnesses are essences. One existentialist thesis—a thesis endorsed by Arthur Prior, Robert Adams, Kit Fine, and others—can be stated as follows: thisnesses are ontologically dependent upon their exemplifications. Take any thisness $t$ and the object $x$ of which $t$ is the thisness; $t$ could not have existed if $x$ had not. If Buckley had not existed, then his thisness would not have existed. Every thisness has *essentially* the property of being exemplified by the object that does in fact exemplify it. More exactly, the thesis in question is that it is *necessary* that every thisness has that property; it is not as if there could have been thisnesses that could have lacked the property in question.

This existentialist thesis can be extended. Let's say that a property is *quidditative* if it is either a thisness or involves a thisness in a certain way. We could try to spell out the way in question in formal and recusive detail; but instead let me just give some examples. *Being identical with Nero* or *being Nero* is a quidditative property; but so are *being more blood-thirsty than Nero, being either Nero or Cicero, being either Nero or wise, being possibly wiser than Nero, being believed by Nero to be treacherous,* and *being such that there is someone more bloodthirsty than Nero.* We may contrast the notion of a quidditative property with that of a *qualitative* property. Again, I shall not try to give a *definition* of this notion; but examples would be *being wise, being 14 years old, being angry, being learned, being six feet from a desk,* and the like. If $P$ and $Q$ are qualitative properties, then so is their conjunction, their disjunction, the complement of each, *being such that there is something that has P,* and *possibly having P.* And the more general existentialist thesis is that while qualitative properties may be necessary beings and exist in every possible world, quidditative properties are ontologically dependent upon the objects whose thisnesses they involve. Of course the thisness of a *necessary* being—God, perhaps, or to use a theologically less dramatic example, the number seven—exists necessarily, just as does the object of which it is a thisness; and the same goes for any quidditative property that involves only thisnesses of necessary beings. But such a quidditative property as *being wiser than Buckley* could not have existed if he had not.

The first existentialist thesis, therefore, is that quidditative properties are ontologically dependent upon the individuals whose thisnesses they involve. And a second existentialist thesis is like unto the first. Consider the propositions

(1)  William F. Buckley is wise

and

(2)  The Lion of Conservativism is wise.

The first, we might think, involves Buckley in a more direct and intimate way than does the second. The second refers to him, so to say, only accidentally—only by virtue of the fact that he happens to be the Lion of Conservativism. (1), on the other hand, makes a direct reference to him, or to use Arthur Prior's term, is "directly about"[1] him. Now it is not easy to say just what *direct aboutness* is or when a proposition is directly about an object; and for our purposes it isn't crucially important. Instead of trying to explain that notion, I shall say that a proposition directly about some object is a *singular* proposition and give some examples: *Buckley is wise, either Buckley is wise or* 2 + 1 = 3, *possibly Buckley is wise, it's not the case that Buckley is wise, someone is wiser than Buckley, Sam believes that Buckley is wise,* and *possibly Buckley does not exist* are all singular propositions. If we think of propositions as having constituents, we may think of a singular proposition as one that has either at least one individual or at least one quidditative property as a constituent. And the second existentialist thesis—accepted again by Adams, Fine, Prior and others—is this: a singular proposition is ontologically dependent upon the individuals it is directly about. So if Buckley had not existed, then, on this view, none of the above propositions would have so much as seen the light of day.

Existentialism, therefore, is the claim that quidditative properties and singular propositions are ontologically dependent upon the individuals they involve.[2] I don't know whether continental *Angst* would be the appropriate reaction to the truth of existentialism, if indeed it were true, but in any event I propose to argue that it is false. First, however, we must try to get a sense of what it is that leads people to accept existentialism.

## II. Why Accept Existentialism?

I wish to consider two lines of argument for existentialism, one for each of the two characteristic existentialist theses. But first we must briefly take note of a doctrine presupposed by both lines of argument. As we have learned at our mother's knees, Meinong and his cohorts held that in addition to all the things that exist—houses, horses, men and mice—there are some more things—golden mountains and round squares, perhaps—that do not. I've argued elsewhere[3] that this claim is mistaken; here let's just agree, for purposes of argument, that the claim is false. Let's agree that there neither are nor could have been any nonexistent objects; it's a necessary truth that there aren't any. This view is sometimes called 'actualism'; I shall follow this custom, but with a *caveat.* 'Actualism' is a misleading name for the view in question; it suggests the idea that whatever is, is *actual.* But that is false. There are many states of affairs—for example *London's being smaller than Los Angeles*—that don't obtain, are not actual. Of course these unactual states of affairs *exist* all right—they exist just as robustly as your most solidly actual state of affairs. But they aren't actual. So there are any number of things that aren't actual; what there aren't any of is things that don't *exist.* 'Existentialism' would be a better sobriquet for the view in question, but of course that name has already been preempted; so 'actualism' will have to do. And let's use '*serious* actualism' as a name for the claim that necessarily, no object could have had a property or stood in a relation without existing—the view, that is, that nothing has any properties in any world in which it does not exist.

Now suppose we return to existentialism. We might initially be inclined to reject it by arguing that singular propositions and quidditative properties are abstract objects and therefore exist necessarily. But not all abstract objects are necessary beings; sets with contingent members, for example, are not—not, at least, if serious actualism is correct. For if it is, then if Quine had not existed, Quine's singleton would not have contained him. But surely Quine's singleton could not have existed but been empty (in which case it would have been the null set); neither could it have contained something distinct from Quine. *Containing Quine* and *containing nothing distinct from Quine* are surely essential properties of Quine's singleton; hence there is no possible world in which it exists but he does not. Quine's singleton, then, is just as contingent as is Quine himself. And of course the same goes for other sets that contain him. If Quine had not existed, the set in fact denoted by the phrase 'the set of human beings' would not have existed. Of course that phrase would have denoted a set, even if Quine had not existed—but a *different* set.

So not all abstract objects are necessary beings. Still, what about properties? It is natural to think, indeed, that a crucial difference between sets and properties lies just here. Sets are ontologically dependent upon their members; hence a set with a contingent member is itself contingent. But properties with contingent exemplification typically aren't ontologically dependent upon those exemplifications. The set of dogs—the set that is in fact the set of dogs—would not have existed had my dog Mischa or any other dog failed to exist; but the property *being a dog* can get by perfectly well whether or not there are any dogs at all. Why suppose it is any different with quidditative properties?

Robert Adams offers an argument: "to be the property of being identical with a particular individual is to stand in a unique relationship to that individual. . . . So if there were a thisness of a non-actual individual, it would stand in a relation to that individual. But according to actualism non-actual individuals cannot enter into any relations. It seems to follow that according to actualism there cannot be a thisness of a non-actual individual.[4] But this statement of the issue isn't wholly accurate. The question isn't whether there are thisnesses of non-actual, that is, non-existent individuals—of course there aren't, because there aren't any nonexistent individuals. In the same way there aren't any shapes of nonexistent individuals—i.e., no shape is the shape of a nonexistent individual. The question is rather whether any thisness could have existed if what it is the thisness of had not. The question is whether, for example, my thisness could have existed if I hadn't. Of course if I hadn't existed, the property that is *in fact* my thisness wouldn't have been my thisness; it would not have been related to me by the relation *being the thisness of*. But it doesn't follow that it couldn't have existed if I hadn't. If I hadn't existed, my brother-in-law would not have been my brother-in-law; he would not have had the property of being related to me by the brother-in-law relation. But it doesn't follow that he couldn't have existed if I hadn't. Having that property is not essential to him; he could have existed whether or not I had. And of course the question about me and my thisness is whether the property of being exemplified by me is essential to it. Since we are given that the property *being exemplified by me if at all* is essential to it, the real question is whether being *exemplified* is essential to it: and it isn't in the least obvious that it *is*. Adams holds that an object may have a *qualitative* essence—an essence that doesn't involve a thisness—and the qualitative essence of an object, he thinks, would have existed even if the object hadn't. Of course, if I had not existed, my qualitative essence wouldn't have been my qualitative essence; it wouldn't have been related to me by the *is-the-qualitative-essence-of* relation. But it could have existed even if I hadn't. Why suppose things are different in the case of my thisness?

Taken as an argument, therefore, the above considerations are inconclusive. I suspect, however, that they aren't really intended as an argument; they are more like an appeal to intuition. Isn't it just clear or obvious that the property *being Socrates* could not have existed if Socrates had not existed? What would my thisness have *been*, if I hadn't existed? But it doesn't seem to me, on reflection, to be the least bit obvious. And would my thisness have been, if I hadn't existed? It would have been an unexemplified essence that could have been the thisness of something.

I turn now to the line of argument for the second existentialist thesis—the thesis that singular propositions are ontologically dependent upon the objects they are directly about. Consider again

(1)  William F. Buckley is wise

and

(2) The Lion of Conservativism is wise.

On the view in question (1) could have failed to exist, and would have done so if Buckley had not existed. (2), on the other hand, is quite impervious to the harrowing vicissitudes besetting contingent objects, and would have existed no matter what. Why the difference?

One line of argument, or at any rate one "consideration determining the intellect," to use John Stuart Mill's phrase, goes as follows. It is plausible to join Mill in supposing that "Proper Names are not connotative; they denote the individuals who are called by them, but they do not indicate or imply an attribute as belonging to these individuals."[5] Proper names, says Mill, have denotation but no connotation: a proper name denotes its referent but does not express a property. He seems to mean that the sole semantic function performed by a proper name is that of denoting its referent; its semantic function is *exhausted* in denoting its referent. The first premise of this argument, then, is that proper names do not express properties. The second premise is the plausible view that sentences containing proper names do in fact express propositions. And the third premise is that a proposition is an articulated structure containing *constituents* standing in relation to each other. It's not at all clear what a constituent of a proposition is supposed to be; but among the constituents of the proposition *all men are mortal* one would find, presumably, the properties *humanity* and *mortality*.

Now suppose you accept these three premises: what sort of proposition will be expressed by a sentence like (1) if the proper name it contains does not express a property? What would be the constituents of such a proposition—what would be, so to speak, its subject-place constituent? What more natural than to take William F. Buckley himself, that fugleman of the right, as a constituent of the proposition expressed by (1)? On this view, singular propositions include among their constituents not just abstracta, such as Buckley's essence, but concreta, such as Buckley himself. If one holds that propositions have constituents, that proper names do not express properties, and that sentences containing them express propositions, then the view that such propositions contain concrete objects as constituents can seem quite compelling.

Now those who think that propositions have constituents, think of the constituency relation as essential to the constitutee, but not, in the general case, to the constituent; that is, if *a* is a constituent of *b*, then *b* couldn't exist without having *a* as a constituent, although it is not true in general that *b* could not have existed with being a constituent of *a*. Both William F. Buckley and Paul X. Zwier are constituents of the proposition *Paul Zwier is more conservative than William Buckley*; so if either of them had failed to exist, the same fate would have befallen that proposition. Obviously, however, Buckley could have existed even if Zwier hadn't; accordingly Buckley could have existed even if that proposition hadn't. And hence (given serious actualism) being a constituent of it is not essential to him. So the fourth premise of the argument is: if a concrete object $O$ is a constituent of a proposition $P$, then $P$ is ontologically dependent upon $O$. To summarize the argument, then: sentences containing proper names express propositions that have concrete and contingent objects as constituents. But the constituency relation is essential to the constituted object; hence singular propositions—many of them, at any rate—are ontologically dependent upon contingent individuals.

Now I think this is at best a weak argument for the existentialist thesis in question; and its weakness results from the obscurity of the premises involving the notion of *constituency*. What exactly, or even approximately, *is* this relationship *being a constituent of*? Do we know or have reason to suspect that propositions *have* constituents? What can we say about the relation that holds between an object—a concept, property, concrete individual or whatever—and a proposition, when the former is a constituent of the latter? Maybe not much. Some philosophers suggest that the sort of proposition expressed by sentences like (1) can be *represented by* or *taken as* a set-theoretical entity of some sort—an ordered pair, perhaps, whose first member is William F. Buckley and whose second is the property of being wise. Of course if this proposition *were* such an ordered pair, then perhaps we could say what its constituents were: perhaps they would be the members of its transitive closure. Presumably, however, the claim is not that such propositions *really are* ordered pairs, but only that we can fittingly *represent* or *take* them as such, in the way in which for some purposes we can take the natural numbers as sets of one kind or another. We have imbibed with our mother's milk the idea that we can 'identify' the natural numbers with any of various sequences of sets. We can also identify them with other things: for example, we could identify zero with Richard Wagner and the rest of the natural numbers with propositions about him: *Wagner has written just one opera*, *Wagner has written just two operas*, and so on. All we need for such identification is a countably infinite set of objects together with a recursive relation under which they form a progression. But of course the fact that natural numbers can be thus identified with sets of one sort or another doesn't at all imply that they really *are* sets, or have as constituents the members of the sets with which we identify them. And the same holds for propositions and ordered pairs of the sort mentioned above. Perhaps for some purposes we can identify the former with the latter; but it doesn't follow that the former have as constituents the members of the latter. It is therefore hard to see that the above suggestion—the suggestion that singular propositions can be represented or taken as certain sets—throws any light on the constituency relation.

Of course there clearly is an interesting relationship between the proposition *All men are mortal* and the properties *being a man* and *being mortal*—a relationship that doesn't hold between that proposition and, say, the number 7 or the Taj Mahal or the property of being a horse. And no doubt we have something of a grasp—inchoate and groping as it may be—of this relation. So, for example, we can grasp enough of the relation in question to see that a proposition couldn't be a constituent of a person. But could a person be a constituent of a proposition? I feel as if I have a grasp of this notion of constituency when I'm told that, say, wisdom but not beauty is a constituent of the proposition *Socrates is wise*; but when it is added that Socrates himself is also a constituent of that proposition, I begin to lose my sense of what's being talked about. If an abstract object like a proposition has constituents, wouldn't they themselves have to be abstract?

But secondly: if we're prepared to suppose something as initially *outré* as that persons can be constituents of propositions, why insist that a proposition is ontologically dependent upon its constituents? Why boggle at the idea that a proposition could exist even if one of its constituents didn't? Perhaps the proposition expressed by (1) has Buckley as a constituent but would have existed even if he had not. If it had, perhaps it would have been slightly ill-formed or even maimed; but couldn't it exist nonetheless?

This argument, therefore, is inconclusive. It's not at all clear what is being claimed when its claimed that propositions have constituents. Insofar as we have a grasp of that notion, however, it is very hard to see how a person could be a constituent of a proposition. And even if propositions do contain persons as constituents, why suppose that containing a given person as constituent is *essential* to a proposition?

## III. An Anti-Existentialist Argument

I want to propose an argument against existentialism—specifically, an argument against the existentialist thesis that singular propositions are ontologically dependent upon contingent objects. The argument begins from an obvious fact. Surely it's possible that Socrates should not have existed; unlike God and the number seven, Socrates is not a necessary being. So the proposition *possibly Socrates does not exist* is true, and the proposition *Socrates does not exist* is possible, that is, possibly true. But that proposition could not have been true without existing. Furthermore, if it *had* been true, Socrates would not have existed. If it had been true, therefore, it would have existed but Socrates would not have existed. It is therefore possible that the proposition *Socrates does not exist* exist when Socrates does not—contrary to the claims of existentialism, according to which that proposition has Socrates as a constituent and hence is ontologically dependent upon him.

Tidying up the argument a bit, we can see it as proceeding from the following five premises:

(3) Possibly Socrates does not exist

(4) If (3) then the proposition *Socrates does not exist* is possible.

(5) If the proposition *Socrates does not exist* is possible, then it is possibly true.

(6) Necessarily, if *Socrates does not exist* had been true, then *Socrates does not exist* would have existed.

and

(7) Necessarily if *Socrates does not exist* had been true, then Socrates would not have existed.

From (3), (4) and (5) it follows that

(8) *Socrates does not exist* is possibly true,

i.e., that proposition could have been true; from (6) and (7) it follows that

(9) Necessarily, if *Socrates does not exist* had been true, then *Socrates does not exist* would have existed and Socrates would not have existed;

and from (8) and (9) it follows that

(10) It is possible that both Socrates does not exist and the proposition *Socrates does not exist* exists,

which contradicts existentialism.

Now I take it that premises (3) and (7) are relatively uncontroversial; so the controversial premises, if any, are (4), (5) and (6). (4), I think, is the next least controversial premise. It has been denied, however, by Lawrence Powers.[6] *Powersian Existentialism*, accordingly, is the sort of existentialist that rejects (4). What can be said for that rejection? Now of course we must grant that "possibly" in (3) is an operator rather than a predicate; and we must also grant that certain natural ways of formalizing the attempt to construct the modal operators as predicates of sentences, rapidly come to grief. State (4) is surely not properly rejectable. Suppose we agree that there are such things as propositions and that propositions are the things that are true or false. (We can say that a *sentence* is true if it expresses a true proposition. Then surely we will regard truth and falsehood as properties of propositions. Furthermore, such a proposition as *It's true that all men are mortal* is true and only if the proposition *all men are mortal* is true—despite the fact that "It's true that" is an operator, not a predicate. Now surely the same goes for

(11) Possibly Socrates does not exist.

Possibility, obviously, is a property of propositions; it is an alethic modality, a mode of truth. How could (11) be true if the proposition *Socrates does not exist* were not possible? What proposition would the sentence (11) express, if it didn't express one entailing that *Socrates does not exist* is possible? (11), surely, is true if and only if *Socrates does not exist* is possible. So (4) should be accepted and Powersian existentialism rejected.

(6), I think, is the next least controversial premise; according to (6), *Socrates does not exist* is such that it couldn't have been true without existing. Another way to put the same point: '*Socrates does not exist*' is *true* entails '*Socrates does not exist*' *exists.* Still another way to put it: every possible world in which *Socrates does not exist* is true, is one in which it exists. This premise has been denied, at least provisionally, by John Pollock; Pollockian Existentialism, therefore, is the sort of existentialism that denies (6).

Now (6) is really a specification of *serious actualism*—the view that no object could have had a property without existing. Stated alternatively, serious actualism is the view that necessarily, for any object *x* and property *P*, it's not possible that *x* should have had *P* but not existed. Stated in terms of possible worlds, serious actualism is the view that necessarily no object has a property in a world in which it does not exist; that is, it is necessary that for any possible world *W* and property *P* and object *x*, if it is true that if *W* had been actual, then *x* would have had *P*, then it is true that if *W* had been actual, *x* would have existed. As our official statement of serious actualism, let's adopt

(12) Necessarily for any object *x*, possible world *W*, and property *P*, if *x* has *P* in *W*, then *x* exists in *W*

where an object *x* has a property *P* in a world *W* if and only if it is not possible that *W* be actual and *x* fail to have *P*.

Now it may be tempting to suppose[7] that serious actualism is a corollary of actualism *tout court.* For suppose, in accord with actualism, that

(13) There are no nonexistent objects

is necessarily true and hence true in every possible world. Then the same can be said for

(14) For any property *P*, there are no nonexistent objects that have *P*

that is,

(15)  Whatever has *P*, exists.

Now consider Socrates, and let *P* be any property and *W* be any world in which Socrates has *P*. Then

(16)  Socrates has *P*

is true in *W*; since (15) is also true in *W*, so is

(17)  Socrates exists.

But then it follows that if Socrates has a property *P* in a world *W*, Socrates exists in *W*; and of course the same goes for everything else.

Now I said it was tempting thus to infer serious actualism from actualism but the above argument represents at best a bit of flocculent thinking. We can see this as follows. If actualism is true, then

(18)  Whatever does *not* exist, exists

is true in every possible world; few would be tempted to infer, however, that if Socrates does not exist in a world *W\**, then he exists in that world. The trouble with the argument, obviously, is the following: (15) is indeed true in *W*, as is (16). To infer that (17) is true in *W*, however, we must suppose that

(19)  If Socrates has *P*, then Socrates exists

is also true there. One thinks of (19) as following from (15) by Universal Instantiation. (15) says that everything there is—everything that exists and everything else as well, if there is anything else—has a certain property *being such that if it has P, then it exists*. (19) (construed *de re* as *Socrates is such that if he has P then he exists*) says just that Socrates has the property. (15) says everything there is has. But then clearly (19) doesn't follow from (15) alone. Another premise is needed: the premise that Socrates is one of the things there are. Of course this premise is true in fact, but perhaps it isn't true in *W*. So from the fact that (15) is true in *W*, we cannot properly infer that (19) is also true in *W*.

From actualism *tout court*, therefore, we cannot properly infer serious actualism. The latter is a separate thesis and requires separate affirmation. And isn't it just false? For consider any world *W\** in which Socrates does not exist: Socrates will not have the property of being wise in *W\**; so

(20)  Socrates is not wise

is true in *W\**; so Socrates has the property of not being wise in *W\**. But of course it won't follow that he exists in *W\**. In the same way, Socrates does not exist in *W\**. But of course it doesn't follow from *that*, that he exists in *W\**. To take another sort of example,

(21)  If Socrates is wise, someone is wise

predicates a property of Socrates: *being such that if he is wise, someone is.* But (21) is also necessarily true; Socrates, therefore, has the property (21) predicates of him in every possible world—even those in which he does not exist.

But the answer to these claims is clear; the sentences (20) and (21) are ambiguous. (20) is ambiguous as between

(20*)  Socrates is unwise

a proposition predicating of him the complement of *being wise,* and

(20**)  It's not the case that Socrates is wise

a proposition that doesn't predicate anything of Socrates but predicates falsehood of the proposition *Socrates is wise.* (20*), we may say, is *predicative* with respect to Socrates; (20**) is *impredicative* with respect to him. A similar comment is to be made about (21). The sentence (21) is ambiguous as between

(21*)  Socrates is such that if he is wise, something is

a proposition that is predicative with respect to Socrates and predicates of him the widely shared property of being such that if he is wise, then someone is, and a proposition equivalent to

(21**)  The propositions *Socrates is wise* and *someone is wise* are such that if the first is true, then so is the second,

which is impredicative with respect to Socrates. (21*) is predicative with respect to Socrates, and contingent, being false in those possible worlds in which Socrates does not exist. (21**), on the other hand, is necessary, but does not predicate a property of Socrates. Exactly similar comments apply to

(22)  Either Socrates is wise or Socrates is not wise.

(23) is ambiguous as between a contingent proposition predicating of Socrates the property *being either wise or not wise,* and a necessary proposition impredicative with respect to Socrates (but predicative with respect to the propositions *Socrates is wise* and *it's not the case that Socrates is wise*). So the proffered examples certainly don't show that serious actualism is false.

Still, isn't there something arbitrary and *ad hoc,* in the present context, about insisting that *Buckley is wise* predicates a property of Buckley while *It's not the case that Buckley is wise* does not? Not really, I think, although *ad hocness* is sufficiently slippery to make it hard to be sure. In any event, let's agree that there are *conditions* as well as properties. For any property $P$, there is the condition of having $P$, and also the condition of not having $P$. Conditions are met by objects, and met by objects in possible worlds. To meet the condition of having $P$ in $W$, an object must have $P$ in $W$; to meet the condition of not having

*P* in *W* an object must not have *P* in *W*. Furthermore, if an object fails to meet the condition of having *P* in *W*, then it meets the condition of failing to have *P* in *W*, although of course it doesn't follow that it meets the condition of having *P̄* in *W*. Still further, there are such conditions as *having P or not having P*, a condition met by everything in every possible world. Then while it may be the case that no object has any *property* in any world in which it does not exist, an object may perfectly well meet *conditions* in worlds in which it does not exist. And while serious actualism may be *true*, from this perspective it looks considerably less substantial.

Now this maneuver, I think, is fruitless. There *really is* an important distinction between failing to have a property *P* in a world and having its complement in that world; failing to have *P* in *W*, furthermore, is not having *P̄*, the complement of *P* in *W*, or indeed any other property. The serious actualist claims that an object exists in any world in which it has a property *P*, but of course she doesn't claim that an object exists in every world in which it *doesn't* have *P*. Furthermore, it isn't at all easy to see what sort of thing a *condition* is, or to state the conditions under which an object meets a condition in a world.

But suppose we waive these considerations and agree that there are conditions. Among the conditions there will be *being wise* and *failing to be wise; being unwise* and *failing to be unwise; existing and failing to exist*. For any condition *C*, the proposition *everything that meets C exists* is necessarily true; but of course it is not true in general that if an object meets *C* in a world *W*, then it exists in *W*. Now some conditions will be *existence entailing*; they will be such that (necessarily) for any object *x* and world *W*, if *x* meets *C* in *W*, then *x* exists in *W*. Others will not; and the serious actualist will hold that any condition of the sort *has P* (where *P* is a property) is existence entailing, while those of the sort *does not have P* are not. Here the serious actualist is correct, I believe; but for present purposes we needn't argue that general point. For suppose we return to

(6) Necessarily, if *Socrates does not exist* had been true, then *Socrates does not exist* would have existed

the premise of the anti-existentialist argument that occasioned our excursion into serious actualism. Our question is really whether *being true* is existence entailing. The question is whether there is a proposition *P* and a possible state of affairs *S* such that if *S* had been actual, then *P* would have been true but nonexistent—i.e., *P* would have been true and there wouldn't have been any such thing as *P*. The answer, it seems to me, is obvious. Clearly there is no such state of affairs and proposition. Clearly no proposition could have been true without existing. Clearly every state of affairs which is such that if it had been actual, *P* would have been true, is also such that if it had been true, then *P* would have existed. (6), therefore, ought to be accepted and Pollockian existentialism, like Powersian, should be rejected.

## IV. Priorian Existentialism

Now suppose we turn our attention to

(5) If the proposition *Socrates does not exist* is possible, then it is possibly true,

the most controversial premise of the anti-existentialist argument. Among those who deny (5) are Arthur Prior,[8] Kit Fine,[9] and Robert Adams.[10] *Priorian Existentialism*, therefore, is the brand of existentialism that denies (5); the Priorian Existentialist believes that a proposition can be *possible* without being *possibly true*. This is initially puzzling—*very* puzzling. If possibility, for a proposition, isn't possible truth, what is it? If a proposition could not have been true, how can it be possible? If someone held that there are many possible worlds, but only the actual world could have been actual, then according to Robert Adams, "we would be left to wonder in what sense the other possible worlds are possible, since they couldn't have been actual." But doesn't the same hold for possibility and possible truth when propositions are the topic of discussion? Indeed, it looks as if there aren't *two* concepts here, but only one; it looks as if '*Socrates does not exist* is possible' (in the broadly logical sense) and '*Socrates does not exist* is possibly true' express the very same proposition. Possibility and necessity, after all, are *alethic* modalities—modalities of *truth*. It looks initially as if 'possible' just *means* 'possibly true'; what else *is* there for it to mean? What can Prior, Fine, Adams *et al.* be thinking of?

One way we can understand this alleged contrast between possibility and possible truth has been suggested (perhaps a bit obscurely) by Arthur Prior possibility, as opposed to possible truth, is *possible nonfalsehood*. To get a grasp of this notion, we must turn to the idea of essential attribution. An object *x* has a property *P* essentially if and only if it is impossible that *x* exist and lack *P*—alternatively (given serious actualism), if and only if it is impossible that *x* have the complement of *P*. Socrates, for example, has essentially the properties *being a person* and *being self-identical*; it is impossible that Socrates should have existed and lacked these properties, and impossible that he should have had either of their complements. On the other hand, there could have been no such thing as Socrates at all, in which case Socrates would not have had these or any other properties. Accordingly it is possible that Socrates should not have had these properties.

Now suppose we agree, for purposes of argument, that the number nine is a necessary being; it could not have failed to exist. (If you think numbers are contingent beings, substitute your favorite necessary being for the number nine.) Like Socrates, the number nine has some of its properties essentially—*being a number,* for example, and *being composite.* In contrast to Socrates, however, nine could not have failed to exist; and hence it is not possible that nine should have lacked these properties. We might mark this difference by saying that Socrates has the property of being a person *essentially,* but nine has the property of being a number *necessarily.* An object *x* has a property *P* necessarily if and only if it is necessary that the former have the latter and only if the state of affairs consisting in *x*'s having *P* could not have failed to obtain. Alternatively, *x* has *P* necessarily if and only if *x* has *P* essentially and *x* is a necessary being. So Socrates has the property of being a person essentially; God, if classical theists are right, has that property necessarily. Everything, trivially, has existence essentially—that is, nothing could have existed but failed to exist. Only such necessary beings as God, however, have existence necessarily.

But now we must not make a similar distinction among propositions. If only some of them are necessary beings, we shall have to distinguish *having truth essentially* from *having truth necessarily.* A proposition *p* has truth essentially if and only if it is not possible that *p* should have existed and lacked truth alternatively (given that no proposition can be neither true nor false) if and only if it is not possible that *p* exist and be false, that is (given (6)), if and only if it is not possible that *p* be false. A proposition will have truth *necessarily* or *be necessarily true,* however, if and only if it has truth essentially and furthermore exists necessarily, could not have failed to exist. So *p* is necessarily true if and only if it is not possible that *p* fail to be true. Every necessary truth is an essential truth; but if the present brand of existentialism is right, the converse does not hold. The proposition *Socrates exists,* for example, could not have been false. It could have failed to exist, however, and hence could have failed to be true; it is therefore essentially but not necessarily true. And now the claim is that to say that *Socrates does not exist* is possible, is only to say that it is possibly non-false—could have failed to be false. But of course that does not entail, say, the Priorian, that it could have been true—that is, is possibly true.

Now I think we can see that Priorian existentialism, like the Powersian and Pollockian varieties, cannot be right. The fundamental reason is that if it *were* right, propositions like

(23) Socrates does not exist

would not be possible after all; and if we know anything at all about these matters, we know that (23) is possible. Let me explain.

First, the Priorian existentialist will concede or rather insist that (23) is not *possibly true.* (23) would be true only if it existed, which it could do only if Socrates also existed; but then of course it would not be true. Nor, furthermore, is (23) true in some possible world. If there were a possible world in which (23) is true, that would be a world in which Socrates does not exist. But (23) does not exist in any world in which Socrates does not; so if (23) is true in some world, it is true in a world in which it does not exist—which, the Priorian concedes, is impossible.

According to Priorian Existentialism, then, (23) is neither possibly true nor true in some possible world. How, then, can it be thought of as possible? The Priorian will reply, of course, that (23) could have failed to be false. It could not have been true; but it could have failed to be false. There are possible worlds in which it is not false: the worlds in which Socrates does not exist. I said that if we know anything at all about modality, we know that (23) is possible; from the point of view of Priorian Existentialism this intuition does not require possible truth. Possible non-falsehood is possibility enough. But surely this is wrong; possible non-falsehood is not possibility enough. In the first place, entirely too many propositions are possibly non-false: for example,

(24) Socrates is self-diverse

and even such explicit contradictions as

(25) Socrates is wise and Socrates is not wise.

According to the existentialist, (24) and (25) are possibly non-false; they would not have existed and hence would not have been false if there had been no such thing as Socrates. But surely there is no sensible conception of possibility at all in which (24) and (25) are possible.

Second, (24) and (25) imply, respectively,

(26) there is at least one thing that is self-diverse,

and

(27) there is at least one thing that is both wise and not wise

in the first order logic. But (26) and (27) aren't even so much as possibly non-false. Possible non-falsehood is therefore not closed under logical implication—a crucially serious impairment for a candidate for possibility.

But the clinching point, I think, is the following. What was the alleged insight behind existentialism in the first place? That it is impossible that objects of which we might say Socrates is a constituent— singular propositions directly about him, possible worlds containing him, his essences, and the like—should have existed if he had not. If $E$ is any entity of that sort, the idea was that

(28) $E$ exists and Socrates does not

is impossible. This is the central existentialist insight. But note that (28), from the Priorian perspective, is possibly non-false; it would have failed to be false if Socrates had not existed. So if possible non-falsehood is possibility enough, (28) is possible after all. The Priorian existentialist is thus hoist on his own petard. His fundamental insight is that (28) is not possible; he therefore argues that propositions such as (23) are not necessary beings. This apparently conflicts with the obvious truth that such propositions are possible. The proffered resolution consists in claiming that possible non-falsehood is sufficient; but then (28) is possible after all.

The moral to be drawn, I think, is that possibility, for a proposition, is possible truth; there is nothing else for it to be. The alleged distinction between possible truth and possibility is a confusion. According to Prior,[11] Jean Buridan distinguished the *possible* from the *possibly true*. Buridan, however, apparently drew this distinction not for *propositions*, but for *sentences*—more exactly, sentence tokens. And here Buridan is correct. A sentence token is true (or true in English) if it expresses (in English) a true proposition; it is possible (we may say) if it expresses a possible truth—if the proposition it express (in English) is possible, i.e., possibly true. The sentence token

(29)  there are not sentence tokens,

then, is possible. It could not have been true (in English), however; for to be true it would have had to exist: in which case it would not have been true. We could therefore say, if we wished, that (29) is possible but not possibly true. But there is no similar distinction in the case of propositions: possibility, for a proposition, is possible truth. Truth and falsehood are the salient characteristics of propositions; it is therefore natural to use 'possible' to abbreviate 'possibly true' (rather than, say, 'possibly existent' or 'possibly Paul's favorite proposition'). But to argue that (23) is possible on the grounds that it could have failed to be false, is like arguing that Socrates is possibly a number or possibly self-diverse on the grounds that he could have failed to have the properties of being a non-number and being self-identical. Indeed he could have failed to have these properties; had he not existed, Socrates would not have had these or any other properties. It is sheer confusion, however, to conclude that he is possibly a number or possibly self-diverse. Similarly, then, for propositions: if some propositions—e.g., (23)—are contingent objects, then those propositions could have failed to be false. It is sheer confusion, however, to conclude that they are possible.

Priorian Existentialism, therefore, is as unacceptable as the Powersian and Pollockian varieties. The conclusion to be drawn is that the anti-existentialist argument is sound and existentialism must be rejected.

## NOTES

1. *Worlds, Times, and Selves* (Amherst: University of Massachusetts Press, 1997), p. 109.

2. Of course the wholehearted existentialist will add that states of affairs (and hence possible worlds) are also ontologically dependent upon the individuals they involve.

3. *The Nature of Necessity* (Oxford, 1974), pp. 121–63.

4. "Actualism and Thisness," *Synthese* 49 (1981), p. 5.

5. *A System of Logic* (New York, 1846), p. 21.

6. In conversation; I'm not certain Powers was altogether serious.

7. As I did in "De essentia," *Grazer Philosophische Studien* (1979), pp. 108–9. I am indebted to John Pollock who helped me see the error of my ways.

8. "Theories of Actuality" in *The Possible and the Actual*, ed. M. Loux (Ithaca: Cornell University Press, 1979), p. 201.

9. "Postscript" in World, Times, and Selves, pp. 116ff.

10. "Actualism and Thisness" (see also note 4).

11. "The Possibly-true and the Possible," in *Papers in Logic and Ethics* (Amherst: University of Massachusetts Press, 1976), p. 202.

# 9

# Replies to My Colleagues

## II. Reply to John L. Pollock

John Pollock's powerful and penetrating essay treats actualism, serious actualism, existentialism, and the basic claim that for any possible state of affairs $S$, there exists a possible world that includes $S$; this is not the order in which Pollock takes up these topics, but it is convenient for my reply. What Pollock says about serious actualism is especially interesting and important, I think, and I shall devote the most space to it.

### A. Actualism

I applaud Pollock's efforts, in this section, to set out the essentials of a modal set theory; this is a topic of great interest. Less promising, however, is his characterization of actualism. I follow Robert Adams in using 'actualism' to name the claim that there neither are nor could have been things that do not exist—the claim that the proposition *there are no things that do not exist* is necessarily true. (As I said above, this name is a bit misleading in that it invites confusing actuality and existence; but it seems to have acquired currency.) According to Pollock, on the other hand, "if actualism is to be claiming something interesting, it must be claiming that there is no reasonable sense in which this sentence ['There are some things that do not exist'] can be understood which makes it true." Taken that way, the prospects for actualism are dim indeed; clearly there are *several* sensible ways of using the sentence in question to express a truth. As

176

Pollock suggests, it can be taken to express what is more perspicuously expressed by "The actual world is such that it is possible that there exist objects that do not exist in *it*."[1] (This may be a bit strained; the latter sentence is more plausibly taken as a clearer rendering of 'There could *have been* some things that do not exist' or 'There could have been some things that do not exist *in fact*'.) And there are other possibilities. We could sensibly use the sentence in question, for example, to state that there are true substitution instances of the form '*t* does not exist' (where '*t*' is a variable ranging over singular terms): 'Faffner does not exist', 'Santa Claus does not exist', 'The man who can beat Botwinnik does not exist'[2] and the like. Taken as the claim that there is no sensible use, in English, for the sentence 'There are some things that do not exist', actualism is very likely false. But why does Pollock believe that if actualism is claiming something interesting, it must be making *that* claim? Because, apparently, he thinks the only *other* sensible understanding of 'There are no things that do not exist' is as expressing what 'There *exist* no things that do not exist' expresses; and *that* proposition is hardly worth asserting. In affirming actualism, however, I mean to affirm neither that triviality nor the falsehood that the sentence 'There are some things that do not exist' cannot plausibly be used to express a truth. What then do I mean? Are there other alternatives?

I think there are. We should note first that philosophers of great intellectual power have asserted that there are things that do not exist; and they haven't taken themselves to be making either the absurd claim that there exist things that do not exist or the trivial claim that the sentence in question can sensibly be used to express a truth. Castañeda, Meinong, and the Russell of 'On Denoting', for example, believe (or, to beg no questions, *claim* to believe) that in addition to all the things that exist, there are some more that do not; among these things that do not exist, furthermore, are some—the round square, for example—such that it isn't even possible that they should have existed. Now Pollock believes, I think, that the sentence 'There are some things that do not exist' taken straightforwardly and literally, expresses the same proposition as 'There exist some things that do not exist' and I am inclined to agree. But how, then, can we avoid saddling Castañeda, Meinong and Russell with the absurd view that there exist things that do not exist, and indeed, things that not only do not but could not have existed? Where can we locate our disagreement with them? Surely not about the proposition *there exist things that do not exist*; they will claim, quite sincerely and no doubt quite accurately, that they believe *that* proposition *false*.

Suppose we call the partisan of nonexistent individuals a "possibilist." This isn't entirely accurate (some such partisans believe not only in possible but nonexistent objects, but also in *impossible* nonexistent objects); but 'anti-actualist' and 'nonactualist' are too unattractive, and no other more appropriate terms seem to be at hand. Now perhaps a good way to put the disagreement between actualist and possibilist is as a disagreement about what sorts of properties and propositions there are. There exist property and proposition descriptions, we might say, such that the actualist believes them empty but the possibilist believes them exemplified. The possibilist believes that there is (and exists) a property that does not entail existence, but is entailed by every property. That is, he believes that there is a property *P*—perhaps he will call it 'being'—that meets two conditions. First, *P* does not entail existence; that is, it is possible that an object exemplify *P* but fail to exemplify existence. And second, every property entails *P*: that is, for any property *P\**, it is necessary that whatever exemplifies *P\** also exemplifies *P*. Furthermore, he will add, the locution 'there is an object such that _____' is related to *P* in just the way that 'there exists an object such that _____' is related to existence; we may say, if we like, that the first locution, the "particular quantifier," *expresses P* just as the existential quantifier expresses existence. According to the possibilist, this property *P*—the property expressed by the particular quantifier—does not entail existence; and if he thinks there are other properties exemplifiable by nonexistent objects—*being the (or a) round square*, for example—these, too, he will say, do not entail existence.

The actualist, of course, will disagree. *He* will hold that there is no such thing as this alleged property *P*. *Every* property, he says, entails existence—that is, for any property *P\**, the proposition *whatever exemplifies P\*, exists* is necessarily true; this is a simple consequence of the fact that the proposition *everything exists* is itself necessarily true. Like Kant (see above, p. 67) the actualist will hold that for any property *P\**, the conjunction of *P\** with existence is equivalent to (entails and is entailed by) *P\**.

Actualists and possibilists, therefore, will disagree as to what properties there are. And this disagreement will engender others; in particular it will engender disagreement as to what propositions there are. The possibilist thinks there is a property *P* that does not entail existence but is entailed by every property; he will also think, no doubt, that there exists a proposition *A* such that necessarily, *A* is true if and only if something exemplifies *P* but not existence. This proposition (or one equivalent to it), he claims, is the proposition expressed by "There are some things that do not exist." Actualist and possibilist, therefore, differ as to what propositions and properties there are. If we see the disagreement between actualist and possibilist in this light, then perhaps a more revealing way to characterize actualism is as the view that there is no property that is entailed by but does not entail existence.

## B. Serious Actualism

*Serious* actualism, as I use the term, is the view that (necessarily) no object has a property in a world in which it does not exist. That is, every object $x$ is such that for any possible world $W$ and property $P$, *if* necessarily, if $W$ had been actual, then $x$ would have had $P$, *then* necessarily, if $W$ had been actual, $x$ would have existed. More exactly, serious actualism is the necessity of this proposition. More simply, it is the claim that no object could have had a property without existing. (*Frivolous* actualism is the conjunction of actualism with the denial of serious actualism.) Pollock accepts actualism, but proposes *not-existing* as a counterexample to serious actualism; Socrates, he says, has the property of not-existing in worlds in which he does not exist. He then reports me as holding that "there is no such property as that of *not existing*" and as adding that "There is a property of *non-existence*, but that is a property nothing can have because in order to have it, an object would have to exist without existing." Bewildered by this unexpected turn of events, he asks, "Why would anyone say this?" and replies as follows:

> There is a very seductive modal fallacy to which I have found myself succumbing on occasion and I suspect that Plantinga is succumbing to it here. The fallacy consists in endorsing instances of the following modal principle:
>
> (13) $\Box(x)\ (Fx \supset Gx) \supset \Box(x)\ \Box(Fx \supset Gx)$.
>
> To see that this principle is invalid, let $F$ be 'does not exist' and $G$ be 'exists'. Assuming that our quantifiers range only over existing objects . . . , the antecedent of (13) is true, . . . , but the consequent is false because it says that everything has necessary existence (p. 126).

Now our first problem is to understand (13). Suppose we treat occurrences of '$\Box Fx$' as expressing modality *de re*, so that '$\Box Fx$', to put it very informally, says that $x$ has essentially the property expressed by F and '$(x)\Box Fx$' says that everything has essentially the property expressed by F[3]; suppose furthermore that an object has a property essentially if and only if it has it in every world in which it exists; and suppose finally that actualism is true, so that there neither are nor could have been any nonexistent objects. Then (13) is a special case of

(14) $\Box(x)\ Fx \supset \Box(x)\Box Fx$

which (understood as above) is a correct modal principle. What (13) so construed says is

(13\*) If necessarily everything is such that if it is F, then it is G, then necessarily everything has essentially the property of being such that if it is F, then it is G

which has no false instances. Specified, as Pollock suggests, to 'does not exist' and 'exists' the result is

> If necessarily, everything is such that if it does not exist, then it exists, then necessarily, everything has essentially the property of being such that if it does not exist, then it exists.

It is easy enough to see that this is true: everything has essentially the property of existing (nothing has existence in any world in which it does not exist); hence everything has essentially the property of being such that if it does not exist, then it exists. This last, furthermore, is necessarily true; so the proposition in question has a true consequent and is therefore true.

Pollock, however, does not understand (13) in this way. How does he understand it? As follows. Let us suppose that for any proposition *P*, there is such a thing as its denial, and for any object *x* and property *P*, there is such a thing as the proposition that *x* has *P*. (The proposition that *x* has *P* will be true in a world *W* if and only if some individual essence of *x* is coexemplified with *P* in *W*; its denial (the proposition that it is not the case that *x* has *P*) will be true in *W* if and only if no essence of *x* is coexemplified with *P* in *W*.) What '$\Box Fx$' says (again, very informally) is that the proposition that *x* is *F* is necessarily true. Then both (14) and the weaker

(14*)  $\Box(x)Fx \supset (x)\Box Fx$

have false substitution instances; for while it is necessarily true that everything exists, it is false that everything is such that the proposition that it exists is necessary (and *a fortiori* false that *necessarily*, everything that exists is such that the proposition that it exists is necessary). And taken this way, (13) will indeed have false instances: what it says, so taken, is

> (13**)  If necessarily everything is such that if it is F, then it is G, then necessarily everything is such that necessarily, if the proposition that it is F is true, then the proposition that it is G is true.

The specification of this to 'does not exist' and 'exists,' as Pollock rightly says, is clearly false.

So far, so good; there is so far no disagreement between us. But Pollock goes on to suspect that I endorse serious actualism just because I mistakenly endorse false instances of (13) taken his way; to this I plead innocent. Why then *do* I endorse serious actualism? Because it follows from actualism, a view that both Pollock and I endorse with unrestrained enthusiasm. The argument is simple enough. I shall begin by explaining why I believe Pollock is mistaken in proposing *nonexistence* (which, I take it, is the complement of existence) as a counterexample to serious actualism. Now first, there is a perfectly straightforward argument from actualism to the conclusion that non-existence (call it 'Ē') is not exemplified. Consider

(1) For any property $P$, if $P$ is exemplified, then there is something that exemplifies $P$

and

(2) For any property $P$, whatever exemplifies $P$ exists.

Here the quantifiers are to be taken as widely as possible; if you think there are things that do not exist, then read the quantifiers as ranging over those things as well as the more conventional existent sort. (1), I take it, is obviously true. (2) is a consequence of actualism, according to which it is necessary that whatever there is, exists. (1) and (2) together entail

(3) If nonexistence is exemplified, then nonexistence is exemplified by something that exists.

Since the consequent of (3) is clearly (necessarily) false, it is false that nonexistence is exemplified. And since (given the truth of actualism) each of the premises of this argument is necessarily true, it follows that nonexistence is necessarily unexemplified; that nonexistence is not exemplified is a necessary truth.

But then nonexistence is not a counterexample to serious actualism. According to the latter, nothing exemplifies a property in a world in which it does not exist. But nothing exemplifies nonexistence in a world in which it does not exist, because nothing exemplifies nonexistence in *any* world. Alternatively: it's necessary that if any object had exemplified nonexistence, then nonexistence would have been exemplified. Therefore it is necessary that nothing could have exemplified nonexistence.

It is easy to see, I think, that we can go on to deduce serious actualism from actualism. For suppose an object—Socrates, let's say—exemplifies a property $P$ in a world $W$. Then (necessarily) if $W$ had been actual, Socrates would have exemplified $P$. Now (necessarily) if Socrates had exemplified $P$, then either Socrates would have exemplified $P \, \& \, E$, the conjunction of $P$ with existence, or Socrates would have exemplified $P \, \& \, \bar{E}$ (where $\bar{E}$ is the complement of existence). As we have just seen, it is impossible that Socrates exemplify $\bar{E}$, and hence impossible that Socrates exemplify $P \, \& \, \bar{E}$. It is therefore necessary that if Socrates had exemplified $P$, then Socrates would have exemplified existence. In terms of possible worlds; suppose Socrates exemplifies $P$ in $W$. Then either Socrates exemplifies $P$ *and existence* in $W$ or Socrates exemplifies $P \, \& \, \bar{E}$ in $W$. There is no world in which Socrates exemplifies $P \, \& \, \bar{E}$. So Socrates exemplifies existence (that is, exists) in $W$.[4]

The above arguments both seem to me to be entirely solid. I am

at a loss to explain why Pollock does not accept them—unless perhaps, it is that his intellect has been clouded by excessive euphoria
induced by an unduly sybaritic, southwestern style of life. But there is
another, less censorious explanation. Pollock suspects I'm just *defining*
'property' in such a way that serious actualism is (trivially) true; he
proposes, therefore, that we speak of *conditions:*

> Suppose we give Plantinga his use of the term 'property', agreeing
> that (19b) and serious actualism are true by stipulation for proper-
> ties. Then it is natural to want a more general term which includes
> both properties and things like *not existing.* I want to say that al-
> though objects cannot have properties at worlds in which they do
> not exist (by the definition of 'property'), they can *satisfy conditions*
> at worlds in which they do not exist, and one such condition is that
> of *not existing.* Another such condition is that of being such that *if*
> *one existed then one would be sentient.* Socrates satisfies the latter at
> worlds in which he does not exist (p. 128).

Pollock goes on to explain that conditions are or determine functions
from individuals to states of affairs (and, we might add, propositions):

> Conditions and properties alike can be regarded as determining
> functions from individuals to states of affairs. For example, the prop-
> erty of *being snubnosed* determines the function which to each indi-
> vidual *x* assigns the state of affairs *x's being snubnosed.* Similarly, the
> condition of *not existing* determines the function which to each in-
> dividual *x* assigns the state of affairs *x's not existing.* These functions
> are functions *in intension* rather than functions *in extension.* . . . If it
> is denied that conditions make sense in any other way, then they
> can simply be identified with the corresponding functions. That is,
> a condition becomes any function from objects to states of affairs
> (p. 128).

Then we can say that

> C  An object *x* satisfies a condition *C* at a world *W* if and only if
> C(*x*) (the value of *C* for *x*) is true at *W*.

"In this way," Pollock adds, "we make perfectly good sense of conditions and of objects satisfying conditions at worlds in which they do
not exist" (p. 129).

Now all of this seems quite correct. Indeed there are conditions;
conditions are just propositional functions (functions in intension)
from individuals to propositions. Since there is such a thing as the
denial of the proposition *Socrates exists* (the proposition *Socrates does*
*not exist* or *it's false that Socrates exists*) there is a propositional function—call it '$\sim$(*x exists*)'—whose value for Socrates is that proposition; and since that proposition is true in worlds in which he does
not exist, Socrates satisfies $\sim$(*x exists*) at worlds in which he does not
exist. In the same way he satisfies the condition *x is wise or* $\sim$(*x is wise*)

at worlds where he does not exist. So an individual $x$ can perfectly well satisfy a condition at a world in which $x$ does not exist.

Then Pollock points out that *some* conditions are such that an object $x$ cannot satisfy them at a world without existing in that world; *other* conditions, however— $\sim(x\ exists)$, for example—can perfectly well be satisfied by $x$ at worlds in which $x$ does not exist. And Pollock suspects that I'm just *defining* 'property' as 'condition that can't be satisfied at a world by an object that doesn't exist in that world', thereby making serious actualism trivially true. But here, I believe, Pollock is falling into a confusion (a confusion I was guilty of on p. 14 of "On Existentialism"): he is confusing satisfaction of a condition *at* a world with satisfaction of a condition *in* a world. The truth of the matter is that while an object can perfectly well satisfy a condition *at* a world in which it does not exist, it cannot satisfy a condition *in* a world in which it does not exist. We may see this as follows.

First (as I've already said), the proposition *Socrates does not exist* is true in worlds in which Socrates does not exist: hence the value of the condition $\sim(x\ exists)$ for Socrates taken as argument is true in worlds in which Socrates does not exist; hence Socrates satisfies this condition *at* such worlds.

But second, Socrates does not satisfy this condition *in* a world in which he does not exist, where

C\* an object $x$ satisfies a condition $C$ in a world $W$ if and only if necessarily, if $W$ had been actual, then $x$ would have satisfied $C$.

For Socrates does not satisfy $\sim(x\ exists)$ in any worlds at all. Here we can give an argument exactly paralleling the earlier argument for the conclusion that Socrates does not exemplify $\bar{E}$ in any possible world. For first, it is impossible that $\sim(x\ exists)$ is satisfied. An object $x$ satisfies a condition or propositional function $C$ if and only if the value of $C$ for $x$ as argument is true. A condition is therefore satisfied only if some object satisfies it—only if, that is, there is an object that satisfies it. Consider therefore

(4) For any condition $C$, if $C$ is satisfied, there is something that satisfies $C$

and

(5) For any condition $C$, whatever satisfies $C$ exists.

(4), once more, is obviously true; and (5), like (2), is an immediate consequence of actualism.[5] (And again, take the range of the quantifiers as wide as possible.) From (4) and (5) it follows that

(6) If $\sim(x\ exists)$ is satisfied, then $\sim(x\ exists)$ is satisfied by something that exists.

The consequent of (6), however, is impossible; so the condition $\sim(x$ *exists*) is not satisfied. Each of the premises, furthermore, is necessary; so it is necessary that $\sim(x$ *exists*) is unsatisfied. You may think it a bit peculiar that some conditions—$\sim(x$ *exists*) for example—could not have been satisfied even though there are worlds at which they are satisfied. But this peculiarity is only verbal, and is due to a quirk in our definition of 'satisfies at'. $C$ is indeed satisfied *in* some possible world only if $C$ is possibly satisfied; the same cannot be said for satisfaction *at*.

But now it follows that there is no possible world in which Socrates satisfies $\sim(x$ *exists*). For suppose he satisfies it in some world $W$: then if $W$ had been actual Socrates would have satisfied $\sim(x$ *exists*); but if Socrates had satisfied $\sim(x$ *exists*), that condition would have satisfied—which, as we have just seen, is impossible. So if Socrates satisfies $\sim(x$ *exists*) in $W$, then $W$ is not possible after all, contrary to hypothesis. Neither Socrates nor anything else, therefore, satisfies $\sim(x$ *exists*) *in* any possible world (although Socrates and many other things satisfy $\sim(x$ *exists*) *at* many possible worlds). And as before, we can easily go on to show that Socrates doesn't satisfy any condition in a world in which he doesn't exist. For suppose Socrates satisfies $C(= x$ *is $C$*) in $W$. Then either Socrates satisfies *x is $C$ & x exists* in $W$ or Socrates satisfies *x is $C$* and $\sim(x$ *exists*) in $W$. As we have seen the latter is impossible; so if Socrates satisfies $C$ in $W$, then he also satisfies *x exists* in $W$, in which case he exists in $W$.

Now for the less censorious explanation of our differences. Pollock has, I think, overlooked the difference between 'satisfies at' and 'satisfies in.' It is indeed true that objects can satisfy conditions *at* worlds in which they do not exist; it doesn't follow (and isn't true) that they can satisfy conditions *in* worlds in which they do not exist. *A fortiori*, it doesn't follow that objects can have properties in worlds in which they do not exist. Pollock is entirely correct, therefore, in pointing out that there are conditions, and that objects can satisfy conditions *at* worlds in which they do not exist. What he says, however, does nothing to show that an object can satisfy a condition or have a property *in* a world in which it does not exist; and that question, after all, is the one to which serious actualism is addressed. Serious actualism has nothing to do with the question whether objects have properties or satisfy conditions *at* worlds in which they do not exist; it has everything to do with the claim that no object has a property or satisfies a condition *in* such worlds.

The distinction between satisfaction in and satisfaction at deserves a little more by way of exploration. As we have seen, it is not in general true that if a condition is satisfied at a world $W$, then it is satisfied in that world. Some conditions, however—wisdom, being snub-nosed, for example—do display this feature. If an object $x$ satisfies wisdom at a given world $W$, then $x$ satisfies wisdom in $W$. A *property*, we may say, is just a condition that is satisfied by an object $x$ *at* a world $W$ only if it is satisfied *in* $W$ by $x$. Alternatively, suppose we say that a condition $C$ is *existence-entailing* if (necessarily) whatever satisfies it at a given world $W$ exists in $W$. To say that a condition $C$ is existence-entailing is not merely to remark that necessarily, whatever satisfies $C$ exists; *that* much is a trivial consequence of serious actualism. It is instead to say something much stronger: for any $x$, if $C(x)$ had been true, then $x$ would have existed. $x$ *is wise* is thus existence-entailing; any world in which *Socrates is wise* is true is one in which Socrates exists. $\sim(x\ is\ wise)$ on the other hand, is not; for the proposition *it is false that Socrates is wise* is true in worlds in which Socrates does not exist. $x$ *exists*, obviously, is existence-entailing; $\sim(x\ exists)$, just as obviously, is not. And then we may say that properties are just the existence-entailing conditions. So properties are those conditions for which *satisfaction at* coincides on any possible world with *satisfaction in*; equivalently, a property is any existence-entailing condition.

We must note further that for any property $P$ and its complement $\bar{P}$ there are four conditions: $x$ *has P, x has* $\bar{P}$, $\sim(x\ has\ P)$, and $\sim(x\ has\ \bar{P})$. (The distinction between $x$ *has P* and $\sim(x\ has\ P)$ corresponds to and underlies what is sometimes called the distinction between external and internal negation.) Thus wisdom and its complement $\bar{W}$ are properties; $\sim(x\ has\ wisdom)$ and $\sim(x\ has\ \bar{W})$—conditions that respectively map Socrates onto *it is false that Socrates has wisdom* and *it is false that Socrates has* $\bar{W}$—are not. The value of an existence-entailing condition for an object $x$ as argument is *predicative*, with respect to $x$; it predicates a property of $x$, and is true only in those worlds in which $x$ exists. On the other hand, $C(x)$ is *impredicative* with respect to $x$ if $C$ is a condition that does not entail existence;[6] a proposition that is impredicative with respect to an object $x$ does not predicate a property of $x$ and can be true in worlds in which $x$ does not exist.

Whether we propose to use the word 'property' in the way I have suggested (thus distinguishing between properties and conditions) is, of course, a merely verbal matter. What is substantive here are two points: (1) some conditions are existence-entailing and some are not, and (2) necessarily every object $O$ and condition $C$ are such that if $O$ had satisfied $C$, then $O$ would have existed (serious actualism).

## C. Existentialism

As I use the term, *existentialism* is the view that singular propositions, singular states of affairs, and haecceities are all ontologically dependent upon the individual they 'involve', as are other propositions, properties and states of affairs appropriately related to those of the first sort. Thus, for example, if William F. Buckley had not existed, then such singular propositions as *William F. Buckley is wise* would also have failed to exist; and the same holds for his haecceity, for the proposition *either William F. Buckley is wise or someone is wise*, for possible worlds in which he exists, and the like. In chapters in this volume, I argued that existentialism is false. Pollock rejects this argument. He then claims that the question of existentialism "makes no difference" to our modal intuitions and he proposes, finally, two analyses of *states of affairs*: one vindicating existentialism and one vindicating its denial (which, to continue my terminological metaphor, I shall call 'essentialism'). He concludes that "our conceptual scheme is simply indeterminate in this respect." I shall comment briefly on each point.

1. Where *S* is the state of affairs consisting in Socrates' not existing, one premise in my argument against existentialism is

(3) Necessarily, if *S* had obtained, *S* would have existed.[7]

(In the original argument I spoke of propositions rather that states of affairs; here I follow Pollock in switching to states of affairs.) Pollock finds this premise "suspect." But *why*? It seems utterly obvious that if *S* had obtained, then there would have *been* such a thing as *S*; but if there had been such a thing as *S*, then (given actualism) *S* would have existed. Pollock points out that (3) does not appropriately follow from

Necessarily, every state of affairs that obtains, exists.

This is quite correct; nonetheless, I can't see how (3) could have been false. If we need something from which to infer it, I suggest

Necessarily, every state of affairs is such that it could not have been actual without existing

or, alternatively,

Necessarily, every state of affairs is such that the proposition that it obtains entails the proposition that it exists.

These seem to me wholly obvious, and I am at a loss to account for Pollock's finding them dubious. How could a state of affairs *S* have obtained if there hadn't been any such state of affairs as *S*? How could *S obtains* have been true if *S exists* had not been true? I say it can't, and that (3) has powerful intuitive support.

To help us see that (3) is after all dubious, Pollock bids us to consider pictures. A picture can represent a state of affairs in which it does not exist: "We can even have a picture which correctly depicts a state of affairs in which there are no pictures (e.g., a picture of a big empty Louvre) and hence in which it does not itself exist" (p. 135). Quite right; in the same way a sentence token *t* can express a proposition—*there are no sentence tokens*, for example—in which it does not exist. But is the analogy relevant? The claim Pollock is defending is that it is at least plausible to suppose that some states of affairs could have been actual without existing—that is, could have been both actual and nonexistent. The fact about pictures to which he draws our attention, however, is that they can represent states of affairs in which they don't exist. How is this relevant? What would be more relevant, I think, would be some property a picture could have had without existing. Say that a picture is *accurate* if it depicts a state of affairs that obtains. Could a picture have been accurate without existing? Surely not. Similarly for sentence tokens. A sentence token *t* can express a proposition in which it does not exist—that is, it can express a proposition *P* that is true only if *t* does not exist. But how is this relevant? What would be relevant would be an example of a property a sentence token could have had without existing. Say that a sentence token is *true* if it expresses a true proposition: it is obvious, I think, that a sentence token couldn't have been true without existing.

Here as earlier there lurks a possible confusion between satisfying a condition (or having a property) *at* a world as opposed to *in* a world. A picture *P*, we may say, is accurate *at* a world *W* if *P* depicts a state of affairs that obtains in *W*; it is accurate *in* a world *W* if (necessarily) if *W* had been actual, *P* would have been accurate. Similarly, a sentence token *t* is true at a world *W* if and only if *t* expresses a proposition true in *W*; *t* is true *in* *W*, however, if and only if (necessarily) if *W* had been actual, then *t* would have expressed a true proposition. What Pollock points out, in these terms, is that pictures and sentence tokens can be accurate or true *at* worlds in which they do not exist. What he needs for his analogy to be convincing, however, is their truth or accuracy *in* worlds in which they do not exist; and that is not forthcoming. Pollock claims that a state of affairs "can be said to represent part of the structure of a possible world at which it obtains, and just as in the case of pictures, there is no obvious reason why it must exist in that world in order to achieve the representation" (p. 136). I don't see how the first part of this claim is true; a state of affairs *S just is* part of the structure of a world in which it obtains; but how can it be said to *represent* it? Does it represent itself? But suppose we waive this quibble and agree that a state of affairs can thus represent a world. If we think (as I do not) that states of affairs can fail to exist, then perhaps we will also think that a state of affairs can represent a world or part of a world in which it does not exist. Perhaps so; but it wouldn't follow that it can obtain *in* a world in which it does not exist, or that it could obtain without existing; and that is what is presently relevant.

2. I am therefore left with the conviction that (3) is true. This gives me a reply to Pollock's second point: that the existentialism/essentialism issue has no bearing on our other modal intuitions. I

believe this is false, because I endorse the essentialist argument. If we accept existentialism, we must give up one of the premises of that argument—all of which, it seems to me, are clearly true. Pollock, as we have seen, suggests we give up the claim that a state of affairs could not have been actual without existing; if I am right, however, his argument for the dubiety of this claim is unsuccessful.

3. Pollock is convinced that all talk of abstract entities "must be analysable in terms of (possibly modal) talk of non-abstract entities". He observes that it is in general difficult to give analyses of abstract objects; but "one case in which the program can be carried out with relative ease," he says, "is the case of states of affairs and possible worlds." To give the analysis, Pollock specifies certain set theoretical structures some of whose elements "correspond" to states of affairs and possible worlds; talk about states of affairs and possible worlds is then correlated with talk about these structures or about members of their transitive closures. Such an analysis does not *identify* states of affairs with sets of the relevant type; rather it analyzes talk of the former in terms of talk of the latter. The analysis, he continues, does not (and is not intended to) tell us

> what states of affairs are. That strikes me as a non-sensical enterprise.
> Rather, this is an analysis of talk of states of affairs in the same sense
> as the analysis of number-theory in terms of higher-order logic is an
> analysis of talk about numbers. The analysis tells us what it is for
> there to be states of affairs of certain sorts, but not what states of
> affairs are. (p. 137)

Deep issues lurk here; I have no space to explore them. I shall therefore confine myself to a couple of discussion-directing questions. First: the analysis of a claim about states of affairs is said to tell us *what it is for there to be* states of affairs of a certain sort. We say: there is such a state of affairs as *Pollock's being a rockclimber*; the analysis of this claim is that there is such a thing as the ordered pair (Pollock, *being a rockclimber*). But how does the latter tell us what it is for there to be such a thing as the former? What does it tell us that we didn't already know? How does it increase our understanding of what it is for there to be such a thing as the state of affairs in question? Couldn't we just as sensibly say that the former tells us what it is for there to be such a thing as the latter? Furthermore there are other sets that we could correlate with the state of affairs in question—for example, an ordered pair of an individual essence or haecceity and a property. Why wouldn't that do just as well? Clearly there are many set-theoretical models of our talk about states of affairs and individuals. Why pick any one of them as more revealing than the others?

A second question: as Pollock points out, we can give different set theoretical analyses of our talk about individuals and states of affairs;

under some of these existentialism comes out true and under others it comes out false. Pollock apparently concludes that "our conceptual scheme is simply indeterminate in this respect." I'm not sure just what this means, but I suspect it implies that there is no question of truth here—that neither existentialism nor essentialism is "determinately true" (i.e., true). But how does this follow? I can't see that the fact in question so much as plausibly suggests that there is no truth of the matter with respect to the issue between existentialism and essentialism.

D. Possible Worlds

First, I agree with Pollock that there are what he calls *transient* states of affairs: states of affairs which, like *Reagan's being president*, can obtain at some times but not at others. Second, Pollock is quite right in pointing out that a possible world must be thought of as a maximal possible *non-transient* state of affairs; otherwise a possible world would have a brief tenure indeed. Thirdly, Pollock is right in pointing out the non-triviality of the claim that there is at least one possible world (even given that there are states of affairs and that every state of affairs has a complement). Still further, Pollock is right in pointing out that even if we agree there are possible worlds, it doesn't trivially follow that

(1) For any state of affairs S, S is possible iff then there is a possible world in which S obtains.

Now Pollock gives an argument for (1) that essentially employs

(11) Necessarily, every possible world is necessarily a possible world.

He gives an argument for (11) that takes as premises

(8) Necessarily, every non-transient state of affairs has necessary existence

and

(9) Necessarily, every non-transient state of affairs is necessarily a non-transient state of affairs;

And the argument from (8) and (9) to (11) employs the full resources of $S_s$. In essence, then, Pollock argues for (1) by assuming as premises the principles that non-transient states of affairs (and hence possible worlds) exist necessarily and have their modal properties—possibility, necessity, etc.—necessarily; it then follows that every possible world is necessarily a possible world—i.e., exists necessarily and couldn't have failed to be maximal and possible. If W exists necessarily and has its modal properties necessarily, furthermore, then there couldn't have been a state of affairs S distinct from each of the states of affairs that do in fact exist. So these are strong assumptions indeed. I believe they are *true* but I think we can give an argument for (1) that doesn't rely on assumptions as strong as these.

For take any possible state of affairs $S$, and let $A$ be the set of states of affairs that are possible and include $S$. (That there *is* such a set is perhaps controversial, but presumably not controverted by Pollock, who agrees that there is such a thing as the set of states of affairs that are actual.) $A$ is partially ordered by the proper inclusion relation—that is, by the relation $R$ that a state of affairs $S$ bears to $S^*$ iff $S$ includes but is not included by $S^*$. According to the Hausdorff maximal principle (which is equivalent to the axion of choice) $A$ has a maximal linearly ordered subset $B$—a subset that is linearly ordered by the proper inclusion relation and is such that no linearly ordered subset of $A$ properly includes it. Let $\&(B)$ be a conjunction of $B$—that is, a state of affairs that obtains if and only if every member of $B$ is actual. Now assume

(2)  For any set of possible states of affairs $S$, if $S$ has a maximal linearly ordered subset, then $S$ has a maximal linearly ordered subset $S^*$ which is such that if every finite subset $S^{**}$ of $S^*$ is possible—that is, such that $\&\,(S^{**})$ is possible—then so is $S^*$ itself (Quasi-compactness).

It follows that $A$ has a maximal linearly ordered subset $B^*$ which is such that if every finite subset of it is possible, then so is $\&(B^*)$. But every finite subset of $B^*$ is possible, since (by the linear ordering) every such subset has a last member which is possible and which includes the other members. Hence $B^*$ is possible and includes $S$.

It is easy to show that $\&(B^*)$ is a possible world. Since $\&(B^*)$ is possible it suffices to show that for every state of affairs $S^*$, either $\&(B^*)$ includes $S^*$ or $\&(B^*)$ includes $\bar{S}^*$. Suppose not—i.e., suppose there is a state of affairs $S^*$ such that $\&(B^*)$ does not include $S^*$ and $\&(B^*)$ does not include $\bar{S}^*$. Either $\&(B^*)\&S^*$ is possible or $\&(B^*)\&\bar{S}^*$ is possible. Each includes $S$; so at least one of them is a member of $A$. But then there is a linearly ordered subset $C$ of $A$ that properly includes $B^*$: either $B^* \cup (\&(B^*)\&S^*)$ or $B^* \cup (\&(B)\&\bar{S}^*)$; and then $B^*$ isn't maximal. So for any state of affairs $S^*$, either $\&(B^*)$ includes $S^*$ or $\&(B^*)$ includes $\bar{S}^*$; but then $\&(B^*)$ is a possible world.

This argument has weaker premises than Pollock's: in particular, it doesn't require the premise that states of affairs have their modal properties essentially.

NOTES

Internal references to pagination are from the original version of this essay.

1. Equivalently: "Possibly there are objects that do not exist in $\alpha$" or "in some possible world there exist objects that do not exist in fact."

2. Richard Cartwright, "Negative Existentials," *Journal of Philosophy* 31 (1960): 628.

3. See Thomas Jager, "An Actualistic Semantics for Quantified Modal Logic," *Notre Dame Journal of Formal Logic* 23 (1982): 335–49.

4. Accordingly, when I said (in "On Existentialism," p. 13) "From actualism *tout court*, therefore, we cannot infer serious actualism," I erred by overlooking the above argument.

5. If, as the actualist claims, it is necessary that everything exists, then it is necessary that anything meeting any condition exists.

6. See *The Nature of Necessity*, pp. 150–51, and "Actualism and Possible Worlds" in *The Possible and the Actual*, ed. Michael Loux (Cornell, 1979), pp. 269 ff.

7. This (3) is from a section of the volume from which this chapter is taken.

# 10

## Two Concepts of Modality

*Modal Realism and Modal Reductionism*

Necessary and contingent propositions, objects with accidental and essential properties, possible worlds, individual essences—these are the *phenomena of modality*. I shall contrast two opposed conceptions of modal phenomena[1]; one of them, as I see it, is properly thought of as *modal realism*; the other is *modal reductionism*. 'Modal realism', as I use the term, has nothing to do with whether certain sentences or propositions have truth values; it has equally little to do with the question whether it is possible that our most cherished theories should in fact be false. I speak rather of *existential* realism and antirealism.[2] The existential realist with respect to universals, for example, holds that there really are such things as universals; the antirealist holds that there are no such things, and may add that the role said by some to be played by them is in fact played by entities of some other sort. The existential realist with respect to so-called theoretical entities in science—quarks or chromosomes, say—claims that there really are things with at least roughly the properties scientists say such things have; the antirealist denies this. In the first part of this chapter, I shall sketch a version of modal realism; in the second, I shall outline and briefly explain modal reductionism. My chief example of reductionism will be the important modal theory of David Lewis: I shall argue that Lewis is a modal realist and/or a realist about possible worlds in approximately the sense in which William of Ockham is a realist about universals: namely, not at all.

# I. Modal Realism

## A. Grade 1: Accidental and Essential Properties

There are three grades of modal realism (to adapt a famous claim); so let us begin at the beginning and turn to the first. Here we may conveniently start with modality *de dicto* and the familiar distinction between necessary and contingent propositions. According to the modal realist, there are *propositions*: the things that are both true or false and capable of being believed or disbelieved. Every proposition is true or false (we may ignore the claim—misguided as I see it—that some propositions are neither); and every proposition is such that it is possibly believed or possibly disbelieved or both.[3] It is the *intentional* character of propositions that is most fundamental and important. Propositions are *claims or assertions*; they *attribute* or *predicate* properties to or of objects; they represent reality or some part of it as having a certain character. A proposition is the sort of thing according to which things are or stand a certain way.

The modal realist therefore holds that there are propositions. What is specific to him as a *modal* realist, however, is the claim that true propositions come in two varieties: those that could have been false, and those that could not. Some but not all true propositions exclude falsehood by their very natures. In the first group would fall the theorems of first order logic, the truths of mathematics and perhaps set theory, and a miscellaneous host of less well regimented items, such as **no one is taller than himself, red is a color, no human beings are prime numbers**, and (at any rate according to some) **there is a being than which it is not possible that there be a greater**. Such propositions are necessarily true; they have the property of being true and have it essentially—that is, they have it in such a way that they could not have lacked it. Other propositions, on the other hand, have the property of being true, all right, but have it accidentally: they could have lacked it. These are contingent propositions: for example, **Socrates was the teacher of Plato** and **Armidale, Australia, is about the same size as Saskatoon, Saskatchewan**. Necessary propositions are absolutely necessary; they are necessary in the strongest sense of the term. This sort of necessity—suppose we call it 'broadly logical necessity'[4]—is to be distinguished from causal or natural necessity (presumably our natural laws and physical constants could have been different in various subtle and not so subtle ways) as well as from self-evidence (in either the narrow or extended sense), from what is known or knowable a *priori*, and what (if there is any such thing) we cannot give up.[5]

A necessary proposition, therefore, has truth (the property of being true) essentially; a (true) contingent proposition has it accidentally. Here we have a special case of a more general distinction: that between an object's having a property essentially, on the one hand, or accidentally on the other. Modality *de dicto* is an important special case of modality *de re*: the special case where the object in question is a proposition and the property in question is truth. But it is only a special case; for according to the modal realist of the first grade, *all* objects have both essential and accidental properties: there are objects and there are properties and all of the first have some of the second accidentally and some of the second essentially. The properties **being self-identical, being a person**, and **being possibly conscious** are essential to me; the properties **wearing shoes** and **liking mountains** are accidental to me. Nine, to take a famous example, has the property of being odd essentially but the property of numbering the planets accidentally. Of course there are variations on the theme of modal realism of the first grade; instead of saying that all objects have both essential and accidental properties, we could have said that *some* objects have both essential and accidental properties. More weakly still, we could have taken modal realism of the first grade as the claim that (*pace* Quine and others) there really is a distinction between necessity and possibility, counting as a modal realist anyone who affirms this, even if he also affirms (perhaps with Brand Blanshard and other idealists) that all objects have all their properties essentially.

## B. Grade II: Possible Worlds

Not content with the claim that all objects have both essential and accidental properties, the modal realist of the second grade asserts that there are such things as *possible worlds* and that for any (temporally invariant) state of affairs or proposition **S, S** is possible if and only if there is a possible world that includes or entails it. She may think of possible worlds in more than one way. She may hold, for example, that there are states of affairs as well as propositions, where a state of affairs is such an item as **Socrates' being wise, 7 + 5's** equaling 12, and **there being no lions in Australia**. A state of affairs is *actual* and *obtains*, or else is not actual and fails to obtain; and a state of *affairs* **S** *includes* a state of affairs **S\*** if and only if it is not possible that **S** be actual and **S\*** fail to be actual. Like propositions, states of affairs have complements or negations: indeed, states of affairs and propositions are isomorphic, with **actuality** and **inclusion** for states of affairs replacing **truth** and **entailment** for propositions. She may also think, as I do, that some propositions (and states of affairs are) *temporally variant*; their truth values can vary over time. Thus the proposition **Paul is eating** is true at the present time, but not, fortunately enough, at every time. As I see it, a sentence like 'Paul is eating', assertively uttered at a time **t**, does not express the temporally invariant proposition **Paul eats at t** but a temporally variant proposition true at just the times Paul eats. Since states of affairs are isomorphic to propositions, there are also temporally variant states of affairs—**Paul's eating**, for example—which obtain at some times but not at others.[6] Possible worlds, then, are possible states of affairs: more specifically, they are temporally invariant states of affairs. Still more specifically, a possible world is a *maximal* possible state of affairs, where a state of affairs **S** is maximal if and only if for every state of affairs **S***, either **S** includes **S*** or **S** includes the complement ~**S*** of **S***. Alternatively, we could say that a possible world is a maximal possible *proposition*: a proposition that is possible, and for every proposition **p** either entails (in the broadly logical sense) **p** or entails ~**p**. (Of course if states of affairs just *are* propositions, then my "alternatively" was not appropriate.)

It is clear that the second grade is indeed a step beyond the first: even if there are both necessary and contingent states of affairs, both necessary and contingent propositions, it doesn't follow, at any rate just as a matter of logic, that there are *maximal* possible propositions or states of affairs.[7] Perhaps for every possible proposition **p**, there is a possible proposition **q** that properly entails it, but no proposition **q** that for every proposition **p** entails either **p** or its complement. (Or perhaps there are possible propositions or states of affairs that are not properly entailed or included by any propositions or states of affairs, but nonetheless are not maximal.) Further, suppose we agree that there is at least one possible world: it still requires a nontrivial argument to show that for any (temporally invariant) state of affairs or proposition **S, S** is possible if and only if there is a possible world that includes or entails it.[8]

According to the modal realist of the second grade, then, for every (possible) temporally invariant proposition or state of affairs there is a possible world in which it is true or obtains. Further, there is one possible world which includes every actual state of affairs[9]; this is the actual world, which I shall call 'alpha'. Alpha alone is actual, although of course all the worlds exist and indeed *actually* exist. Still further, this vast assemblage of worlds is complete and world invariant: each of the worlds exists necessarily, and there could not have been a world distinct from each of the worlds that does in fact exist. (At any rate so I say; the existentialist[10] would disagree.) We can now make the traditional assertion connecting truth in worlds with modality *de dicto*: a proposition is necessarily true if and only if true in every possible world.

## C. Grade Three: Things Have Properties in Worlds

According to the modal realist of the third grade, concrete objects such as you and I have properties in worlds. This isn't as trifling as it sounds. An object **x** has a property **P** in a world **w** if and only if it is not possible that **w** be actual and **x** exist but fail to have **P**—alternatively, if and only if **w** includes **x**'s having **P**. An object's having a property in a world, obviously enough, is no more than a special case of an object's having a property in a proposition or state of affairs, where **x** has **P** in a proposition **A** if and only if it is not possible that **A** be true and **x** exist but fail to have **P**.

But isn't it just obvious and uncontroversial that Socrates, for example, has the property of being wise in the proposition **Socrates is wise**? It isn't obvious and non-controversial, because it isn't uncontroversial that there is such a proposition as **Socrates is wise** (or such a state of affairs as **Socrates' being wise**). More exactly, what isn't uncontroversial is that Socrates and the proposition expressed by 'Socrates is wise' are such that it isn't possible that the second be true and the first fail to be wise. For suppose a view of names like Frege's is true: such a proper name as 'Socrates', on this view, is semantically equivalent to such a definite description as 'the teacher of Plato' or 'the shortest Greek philosopher'. A proper name therefore expresses a property; it expresses such a property as **being the (sole) teacher of Plato** or *being the shortest Greek philosopher*. Such a property, of course, is accidental to Socrates—he could have existed but lacked it. If so, then the proposition expressed by the sentence 'Socrates is wise' could have been true even if Socrates (the person who actually *is* the teacher of Plato) were not wise, provided there existed someone who was wise and the sole teacher of Plato. If this view of names were correct, then the sentence 'Socrates is wise' would not express a proposition in which Socrates has wisdom. It could be held, more generally, that there are no sentences at all that express a proposition so related to Socrates, and that indeed there aren't any propositions so related to him. To hold this view is to hold that there is no proposition which is *singular* with respect to Socrates; for a proposition is singular with respect to an object **x** only if it is a proposition in which **x** has some property or other. So suppose there aren't any propositions singular with respect to concrete, contingent beings such as you and I: then there are no worlds singular with respect to us, and hence no worlds in which we have properties. On this view, worlds will be *Ramsified*: they will be general propositions or states of affairs specifying that certain properties and relation—certain *qualitative* (as opposed to *quidditative*[11]) properties and relations—are exemplified. Such worlds will specify, for each of us individually and all of us collectively, various roles we could have played; but no world will specify that you or I play a given role. An object **x** has a property **P** in a world, therefore, only if there are propositions singular with respect to **x** and **P**. But clearly if there is a proposition singular with respect to **x**, then there is a world in which **x** has **P**. Objects have properties in worlds, therefore, if and only if there are singular propositions.

Further, objects have properties in worlds if and only if there are *individual essences*: properties essential to an object and essentially unique to that object.[12] First, it is obvious that if an object has an individual essence, then there are worlds in which it has properties. For suppose Socrates has an essence **E**: then there is a proposition and a state of affairs in which Socrates has wisdom: **E and wisdom are coexemplified** and **E's being coexemplified with wisdom**. And then, of course, there would be possible worlds in which Socrates has wisdom, those worlds including the states of affairs or propositions in question. So if there are individual essences, there are also singular propositions.

But it is also easy to see that if there are singular propositions, then (given certain plausible assumptions) there are also individual essences. For suppose we know what it is for a proposition to predicate a property of an object. A proposition **A** predicates a property **P** of an object **x** only if necessarily, if **A** is true then **x** has **P**.[13] Given this notion, we can see that if there are singular propositions, there will also be essences. For consider the singular proposition **Socrates is wise**. This proposition predicates wisdom of Socrates and nothing else. So there is the property **being the person the proposition *Socrates is wise* predicates wisdom of** (or the property **standing to the proposition *Socrates is wise* in the relation in which an object stands to a proposition if and only if the latter predicates wisdom of the former**); and this property is an essence of Socrates. Clearly it is *essential* to him: he could not have existed and been such that this proposition did not predicate wisdom of him. But it is also essentially unique to him; there could not have been someone distinct from Socrates who was such that this proposition predicated wisdom of him. It is therefore an essence of Socrates.

According to the modal realist of the third grade, then, objects have properties in worlds. In view of the above equivalences, he might as well have said that there are singular propositions; for objects have properties in worlds if and only if there are singular propositions. Or he might have said that there are individual essences; for objects have properties in worlds if and only if there are individual essences. And given that objects have properties in worlds, we can make the traditional assertions connecting essential property possession with having properties in worlds: an object **x** has a property **P** essentially if and only if **x** has **P** in every world in which **x** exists; **x** has **P** accidentally if and only if **x** has **P** and there is a world in which **x** exists but lacks **P**.

Now suppose we agree that things do in fact have properties in worlds, so that in fact there are individual essences. Then fascinating questions arise: questions I can only mention, not discuss. First: do objects have *qualitative* essences, i.e., essences constructible out of purely qualitative properties? Infinite disjunctions of infinite conjunctions of such properties, perhaps? Second: are there *haecceities*, where a haecceity of an object is the property of being that very object? If so, are haecceities non-qualitative? If they are, will there also be other non-qualitative essences? Third: an unusually interesting alleged special case of individual essences is presented by *unexemplified* individual essences: individual essences that could have been exemplified, but in fact are not. *Existentialists*—such philosophers as Robert Adams,[14] Kit Fine,[15] and Arthur Prior[16]—deny that there are any such things, although at the high cost of denying one or more of three exceedingly plausible premises.[17] Singular propositions and quidditative properties, they say, are dependent upon the individuals they involve; so if Socrates had not existed, then the same would have held for this individual essence.

## D. Actualism and Serious Actualism

But what about possibilia—i.e., mere possibilia? A *possibile* would be a thing that does not exist although it could have; a thing that does not exist in the actual world but does exist in some other world. Should we not add a fourth grade of modal realism, a grade occupied by those who hold that in addition to all the things that exist, there are some more that do not? I doubt it. There is nothing specifically modal about these alleged things that do not exist—or rather there is nothing any more modal about them than about anything else. Anything that does exist is a *possibile*; the claim to fame of these alleged nonexistents is not the modal claim that they possibly exist, but the ontological claim that while indeed there *are* such things, they do not *exist.* I therefore do not believe that we should spend a grade of modal realism on these disorderly elements. The compleat modal realist, however, must take a stand on the question whether there are any such things as mere possibilia. I suggest he reject them as a snare and a delusion and embrace what is sometimes called 'actualism'. Actualism is the view that there neither are nor could have been any entities that do not exist, (where our quantifiers are taken wholly unrestricted). 'Actualism' is not a good name for actualism; it slyly encourages a confusion that is apparently all too attractive on its own demerits: the confusion between actuality and existence. The actualist does not hold that everything is *actual* (he recognizes, of course, that some states of affairs are not actual and some propositions are false); what *he* holds is that everything *exists* (again, quantifier taken unrestrictedly); there are no things that do not exist. But the name seems to have become entrenched, so 'actualism' it shall be. The compleat modal realist, therefore, will be an actualist. There may be more things than are dreamt of in our philosophy, but there aren't more things than all the things that exist; and while there could have been things distinct from each of the things that exist, it does not follow that there are some things that do not exist but could have.[18] What does follow (as I see it) is that there are some unexemplified essences.

Let us therefore embrace actualism. We can take a further step; we can also embrace *serious* actualism. The serious actualist holds, naturally enough, that everything whatever exists, but he adds that nothing has properties in worlds in which it does not exist. That is, for any world **w**, if Socrates has a property in **w**, then Socrates exists in **w**; for any world **w**, if **w** is such that if it had been actual, then Socrates would have had **P**, then **w** is such that if it had been actual Socrates would have existed. Still another way to put it: Socrates could not have had a property without existing.

On the face of it, serious actualism certainly looks to be *de rigueur* for the actualist. If there could have been no objects that do not exist, how could it be that Socrates should have had some property but not existed? If he had had some property or other, then there would have been such a thing as Socrates, in which case (by actualism) there would have *existed* such a thing as Socrates. Still, there are actualists who deny serious actualism. Kit Fine[19] and John Pollock,[20] both sturdy actualists, maintain that Socrates does have properties in worlds in which he does not exist: they say he has *nonexistence*, the complement of existence, in such worlds. We all agree, say they, that there are worlds in which Socrates does not exist; what could be more sensible, then, than to say that in those worlds he has the property of nonexistence? I concede a certain surface plausibility to this opinion; on a closer look, however, we can see, I think, both that serious actualism is a corollary of actualism *tout court*, and that the apparent plausibility of the contary opinion is merely apparent.

First, then, I propose to argue that if actualism is true, then Socrates has neither the property of existence nor the complement of that property in worlds in which he does not exist. My argument has the following two premises:

(1) Necessarily, for any property **P**, if **P** is exemplified, then there is something that exemplifies it,

and

(2) Necessarily, for any property **P**, whatever exemplifies **P** exists.

(1), I take it, is obvious; and (2) is an immediate consequence of actualism. (If, as actualism testifies, necessarily, everything exists, then necessarily, everything that meets any condition exists.) But (1) and (2) entail

(3) Necessarily, if nonexistence is exemplified, it is exemplified by something that exists.

Clearly enough, it is impossible that nonexistence (the complement of existence) be exemplified by something that exists; it is therefore impossible that nonexistence be exemplified. So suppose Socrates has a property **P** in a world **w** in which he does not exist: then if **w** had been actual, Socrates would have exemplified **P**. So if **w** had been actual, then either Socrates would have exemplified **P & existence** (the conjunction of **P** with existence) or **P & nonexistence**. He could not have exemplified the latter; for if he had, then nonexistence would have been exemplified, and we have seen that this is impossible. Therefore he would have exemplified the former; hence he would have exemplified existence. But then Socrates exemplifies existence in any world in which he exemplifies any property at all, just as the serious actualist claims.

If this is so, however, whence the plausibility of the contrary opinion? Why does it seem no more than common sense to say that Socrates exemplifies nonexistence in worlds in which he does not exist? We can see why as follows. As realists of the third grade, we agree that there are singular propositions. Associated with every property **P**, therefore, is a propositional function: a function whose value, for a given object **x**, is the singular proposition that **x** has **P**. Call these functions *conditions*. Associated with the property **being wise**, then, is a condition that maps an object—Socrates, let's say—onto the proposition that it is wise. Of course there is also the condition that maps Socrates onto the proposition that he is unwise, has the complement of wisdom. But there is also a condition that maps Socrates onto the proposition **it is false that Socrates is wise**—which proposition, according to the serious actualist, is distinct from the proposition **Socrates is unwise**. (The latter proposition is true only in worlds in which Socrates exists and has the complement of wisdom; the former is true in those worlds, but also in the rest of the worlds in which Socrates does not have that property, namely, the worlds in which he does not exist.) So we have four conditions:

>**x is wise**
>**x is unwise**
>**~(x is wise)**

and

>**~(x is unwise)**.

The first two of these, says the serious actualist, are *predicative*—i.e., their values, for any object **x** taken as argument, predicate a property of **x**; their values, for Socrates taken as argument, respectively predicate wisdom and unwisdom of him. The second two, on the other hand, are impredicative. Their values, for Socrates taken as argument, do indeed predicate a property (namely, falsehood) of the *propositions* **Socrates is wise** and **Socrates is unwise**; but they predicate no property of Socrates himself. More generally, the value of an impredicative condition for an object **x** predicates no property of **x** although it may predicate a property of some proposition predicating a property of **x**.

Now perhaps it is plausible to think that properties just are con-ditions—or at any rate are so intimately connected with them that for each distinct condition there is a distinct property: the property the value of that condition, for a given object **x** taken as argument, predicates of **x**. That is, it is plausible to think that *predicative* condi-tions are or are intimately connected with properties; as we have seen, says the serious actualist, the value of an impredicative condition, for an object **x** does not predicate a property of **x**. But clearly actualism implies (by the above argument) that no object can satisfy a predi-cative condition in a world in which it does not exist; thus serious actualism is vindicated.

Now here the actualist opponent of serious actualism (call him a 'frivolous actualist') is not without reply. "Is it so clear," he says, "that such a proposition as **it is false that Socrates is wise** predicates no property of Socrates? True, it predicates falsehood of the proposition **Socrates is wise**; but why should that prevent its also predicating a property of Socrates—the property, perhaps, of being such that the proposition that he is wise is false? But if this is correct, then the conditions you call impredicative are not really impredicative after all; and surely Socrates can satisfy *those* conditions in worlds in which he does not exist. Surely, for example, he can satisfy such conditions as ∼(**x exists**) and ∼(**x is wise**) in worlds in which he does not exist; after all, the values of those functions for Socrates taken as argument are true in those worlds."

But here we must pay careful attention to this idea of an object's satisfying a condition in a world—or rather, we must distinguish two related notions, both of which lurk in this area. On the one hand there is the idea that an object **x** satisfies a condition **C** in a world **w** if and only if necessarily, if **w** had been actual, then **x** would have satisfied **C**. On the other hand, there is the idea that an object **x** satisfies a condition **C** in a world **w** if and only if necessarily, **C(x)** is true in **w**—if and only if, that is, necessarily, if **w** had been actual, then the value of **C** for **x** taken as argument would have been true. We can put these two as follows:

D1 **x** satisfies **C** in **w** iff necessarily, if **w** had been actual, then **x** would have satisfied **C**.

and

D2 **x** satisfies **C** in **w** iff necessarily, **C(x)** is true in **w**.

To mark the difference between these two, let's say that **x** satisfies **C** *in* **w** if **x**, **C** and **w** are related as in D1, and that **x** satisfies **C** *at* **w** if they are related as in D2. Then the thing to see is that if actualism is true, no object satisfies a condition (or has a property) *in* a world in which it does not exist, although an object such as Socrates satisfies a condition such as ~**x is wise** *at* worlds in which it does not exist. We can see this via an argument that exactly parallels the argument I gave earlier for the conclusion that Socrates has no properties in worlds in which he does not exist. My premises are

(4) Necessarily, for any condition **C**, if **C** is satisfied, then there is something that satisfies it

and

(5) Necessarily, for any condition **C**, whatever satisfies **C** exists.

Again, (4) is obvious and (5) follows from actualism. But (4) and (5) together entail

(6) Necessarily, if the condition ~(**x exists**) is satisfied, then it is satisfied by something that exists.

The consequent of (6), however, is impossible; it is therefore impossible that ~(**x exists**) be satisfied. It may seem a bit bizarre that there are conditions that cannot be satisfied, even though there are worlds at which they are satisfied. This peculiarity is merely verbal, and is due to a quirk in our definition of 'satisfies at'. **C** is indeed satisfied in some possible world only if **C** is possibly satisfied; the same cannot be said for satisfaction *at*.

But now it follows that there is no possible world in which Socrates satisfies ~(**x exists**). For suppose he satisfies that condition in some possible world **w**: then if **w** had been actual, Socrates would have satisfied that condition, in which case it would have been satisfied—which, as we have just seen, is impossible. So if Socrates satisfies ~(**x exists**) in **w**, then **w** is not possible after all, contrary to hypothesis. Neither Socrates nor anything else, therefore, satisfies ~(**x exists**) *in* any world (although of course Socrates and many other things satisfy ~(**x exists**) *at* many possible worlds). And as before we can easily go on to show that Socrates does not satisfy any condition at all in a world in which he does not exist. For suppose Socrates satisfies **C** (= **x is C**) in **w**. Then either Socrates satisfies **x is C & x exists** in **w**, or Socrates satisfies **x is C and** ~(**x exists**) in **w**. As we have seen, the latter is impossible; hence if Socrates satisfies **C** in **w**, then he also satisfies **x exists** in **w**, in which case he exists in **w**. It is therefore a mistake to think that an object can satisfy any conditions at all, predicative or impredicative, in worlds in which it does not exist. An object satisfies a condition or exemplifies a property in a possible world, therefore, only if it exists in that world, just as the serious actualist claims. Serious actualism, therefore, follows from actualism *simpliciter*; the temptation to think otherwise, I believe, stems from a tendency to confuse *satisfaction at* with *satisfaction in*. It is easy to confuse these two, and this confusion leads immediately to the idea that Socrates satisfies nonexistence in worlds in which he does not exist. The modal realist of the first grade, therefore, holds that individuals in general and propositions in particular have both essential and accidental properties; the modal realist of the second grade adds that there exist possible worlds. According to modal realism of the third grade, objects have properties in worlds—alternatively, objects have essences. The modal realist will also hold, I hope, that there are no things that do not exist, although there could have been things that do not exist in the world that is in fact actual. Finally, since he is an actualist, he should also embrace serious actualism.

## II. MODAL REDUCTIONISM

Suppose you, like (say) W. V. Quine, are a lover of desert landscapes: you believe in nothing but concrete individuals and set-theoretic constructions on them. Suppose you are also inclined to accept our common modal opinions: you believe that things might have been different in many ways, that if things had been appropriately different, then you would have had some properties that in fact you lack, and that there could have been people distinct from each of the people there actually are. Then you have something of a problem: how to construe these modal facts without recourse to propositions that are true but possibly false, properties an object has accidentally, possible worlds that are merely possible, and essences that are not exemplified. For none of these things seems to fit with the idea that whatever there is, is either a concrete individual or a set.

So what to do? Well, you could *quine* the whole disorderly crew: there simply *are* no essences, possible worlds, properties, propositions, and the like, you say. Serious science, you proclaim, has no place for such unwholesome elements, and you go on to blame a bad upbringing for our powerful tendency to think in modal terms. But there is a more subtle alternative; you could embrace the whole motley menagerie with an outward show of enthusiasm, but seek to introduce order and domesticity by analyzing them in terms of the objects you favor; you could *model* them and their properties in concreta and sets. That is the course taken by David Lewis, whose powerfully subtle modal thought will be my chief example of modal reductionism.

### A. Lewis's Modal Theory

Lewis's theory of modality and possible worlds began life as "Counterpart Theory":

> The counterpart relation is our substitute for identity between things in different worlds. Where some would say that you are in several worlds, in which you have somewhat different properties and some-

what different things happen to you, I prefer to say that you are in the actual world and no other, but you have counterparts in several other worlds. Your counterparts resemble you closely in content and context in important respects. They resemble you more closely than do the other things in their worlds. But they are not really you. For each of them is in his own world, and only you are here in the actual world. Indeed we might say, speaking casually, that your counterparts are you in other worlds, that they and you are the same; but this sameness is no more a literal identity than the sameness between you today and you tomorrow. It would be better to say that your counterparts are men you would have been, had the world been otherwise.[21]

On this account, you and I exist in just one possible world: the actual world. Now why would Lewis say a thing like that? Why would he thus sharply diverge from the modal realist, who typically holds that each of us exists in many different possible worlds? His answer in "Counterpart Theory and Modal Logic" (Lewis 1968): "P2, the postulate according to which nothing exists in more than one world, serves only to rule out avoidable problems of individuation" (*Op. Cit.* p. 114). We can see a better answer, however, once we see clearly how Lewis thinks of possible worlds. Possible worlds, he says, are spatiotemporally isolated concrete individuals: concrete individuals that are spatiotemporally related only to themselves and their parts. This wasn't entirely clear from his early accounts. Consider this famous passage from *Counterfactuals* (Lewis 1973):

> I believe that there are possible worlds other than the one we happen to inhabit. If an argument is wanted, it is this. It is uncontroversially true that things might have been otherwise than they are. I believe, and so do you, that things could have been different in countless ways. But what does this mean? Ordinary language permits the paraphrase: there are many ways things could have been besides the way they actually are. On the face of it, this is an existential quantification. It says that there exist many entities of a certain description, to wit "ways things could have been." I believe that things could have been different in countless ways; I believe permissible paraphrases of what I believe: taking the paraphrase at its face value, I therefore believe in the existence of entities that might be called 'ways things could have been'. I prefer to call them 'possible worlds'.[22]

This suggestion seems more than compatible with the idea that possible worlds are not concreta, such as you and I and God, but abstracta, like the null set and the number 7. "Ways things could have been," one might sensibly think, would be properties, perhaps, or possibly propositions, or states of affairs, or other abstracta.[23] But Lewis has recently clarified his view:

Are there other worlds? I say there are. I advocate a thesis of plurality of worlds, or *modal realism* . . . that holds that our world is but one world among many. There are countless other worlds, other very inclusive things. Our world consists of us and all our surroundings, however remote in time and space; just as it is one big thing having lesser things as parts, so likewise do other worlds have lesser other-worldly things as parts. The worlds are something like remote planets; except that most of them are much bigger than mere planets and they are not remote. Neither are they nearby. They are not at any spatial distance whatever from here. They are not far in the past or future, nor for that matter near; they are not at any temporal distance at all from now. They are isolated: there are no spatiotemporal relations at all between things that belong to different worlds. Nor does anything that happens at one world cause anything to happen at another.[24]

So worlds are concrete particulars—many of them enormous, but some no larger than a flea. (In fact, some of them *are* fleas; Lewis holds that every concrete particular has a duplicate that is coextensive with its world and hence *is* that world.) Each world, furthermore is *maximal* in the sense that each of its parts is spatiotemporally related to each of its parts and only to its parts. (So suppose we call them 'maximal objects'.) Maximal objects, of course, are not individuals that do not exist but could have; each of them exists, all right, although (except for the one of which we are a part) they are not spatiotemporally related to you and me. What we ordinarily refer to as "the universe" is one of these maximal objects; Lewis calls it 'the actual world'. But if possible worlds are maximal objects and you and I are parts of such a maximal object, then it is easy to see a good reason for thinking you and I exist in just one maximal object: if we existed in more than one, then each would be spatiotemporally related to the other (by virtue of sharing us as parts) and hence would not be maximal after all.[25]

So I exist in just one world; how can it be, then, that I have accidental properties? If there is no other world in which I exist, then for any property I do not have, there is no world in which I have it; so how could I have such a property? Lewis's answer: I possibly have a property if I have a counterpart—someone in this world[26] or another who is sufficiently similar to me—who has it.[27] I am possibly going barefoot today; that is, in some world there is someone who appropriately resembles me and is going barefoot. An object has a property accidentally if and only if it has it and has a counterpart that lacks it; an object has a property essentially if and only if it and all its counterparts have it.

Possible worlds, therefore, are maximal objects. The actual world is the maximal object of which we are parts; other maximal objects and their parts are *possibilia*. On Lewis's view a *possibile* is a concrete individual that is part (or the whole) of a world and spatiotemporally unrelated to us. *Pace* Meinong, Castañeda and Parsons, possibilia are not things that do not exist but could have; instead they are things that exist as solidly as you and I, though (except for our worldmates) at no spatiotemporal distance from us. *Properties* are sets—any sets; and an object *has* a property if and only if it is a member of it. An *individual essence* is the set of some individual and its counterparts. *Propositions* (or states of affairs: Lewis does not distinguish them) are sets of possible worlds: a proposition is true if and only if the actual world is a member of it, *possibly true* if and only if it is not empty, *necessary* if and only if it is the set of all possible worlds, and *impossible* if and only if it is the null set. Some propositions, of course, are unit sets; and since some worlds are donkeys or fleas, some propositions are unit sets of donkeys or fleas.

B. Modal Realism?

At first glance Lewis looks like a paradigm modal realist; indeed, Robert Stalnaker and others call him an *extreme* modal realist. Take the first grade of modal realism, the view that there are objects that have both accidental and essential properties. Surely Lewis endorses this view? An object has a property **P** *essentially*, he says, if and only if it is a member of **P** and so are all its counterparts; it has **P** *accidentally* if and only if it is a member of **P** but has a counterpart that is not. He holds that each of us has counterparts that have properties we don't; he also holds that each of us and all our counterparts are members of the universal set of individuals; should we not conclude that on his view objects have properties essentially and accidentally? Take modality *de dicto*, that special case of the first grade. Lewis holds that among the sets of maximal objects containing the maximal object of which we are a part, some contain fewer than all those objects and some (one) contain them all; shouldn't we conclude that on his view some true propositions are contingent and some necessary? Turn to the second grade of modal realism: don't we find Lewis claiming (indeed, stubbornly insisting) that there are possible worlds? Turn finally to the third grade of modal realism: don't we find Lewis affirming both that there are individual essences (the set of an individual and its counterparts) and that objects have properties in worlds (where an object has a property in a world if and only if it is a member of that property and is part of that world)? So doesn't it follow that Lewis's view is a case of modal realism and a case of realism about possible worlds?

It doesn't follow. Lewis's modal theory is *apparently* realistic; in fact, however, it is not realist at all—or so, at any rate, I shall argue. (Of course this is nothing against the view; nobody says you have to be a modal realist.) Turn first to modality *de dicto*, that special case of modal realism of the first grade according to which some true propositions are contingent and some necessary; and say that a theory is *realist*, if it asserts that indeed there are some things of this sort, *antirealist* if it asserts that there are no such things, and *nonrealist* if it is not realist. I believe Lewis's theory is an example of antirealism here. True enough, Lewis seems to *say* that there are necessary and contingent propositions, but he also says that they are *sets*. There are many contingent propositions; each is a set of maximal objects. There is just one necessary proposition: the set of all the maximal objects; there is just one necessarily false proposition: the null set.

My complaint is not just that on this view there is only one necessary (or necessarily false) proposition, when it is clear that in fact there are many. That is indeed a legitimate complaint: surely a person could know that $2 + 1 = 3$ even if he does not know that arithmetic is incomplete or that Goldbach's conjecture is true (if it is) or that there is such a person as God. This complaint is legitimate; but if it is multiplicity we want, Lewis is prepared to oblige. He has other set-theoretic constructions on offer to "play the role" of propositions, and among them are some with as much multiplicity as you please (Lewis 1986, p. 57). But my complaint comes right at the beginning and is both much more obvious and much more radical: sets, as we all know, are not the sort of things that can be true or false at all. You are teaching a course in set theory. The first day an agressive but confused student demands to know your view of the null set: is it true, he asks, or is it false? He adds (a bit truculently) that in his opinion it is clearly false. Your reply, appropriately enough, is that it is neither; sets aren't the sort of things that can be either true or false. When this student claims that the null set is false, what he says is obviously mistaken; and isn't that claim obviously mistaken, even if made, not by confused student, but by first-rate philosopher?

Perhaps Lewis's reply to this line of argument would go as follows: that there *are* such things as propositions—i.e., the things that are true or false and can be believed and disbelieved—that is a matter of common opinion and something we all know pretheoretically. But we don't know pretheoretically what these things are like, or what their nature is: *that* is a matter, not for common opinion, but for the theoretician.[28] (Perhaps Lewis would say here, as he does in another context, that "if naive intuition claims to decide such a recondite matter, we ought to tell it to hold its tongue" (246)). Here theory is under little pressure from common opinion or pretheoretical knowledge. But then no theory can be anti-realistic with respect to propositions just by saying that propositions are sets (or by attributing to them any other kind of nature).

Clearly this is partly right: there is much about the nature of propositions we don't pretheoretically know. Are they, as some have thought, sentences in some very large powerful language? Are they instead, as Augustine and the bulk of the medieval tradition insist,

divine thoughts? Do they have an internal structure? Do they have
properties as constituents? Do they have concrete objects as constituents? Are there singular propositions? Lewis is right; we don't pretheoretically know the answer to these questions. But we do know *something* about the nature of propositions, prior to theory. (By virtue of
this pretheoretical knowledge we know, for example, that propositions couldn't be sentences of English or German.) Conceivably they
could turn out to be idealized sentences or divine thoughts; but they
couldn't turn out to be just *anything*—donkeys, or fleas, or tables,[29]
for example. We know that no propositions are donkeys, and we know
that none are fleas. We know that no one believes fleas or donkeys
(and not because of a depressing tendency on their parts to prevari-
cate).

Now on Lewis's view, no propositions are donkeys or fleas (although some possible worlds are); but some of them—uncountably
many of them—are unit sets of donkeys and fleas. I say this is something we pretheoretically know to be false. Even as we can see that a
proposition can't be a donkey or a flea, so we can see that a proposition can't be the unit set of a flea, or any other set of fleas or
donkeys, or other livestock—or a set of concrete objects of any sort.
You can't believe a set, and a set can't be either true or false. The
problem, fundamentally, is that sets, like donkeys, obviously lack the
relevant intentional properties—the intentional properties propositions have. A set is neither a claim nor anything like a claim; it doesn't
represent its members or anything else as being thus and so; it neither
is nor makes a claim as to what things are like.[30] The unit set of a
donkey, for example, doesn't represent its member as being a donkey,
or a nondonkey, or anything else; it is mute on that topic, as on every
other. It certainly doesn't represent things as being such that there
are no horses and that all pigs can fly, as it would, on Lewis's theory,
if its member were a maximal object. On Lewis's theory, the null set
is the impossible proposition. (If it is necessary that there be a null
set, then the null set, on his view, is the proposition that there is no
null set!) But why say it is *that* proposition? If the null set is a proposition, why couldn't it be a necessary proposition, or any other proposition? I say it is obvious that the null set isn't any proposition at all.
It isn't the claim that there are married bachelors or that $3 + 1 = 7$
or that there is no such thing as the null set; nor is it the denial of
these claims. A set isn't a claim; it no more represents things as being
a certain way than an elephant has subsets. On Lewis's view there are
concrete *possibilia* and sets and nothing else,[31] but if so then on his
view there are no propositions at all, and hence none that are necessary or contingent. I therefore believe that Lewis's theory is nonrealistic and indeed antirealistic with respect to this special case of
modal realism of the first grade.

Now suppose we turn to the more general thesis of modal realism of the first grade: the claim that objects have properties both essentially and accidentally. Is this true, on Lewis's theory? Is it true, on Lewis's view, that Socrates could have had the property of being foolish? Of course he endorses the words 'Socrates could have had the property of being foolish'; on his theory this sentence is true, expresses a truth. But my assertively and sincerely uttering or writing the sentence 'There are X's' is insufficient for my holding that there are X's, as is my theory's assigning truth to this sentence. Perhaps, for example, I use the words involved in such a way that they do not in fact express the proposition in question. Compare the ultraliberal theologian who says that on his theory there is indeed such a person as God, all right—the sentence 'There is a God' expresses a truth— but there are no supernatural beings, and as he uses the word 'God' it denotes the "evolutionary-historical" process that has brought us into being.[32] That theologian's theory, in all probability, is not realistic with respect to God.

On Lewis's theory, then: do individuals have accidental properties? According to the theory, you have counterparts who are members of sets you are not a member of; and this is offered as an analysis of your having some properties accidentally. But is the analysis correct? Suppose there exists a person who is very much like you and is a member of some set you are not a member of: is that so much as *relevant* to your possibly having some property? It is hard to see how. On the face of it, there being a foolish person who is otherwise a great deal like Socrates has nothing whatever to do with the question whether Socrates could have been foolish. Surely it is not relevantly sufficient for Socrates' being possibly foolish; and the fact, if it is a fact, that this person is spatiotemporally unrelated to us and Socrates doesn't help. Nor, of course, is it necessary; even if everyone (even those, if any, who inhabit maximal objects distinct from ours) were wise, it would still be the case that Socrates could have been foolish. The existence of other maximal objects and counterparts who are members of sets I am not a member of is clearly irrelevant to the phenomena of modality. Surely I could have been barefoot even if everyone, even those in other maximal objects if there are any, were wearing shoes. Surely the proposed analysis is incorrect; it flouts the obvious pretheoretical truth that what is a possibility for me does not depend in this way upon the existence and character of other concrete objects.

Lewis sees his theory as "disagreeing with firm common sense opinion" (Lewis 1986, p. 133) especially with respect to his ontology— that uncountable magnitude of donkeys spatiotemporally unrelated to us, and those more than uncountably many maximal objects. Firm commonsense opinion is indeed incredulous here; there is no reason, pretheoretically, to believe that there is more than one maximal object; and considerable pretheoretical impulse to be at least agnostic about the matter. The idea that there are more than uncountably many of them, therefore, seems a great deal to swallow. Still, common opinion tends to be agnostic here and could perhaps be convinced by enough of the right sort of evidence. (A traditional theist will be harder to convince; from his point of view there couldn't be all those donkeys spatiotemporally unrelated to us. Say that **x** has been *created\** by God if either **x** has been created by God or has been created by something that has been created\* by God. According to the traditional theist, it is a necessary truth that every nondivine concrete particular has been created\* by God. All the donkeys there are, accordingly, are causally related to God. But (necessarily) things causally related to the same thing are causally related to each other; so there couldn't be any concrete particulars that are causally unrelated to you and me.) Where firm common opinion sticks in its heels is at the claim that it is *necessary* that there be all those donkeys and maximal objects. It seems clearly *possible* that there be at most one maximal object and only finitely many donkeys; and it is possible that all the donkeys there are be spatiotemporally related to us.

The idea that there are more than uncountably many donkeys and maximal objects is therefore problematic. But the real problem, from a modal point of view, is not with *that* idea but with the claim that a thing possibly has a property if and only if it has a counterpart that has the property. Perhaps I do indeed have a counterpart who can talk French; but clearly enough even if I don't, it is still possible that I talk French. Counterparts, concrete objects spatiotemporally unrelated to us, other maximal objects—these are all quite irrelevant to modality.

Still, even if this analysis is incorrect, it does not follow that Lewis's theory is either nonrealistic or antirealistic with respect to objects that have properties essentially and accidentally; and that, after all, is the question at issue. (Even if my analysis of causation is incorrect, it does not follow that I do not believe in causation.) Nevertheless Lewis's theory, if taken at face value, is (as I see it) a radical rejection of essential and accidental property possession; on his theory, no objects have properties accidentally or essentially. The reason, fundamentally, is that on this theory there are no such things as properties at all. Lewis takes a property to be a set—in the first instance a set of all its this- and otherworldly members; but if we aren't satisfied with *those* sets in the role of properties, he has others on offer (Lewis 1986, pp. 56–59). But clearly enough, properties are *not* sets. As Lewis sees things, we know pretheoretically that there are such things as properties—at any rate we firmly believe that there are entities that deserve the name—but (as in the case of propositions) we don't pretheoretically know much of anything about their nature. And indeed there *is* much we don't know about them. But we do know *something* about their nature, and enough to see that they could not be sets. Take, for example, the property of being a donkey, which Lewis proposes to identify with the set of donkeys (this- or otherworldly donkeys). *That* set, clearly enough, could not have been empty; it could not have been the null set. (Had there been no donkeys, that set would not have existed.) But the property of being a donkey could have been unexemplified; obviously there could have been no donkeys at all, here or on any other maximal object, if there are any others. Donkeyhood is contingently exemplified; the set of donkeys (since there are some donkeys) is essentially nonempty; hence the property of being a donkey is not the set of donkeys.[33] Of course Lewis can *get the effect* on contingency in his model; some but not all maximal objects **w** are such that the set of donkeys-in-**w** is empty. But how does this help? The set of donkeys—i.e., the set of all donkeys— still has a property donkeyhood lacks; hence the former is distinct from the latter. So I say it is obvious that properties are not sets. It is obvious that no property is the unit set of a donkey, or a larger set of donkeys, or any other set of animals or concreta. (It is obvious that no properties are sets; but I must concede that it is not *as* obvious as that no propositions are sets.) But if it is obvious that no property is a set, then Lewis's theory is a rejection of modal realism of the first grade.

I turn now to the second grade of modal realism: the claim that there are possible worlds. How does Lewis's theory stand with respect to this claim? Are there any such things, on his theory? I think not. (Of course there are the things he *calls* possible worlds—at any rate there is *one* such thing.) First, it is clear, I think, that the phrase 'possible world' is philosopher's talk for something like 'way things could have been', or better, 'total way things could have been'. (And so the use of 'world' in 'possible world' is quite different from its use in, e.g., 'God created the world.'[34]) Now this pretheoretical idea of a way things could have been (like the ideas of proposition and property) pretheoretically displays a certain indefiniteness: a way things could have been could be a state of affairs, perhaps, or a property, or a proposition or perhaps even (cardinality problems aside) a set of propositions or states of affairs. But could possible worlds, ways things could have been, turn out to be maximal objects? It is hard to see how. There are at least two central and obvious characteristics of possible worlds (or total ways things could have been). First, they are such that if there is at least one object that has a property accidentally, then it follows that there are at least two possible worlds; if there are **n** properties such that I could have had any combination of those properties, then there are at least $2^n$ possible worlds. Second, possible worlds are such that if there is at least one contingent proposition, it follows that there are at least two possible worlds; more generally, if there are at least **n** appropriately independent propositions then there are at least $2^n$ possible worlds. Not so for maximal objects. If it is possible that there be more than one maximal object (and perhaps it isn't), it will be a contingent matter just how many there are in fact; there could be two, or six, or (less likely) countably infinitely many. (Could there be at least $2^c$, as Lewis's theory requires?) But what is more important in the present context is this: the number of maximal objects, unlike the number of possible worlds, is independent of the number of logically independent propositions (and independent of the number of combinations of properties I could have had). There are objects that have properties contingently and propositions that are contingent; and that is true no matter how many maximal objects there are. I have the property of wearing shoes accidentally; the proposition **Paul is over six feet tall** is contingent; and this is so even if, as most of us believe, there is only one maximal object. So possible worlds can't be maximal objects.[35] Lewis's theory, then, is not a realism with respect to possible worlds.

Still further, this theory, I think, is an *antirealism* with respect to possible worlds. Like propositions, possible worlds have that intentional property: a possible world is such that things are thus and so *according* to it; a possible world *represents* things as being a certain way. But no concrete object or set theoretic construction does a thing like that. So if all there are are concrete individuals and set-theoretic constructions on them, then there are no possible worlds. On Lewis's ontology that is all there are; so on his theory there are no possible worlds; so Lewis's theory is an example of antirealism with respect to possible worlds. Suppose someone says:

> On my theory there is another universe causally and spatiotempo-rally discontinuous with the universe we see around us. This universe contains duplicates of some of us, and things similar to others of us. But all the objects in either that universe or ours or anywhere else are concrete particular or set-theoretic constructions therefrom.

Then on that person's theory there are no possible worlds, and adding more maximal objects won't help. So I believe Lewis's theory is antirealist about possible worlds. But if so, then on this theory it is not the case that objects have properties in worlds; so Lewis's theory is an antirealism of the third grade as well as of the second and the first. The just conclusion, I think, is that Lewis is about as much a modal realist as is W. V. Quine. (Let me hasten to add, once more, that this is no denigration of his views; nobody claims modal realism is *de rigueur* for modal theorists. I mean only to correct what I see as widespread misunderstanding.)

Of course there is *something* in the neighborhood with respect to which Lewis is a realist, and a pretty unusual and interesting thing at that: a plurality of maximal objects. Like Quine, he prefers desert landscapes: concrete objects and sets. Lewis's desert, however, with its $2^c$ or more spatiotemporally isolated maximal objects, is both more extensive and less continuous than Quine's. Lewis is certainly a realist of an interesting kind; but what he isn't is a *modal* realist. On his theory, as I see it, there are no propositions, states of affairs, possible worlds, essences or objects with essential and accidental properties; what there are instead are concrete objects and set theoretical constructions on them, some of which play roles formally similar to the roles in fact played by the phenomena of modality if the modal realist is right.

## C. Lewis and Modal Reductionism

Lewis seems to say some puzzling things: that among the propositions there are some that are unit sets of donkeys, that the property of being a donkey is a set of this- and otherworldly donkeys, and that I could have been going barefoot now only if there is someone sufficiently like me who is going barefot now. These are things I said we know are false. Why, then, would Lewis say them? He seems to say puzzling things: what is most puzzling is that he should say them. But perhaps he isn't really saying them; perhaps there is something more subtle going on. (It's not entirely easy to see just what Lewis's project really is; but I shall do my best.) First, Lewis is a modal *reductionist:* He offers reductive analyses of the phenomena of modality: he reduces possible worlds to maximal objects, propositions and states of affairs to sets of maximal objects, essences to sets of concrete objects, and essential and accidental property possession to similarity and set membership.

There are at least two kinds of philosophical analysis: *reductive* and *explicative.* The explicative analyst gives analyses of the sort G. E. Moore said could not be given of goodness: he tries to penetrate a concept we already have, to discern the structure of such a concept, to resolve it into its components (if any), and to show the relations in which those components stand.[36] The late lamented analysis of knowledge as justified true belief is of this sort. The *reductive* analyst, however, is stalking different game. One who reduces propositions to sets does not claim that when we reflect on our common concept of propositions, what we see is that propositions after all are really sets, or that the concept of propositions is really the same concept as that of a certain sort of set. Instead, he proposes what from the point of view of that common concept is a *substitute;* the whole point of his analysis is to provide a substitute for the suspect entities, thereby thinking perhaps, to reduce commitment to questionable ontology.

There are at least two kinds of reductive analyses: ontological and semantical. The first kind tells us that there really are such things as A's, but (contrary to what we might have thought) they are really B's: there are such things as houses and horses, but in fact they are really congeries of sense data; there are such things as mental states, but in fact each mental state is identical with some neurological state; there really are such things as propositions, but in fact they are sets of maximal objects. He then uses the relevant terms—'proposition', 'true', and the like—in their ordinary and established ways, and may seem to say quite outrageous things; that some sets are true, that some are necessarily true, that the null set represents Frege as a married bachelor, that the null set is necessarily false, and that Frege believed the null set until Russell showed him the error of his ways. But Lewis's analyses are not like this. He does not tell us that there really are such things as propositions and properties, and that *what* they really are are sets:

> All this is a matter of fitting suitable entities to the various rather ill-defined roles that we rather indecisively associate with various familiar names. Don't think of it as a matter of discovering which entities *really are* the states of affairs, or the ways things might be, or the possibilities, or the propositions, or the structures!

The *semantical* reductionist, by contrast, uses the relevant terms in a nonstandard way. By 'proposition' he might just *mean* 'set of maximal objects'; and by 'is true' he might mean 'has the maximal object of which we are parts as a member'.[37] Sometimes it looks as if this is the course Lewis takes:

> Not everyone means the same thing by the word 'proposition'. I mean a set of possible worlds, a region of logical space. Others mean something more like a sentence, something with indexicality and syntactic structure, but taken in abstraction from any particular language. The word "property" is also used in many senses. I mean a set: the set of exactly those possible beings, actual or not, that have the property in question.[38]

A semantical reductionist doesn't claim that propositions are sets; since by 'proposition' he means sets of maximal objects, when he says "propositions are sets of maximal objects" what he asserts is what the rest of us assert when we say "sets of maximal objects are sets of maximal objects." Then he doesn't really assert such peculiar items as that propositions are sets of maximal objects or that the property of being a donkey is the set of this and other worldly donkeys.

Is Lewis a semantical reductionist? I'm not quite sure. What is clearer, I think, is that he proposes *models*. He models our modal talk, or thought, or the modal phenomena in set-theoretic constructions on concrete individuals; he proposes models whose domains of interpretation contain only the sorts of entities of which he approves. He offers us semantics for our modal discourse, semantical systems that have recourse only to the sorts of things he believes in. Lewis thinks there are various *roles* associated with such words as 'proposition', 'property', 'state of affairs', 'possibility', and the like (and not just the roles of denoting the propositions, properties, states of affairs, possibilities, and the like); and the job of analysis or theory is to find the things that best fill these roles:

> 'Property,' and the rest, are names associated in the first instance with roles in our thought. It is a firm commitment of common sense that there are some entities or other that play the roles and deserve the names, but our practical mastery of uses of the names does not prove that we have much notion what manner of entities those are. That is a question for theorists. I believe in properties. That is, I have my candidates for entities to play the role and deserve the name. My principle candidates are sets of possible individuals. (But I can offer you alternatives—other set-theoretic constructions out of possible individuals—to suit different versions of the role.) (Lewis 1986, p. 189)

And (speaking of states of affairs and ways things might be):

> I suppose it is a firm commitment of common sense that there are some entities or other that fill the roles, and therefore deserve the names. But that is not to say that we have much notion of what sort of entities those are. We can toss the names around and never think what manner of entities we are talking about. Only when we want to improve on common sense and get something more systematic and unified and definite, does the question arise. The entities that deserve the names are the entities best suited to fill the roles. To figure out what those are, we must survey the candidates according to our best systematic theory of what there is. It's no good saying: which are they? Why they are the states of affairs! (Ibid., p. 185)

(To the question "Who shall play Polonius?" says Lewis, it's no good replying, "Why, Polonius, of course!")

Lewis *takes* properties to be certain sets; he *identifies* properties with those sets, in something like the way in which one might take the number 1 to be the unit set of the null set: "I identify propositions with certain properties: namely with those that are instantiated only by entire possible worlds" (ibid., p. 50). To take properties or propositions to be sets is to endorse those sets as suited to play the relevant role:

> If we believe in possible worlds and individuals, and if we believe in set-theoretic constructions out of things we believe in, then we have entities suited to play the role of properties.
>
> The simplest plan is to take a property just as the set of all its instances—*all* of them, this- and other-worldly alike. Thus the property of being a donkey comes out as the set of all donkeys, the donkeys of other worlds along with the donkeys of ours.

Further, there may be several versions of the property role among which our use of the relevant terms does not make a choice. Thus we can't sensibly ask, for example, whether two properties are ever necessarily coextensive. We must recognize instead that the word has become associated with a variety of subtly different roles:

> Here there is a rift in our talk of properties, and we simply have two different conceptions. It's not as if we have fixed once and for all, in some perfectly definite and unequivocal way, on the things we call 'the properties', so that now we are ready to enter into debate about such questions as, for instance, whether two of them are ever necessarily coextensive. Rather, we have the word 'property' introduced by way of a varied repertory of ordinary and philosophical uses. To deserve the name of 'property' is to be suited to play the right theoretical role: or better, to be one of a class of entities which together are suited to play the right role collectively. But it is wrong to speak of *the* role associated with the word 'property' as if it were fully and uncontroversially settled. It comes in many versions, differing in a number of ways. The question worth asking is: which entities, if any, among those we should believe in, can occupy which versions of the property role? (Ibid, p. 55)

Lewis models our modal thought and talk in concrete objects and set theoretical constructions therefrom. There are several different models on offer: the proposition **Sam is happy** could be a set of worlds, for example; but it could also be a pair set consisting of Sam and a property; and of course there are many other possibilities. There is something that represents *de re* of me that I am Fred: we can take Fred himself as the thing that does so (ibid, p. 232). (Under a weaker counterpart relation there are things that represent me as being a poached egg: we can take the poached eggs to be those things.) What isn't wholly clear, however, is just what Lewis, qua theoretician, proposes to do with these models.[39] There they are: all those different models in which different things play the role of a given proposition or property. We are not to ask which really *is* that proposition or property; no model is endorsed to the exclusion of the others; all are acceptable, although some are more suitable for some purposes than for others. If you think there is only one necessary and one impossible proposition, there is an appropriate model; if what you want is multiplicity (many necessary propositions), that is easily arranged; if you think that concrete objects such as you and I are constituents of propositions, that too is no problem: there is a model to fit.

Now I find this puzzling. I'm not sure what claim, if any, is being made about propositions, properties, states of affairs, possibilities, and their like. But perhaps at any rate the following is clear. Lewis accepts what he calls the common opinion that indeed there are such things as propositions, properties, etc. He adds, however, that common opinion has no definite idea as to what these things are; this is up for theoretical grabs; so far as what we pretheoretically know is concerned, these things could be any of the objects presented by the proposed models.

But is this really true? Indeed there are those roles of which Lewis speaks; but aren't they accompanied by much fuller stage directions—e.g., no proposition can be played by a set—than he supposes? Alternatively, don't we know a lot more about what fills them than he supposes? Do we have only those roles Lewis speaks of, so that it is up to theory to say what fills them? Or do we also know something about the sorts of things that occupy them—e.g., that no proposition is the unit set of a donkey, or any larger sets of donkeys, or indeed any set at all? The model realist—my kind of modal realist—says there are such things as proposition, properties, worlds and their like. We know that these things play certain roles, sure enough; but we know more about them than that. We know, e.g., that they are not sets—although there might be interesting isomorphisms between propositions and certain set-theoretic structures, isomorphisms from which we can learn about propositions, even if we know that propositions aren't sets. We know that neither Paul nor any poached egg[40] can represent of me that I am Paul or a poached egg, although there are models of modality in which Paul or a poached egg could play the role of such a representer—models from which we may be able to learn something important about representation.

So I am not quite sure what Lewis's theory says about propositions and their like. But this much seems reasonably clear: according to this theory, any propositions (or property) you pick is at any rate some set or other. And *if* this is so, then I say his theory is antirealistic about these things.

It's Lewis's concretism that is to blame—his view that all there are are concrete individuals and sets (and perhaps also immanent universals or tropes). For there are obvious truths which together with this claim entail that there are no propositions, properties, or possible worlds. It is not that concretism *as such* is incompatible with modal realism. According to another, more moderate if vaguer version of concretism, there are indeed such nonconcreta as propositions, properties, numbers, sets, states of affairs, possible worlds and so on; but all of them must somehow be rooted in or dependent upon concrete objects. Sets, for example, are ontologically dependent upon their members; had Paul Zwier failed to exist, then so would his unit set. (Perhaps sets are also and essentially *collections*—as Cantor thought—and thus dependent upon some kind of collecting activity on the part of some individuals or other.) Propositions depend for their existence upon concrete thinkers: propositions, perhaps, just *are* thoughts (and even that allegedly arch-Platonist Frege called them *Gedanken*); and properties, perhaps, just are concepts. This view is open to obvious and crushing objection if the thinkers involved are *human* thinkers: for then there are far too many propositions and properties. Of course there is no problem here for the Augustinian view according to which propositions are *divine* thoughts (and properties divine concepts). Some might think explaining propositions as God's thought is at best a case of *obscurum per obscurius* (Lewis 1986, p. 58).

But one man's cost is another man's benefit; if you already accept or are inclined to accept theism, then this suggestion may seem not just acceptable, but compelling.

## D. Two Objections

(1) "You say Lewis is not a modal realist; but *he* says he is. And isn't he the authority on his own theory? Who are you to say that this theory is anti-realistic if he says it isn't?"

Reply: similar questions are regularly debated in theology. Someone might claim that according to his theory Christ indeed arose from the dead; what this means, he says, is that the disciples "had an experience of forgiveness, which they expressed in categories of resurrection." It remains a question whether on his theory Christ arose from the dead. He assertively writes and utters such sentences as 'Christ arose from the dead'; on his theory, that sentence expresses a truth; but it doesn't follow that on his theory Christ arose from the dead. An even more liberal theologian might say, "Certainly on my theory there is such a person as God: when I say that, what I mean is that I face the Future with confidence."[41] It remains a question on his theory whether there is such a person as God. Consider a paradigm nominalist: he says that there are no universals, properties, or kinds; he adds that the role the realist thinks is played by such things is in fact played by utterances or inscriptions of words of natural languages. Such a nominalist is a reductionist with respect to universals; he is also an antirealist with respect to them. (Never mind whether his reduction is successful or not.) Compare this nominalist with someone who claims to be a realist with respect to universals but adds that universals are really inscriptions or utterances of words of natural language; that, he says, is what their nature is. This person's ontology, I suggest, is indistinguishable from the paradigm nominalist's views, despite his realist claims and aspirations. Claiming royalty at the font doesn't automatically confer sovereignty; claiming to be a realist with respect to universals is insufficient for being one. Suppose someone says he believes in elephants: only on his theory, he says, elephants are really numbers—numbers equal to the sum of their proper divisors. He adds that there are no material objects. Then according to his theory there are no elephants, despite his assertively writing or uttering "On my theory there are elephants, only as it happens they are perfect numbers." Lewis says he believes in the phenomena of modality—propositions, properties and the like:

> I believe in properties. That is, I have my candidates for entities to play the role and deserve the name. My principal candidates are sets of possible individuals. (But I can offer you alternatives.) (Lewis 1986, p. 189)

No doubt there are indeed set-theoretic constructions on individuals that can play the role of properties (or propositions) in one or another model of our modal talk; but saying so, I submit, is not sufficient for being a realist with respect to properties (or propositions).

(2) "In arguing that Lewis is a modal anti-realist, you employ premises that he doesn't accept—such premises, for example, as the claim that no set can be believed, that no set is a claim or an assertion, that no set represents anything as being thus and so, and that no set could be true or false. But Lewis accepts none of these premises; so you can't properly employ them to determine the commitments of his theory."

Reply: the question is how to tell what a theory is committed to: what premises and argument forms can be used, along with what a theory explicitly asserts, to reach propositions to which that theory is committed? This is a delicate question. Suppose my theory does not contain a given premise: does that show that it is not committed to any conclusion that can be derived from what it explicitly says only with the help of that premise? I don't think so. Consider someone with a theory according to which, oddly enough, there are two uniquely tallest men. You point out that according to his theory, there is more than one uniquely tallest human being; he demurs, replying that on his theory it is not true that two is greater than one. His theory is nonetheless committed, I think, to the proposition that there is more than one uniquely tallest human being. Suppose my theory contains **p** and also **if p then q**; then it is committed to **q**, even if I claim that *modus ponens* is no part of my theory. Return to the ultra-liberal theologian—a peculiarly rigid follower of Bultmann, for example—according to whose theory there is no person who is perfect in knowledge and power and who has created the worlds; in fact there are only material objects and no supernatural beings at all. We characterize his theory as atheism, i.e., anti-realism with respect to God. "Not at all," he says; "on my theory, to accept belief in God is to adopt a certain attitude or policy: it is to resolve to accept and embrace one's finitude, giving up the futile attempt to build hedges and walls against guilt, failure, and death." He adds that he rejects the premise that any theory according to which there are only material objects and no supernatural beings is an atheist theory. The fact is, I think, that his theory is atheist, whether or not he accepts those premises. (In the case of this theologian (and some of the others), there is a certain evasiveness, a certain deplorable deceptiveness, a certain lack of candor. No such thing characterizes Lewis's views; quite the contrary: Lewis is wholly forthright as to what it is he thinks.) In each of these cases, it is quite proper to use a premise not included in the theory in question to determine what that theory is committed to. I say the same goes with respect to the premises that no sets predicate properties of objects, or represent things as being thus and so, or are true or false, or are assertions, or are believed. So I think it is quite proper to use these premises to determine the commitments of Lewis's modal theory, even if he does not accept those premises.

Of course the question what a theory is committed to is delicate. Let **T** be a theory: and suppose **T** entails (i.e., strictly implies) that there are no X's. It doesn't follow that according to **T** there are no X's. For perhaps **T** contains some false (and hence necessarily false) mathematics; it wouldn't follow that according to **T** there are no possible worlds, despite the fact that **T** entails that there are no possible worlds (as well as that there are some). Suppose **T** attributes to X's a property **P** such that every X has the complement of **P** essentially, or a property **Q** such that it is impossible that there be X's that have **Q**; or suppose there is some property **R** such that it is necessary that X's have **R** essentially and such that according to **T** nothing has **R**: it still doesn't follow that **T** is antirealist with respect to X's. Surely I could have a mistaken theory about quarks: a theory according to which there are such things as quarks and according to which quarks have a property **P** such that in fact it is a necessary truth that all quarks have ~ **P** essentially. Then my theory attributes to quarks a property **P** such that every quark has the complement of **P** essentially; it also attributes to quarks a property such that it is impossible that there be any quarks that have that property; and there is a property **R**—namely, **being a quark not having P**—such that it is necessary that quarks have this property essentially, while according to my theory nothing has this property. But it doesn't follow that my theory is antirealist with respect to quarks. Suppose it is a necessary truth that every contingent object has essentially the property of having been created* by God;[42] and suppose someone's theory asserts that human beings have not been created* by God. It doesn't follow that on the theory in question there are no human beings.

On the other hand, as we have already seen, **T**'s (or **T**'s expression) containing a sentence like 'There are X's' is not sufficient for **T**'s being realistic with respect to X's (or even for its not being antirealistic with respect to X's). Still further, even if **T** asserts that according to **T** there are X's, it doesn't follow that according to **T** there are X's. A person might say that on his theory there are angels; it does not follow that on his theory there are angels. For if he goes on to say that on his theory angels are cats (and thinks of cats no differently from the rest of us), then it is not the case that his theory asserts that there are angels.

This question, therefore—the question just what a theory is committed to—is both vexed and delicate. What is it that determines which premises can be used in conjunction with what a theory explicitly asserts to reach propositions to which that theory is committed? I think it's a matter of *obviousness*; wholly obvious propositions can be used in that fashion. Of course there are problems here (problems I don't have the space to enter). We must remember Kreisel's dictum: "it ain't obvious what's obvious"; and to whom must the propositions be obvious? and since obviousness is a matter of degree, does it follow that commitment of a theory to a proposition is a matter of degree? I shall save these questions for another time and turn to a different objection. I say it is obvious that, e.g., no set represents anything as being thus and so; but is that really obvious, or better, is it relevantly obvious? According to some, there is theory, and then there are data, or evidence, or the appearances (the appearances a theory must save). A semantic theory such as Lewis's is accountable to the data—but not of course to other semantic theories.[43] The data are our linguistic intuitions as to which sentences express truths: "Our intuitive judgments, made 'upon reflection' after we have assured ourselves of the nonlinguistic fact, of what is true and what implies what, are the appearances that a semantic theory must save" (ibid., p. 320). On this view, a satisfactory theory will assign the right truth values to the sentences; but if it turns out, on the theory, that these sentences express propositions quite different from the ones we thought they did, that is nothing against it.[44] Further, the relevantly obvious truths, the ones we can properly use along with what a theory explicitly asserts to determine what the theory is committed to, are just those nontheoretical truths of linguistic intuition.

Now Lewis (sensibly enough) endorses no such facile bifurcation of theory and linguistic intuition:

> There is no sharp line between sacrosanct intuition and freewheeling theory. We start where we are—where else?—with a stock of initial opinions, and we try to rework them into something better Any revision of previous theory counts as some cost. But some of our opinions are firmer and less negotiable than others. And some are more naive and less theoretical than others. And there seems to be more tendency for the more theoretical ones to be more negotiable. (Lewis 1986, p. 241)

Among our firm opinions in this area are our "linguistic intuitions" to the effect that certain sentences—such sentences as 'Socrates could have been foolish'—do indeed express truths. Quite right. But aren't some of the "more theoretical" claims equally obvious? Clearly enough, 'Socrates could have been foolish' expresses a truth; but isn't it nearly as obvious that the truth it expresses does not require that Socrates have a foolish counterpart? Isn't it equally obvious that the truth in question is not a set of maximal objects, or of other concrete objects, or indeed a set of any kind at all? Isn't it equally obvious that no proposition is the unit set of a donkey, or the null set? Lewis once said he found it hard to believe that he and all his surroundings were a set of sentences.[45] That seems fair enough; but is it much easier to believe that the proposition **7 + 5 = 13**, say, or **there is no God** (if you are a classical theist) or **there is no null set** (if you are not) is really the null set? Or to believe that uncountably many propositions are unit sets of fleas or donkeys? I doubt it. And the same holds, I think, for the other premises I used to argue that Lewis's view is not a case of modal realism. (I must concede that some of these propositions are more obvious than others; it is clearer that Lewis's view is antirealistic with respect to propositions than with respect to properties, and clearer with respect to properties than with respect to possible worlds.) But even if I am wrong, even if the existence of these obvious truths is not sufficient for the theory's being antirealist, the most important point still remains: the theory in conjunction with obvious truths obviously entails modal antirealism of all grades.

## E. Concluding Reflection

Although Lewis proposes semantical reductionist models for our modal discourse, it is less than clear that he is a semantical reductionist, because it isn't clear what it is he proposes that we do with these models. Still, his theory has some affinities with semantical reductionism, and in conclusion I wish to say briefly why I think semantical reductive analysis is unhopeful. For what is the point of the project? One begins with an ontological conviction—that all there are are concrete particulars and set theoretic constructions on them, perhaps. This conviction seems hard to square with common opinion, (including one's own opinion) about truths and falsehoods, properties, possibilities, and the like. One hopes to remedy the situation by giving the semantical reductive analysis in question. But how does the analysis help? Offering a semantical analysis does little to respect common opinion; for it preserves the sentences typically used to express common opinion, but not the opinion they express. It is common opinion that some propositions are true and others false, and that I could have been wearing my other shoes. The reductionist respects these *sentences*; they come out true on his analysis. But in his mouth what the first means is that some sets of maximal objects include the maximal object of which we are parts and some do not; and what the second means is that there exists (quantifier taken broadly) someone sufficiently like me who is wearing his other shoes. Clearly these are not the common opinions commonly expressed in the sentences he endorses; while he speaks with the vulgar, he thinks with the learned, and his agreement with common opinion is a merely verbal agreement. If divergence from common opinion is costly, semantical analysis does little to help.[46]

Insofar as he is concerned with divergence from common opinion, from what we all know or believe, the reductive analyst faces a dilemma. On the one hand, he can propose his theory as the sober metaphysical truth: there are possible worlds and they are maximal concrete objects; there are such things as propositions, and they are sets of maximal concrete objects. But these suggestions, of course, are wholly at variance with common opinion, according to which no possible worlds are donkeys (or other concreta) and no propositions are sets of concreta. On the other hand, he can propose a semantical analysis: he can assign a meaning to the relevant sentences—the sentences expressing common opinion about truth and modality—by way of a semantics whose domain of interpretation includes only objects of the sorts he approves of. The semantics then assigns propositions to these sentences, and when he affirms the sentences he affirms those propositions. Then, however, he winds up respecting not common opinion, but only the words in which common opinion is commonly expressed.

At the beginning of section II, I said that one who believes only in sets and concreta has at least two options: on the one hand, she can quine what doesn't seem to fit, and on the other she can give a reductive analysis of these things. I implied that the second was subtler than the first. Perhaps it is; but so far as flouting what we pretheoretically know or believe is concerned, there is little real difference between them. The first, futhermore, is more straightforward, more conducive to clarity of thought than the second, at least if the reductive analysis in question is a semantical analysis. Return once more to the hyper-liberal theologian who insists that on his theory there is such a person as God all right, even though there are no supernatural beings: for the word 'God', as he uses it, he says, denotes the evolutionary-historical process (or perhaps "the forces not ourselves that make for goodness"). Suppose such a theologian goes on to model the rest of what theists ordinarily say in nonsupernatural beings: he doesn't share their belief that there is such a person as God, even though on his theory the words 'There is such a person as God' express a truth. His opinion differs from that of the plainspeaking atheist only by virtue of being less plainly spoken. Something similar goes for the semantical reductionist.[47] One who quines the modal phenomena rejects both common opinion and the sentence in which it is expressed; the semantical reductionist endorses the sentences but rejects the opinions. From the point of view of modal realism, it is hard to see a significant difference.

By way of conclusion then: the modal realist believes in necessary and contingent truths, objects with essential and accidental properties, and individual essences. He will also, I hope, accept actualism; and if actualism, then serious actualism. By contrast the modal reductionist, whatever the virtues of his views, is not a modal realist at all.[48]

## NOTES

1. Modal phenomena are not, of course, to be contrasted with modal noumena; my use of the term is Platonic, not Kantian.

2. See my "How to Be an Anti-Realist," *Proceedings of the American Philosophical Association*, vol. 56, pp. 47–49.

3. According to the classical theist, every proposition is *in fact* (and, indeed, *necessarily*) believed or disbelieved—by God, who is a necessary being and essentially omniscient.

4. See my *The Nature of Necessity* (Oxford: Clarendon Press, 1974), p. 2.

5. Ibid., pp. 2–9.

6. See "Self-Profile" in *Alvin Plantinga*, ed. James Tomberlin and Peter van Inwagen (Dordrecht: D. Reidel Publishing Co., 1985) (hereafter *"Profiles"*), pp. 90–91, and John Pollock's "Plantinga on Possible Worlds" (op. cit.), p. 122.

7. See Pollock, pp. 121–26, and my reply in chapter 9 of this volume.

8. Ibid.

9. Given a proposition (or state of affairs) **P**, there will typically be several distinct propositions (or states of affairs) equivalent to it; in the interests of brevity, I ignore the question whether this also holds for possible worlds.

10. See chapter 8 of this volume; see also Pollock, pp. 134–40.

11. See chapter 8 of this volume.

12. Examples of such properties would be **being Socrates, being identical with this very thing** (I am referring to the number 7), and such world-indexed properties unique to an object as **being the first dog to be born at sea in alpha**. (For more about world-indexed properties, see *The Nature of Necessity*, pp. 62–65.)

13. This condition is necessary but not sufficient. The proposition **7 is prime** predicates primeness of the number 7; it does not predicate primeness of the number 5, despite the equivalence, in the broadly logical sense, of **7 is prime** and **5 is prime**. The proposition **Socrates is wise** predicates wisdom of Socrates and does not predicate **being prime** of 7, despite its equivalence, in the broadly logical sense to **Socrates is wise and 7 is prime**.

14. See, for example, "Theories of Actuality" in *The Possible and the Actual*, ed. Michael Loux (Ithaca: Cornell University Press, 1976), and "Actualism and Thisness," *Synthese*, vol. 49 (1981).

15. See his Postscript in A. N. Prior and Kit Fine, *Worlds, Times, and Selves* (Amherst: University of Massachusetts Press, 1977), and "Plantinga on the Reduction of Possibilist Discourse" in *Profiles*.

16. See, for example, "Modal Logic and the Logic of Applicability" and "Supplement to 'Modal Logic and the Logic of Applicability' " in *Worlds, Times, and Selves*, and "The Possibly True and the Possible" in *Papers in Logic and Ethics* (Amherst: University of Massachusetts Press, 1976).

17. See "On Existentialism," pp. 9–20, and "Replies," pp. 340–49. See chapters 8 and 9 of this volume.

18. See my "Actualism and Possible Worlds," *Theoria* 42 (1976), p. 160; reprinted in Loux, *The Possible and the Actual*, p. 272.

19. See "Plantinga on the Reduction of Possibilist Discourse" in *Profiles*, pp. 165–71.

20. Ibid. pp. 126–30.

21. "Counterpart Theory and Quantified Modal Logic," *Journal of Philosophy* (1968), pp. 114–15; reprinted with postscript in Lewis: *Philosophical Papers* (Oxford: Oxford University Press, 1983).

22. *Counterfactuals* (Cambridge, Mass.: Harvard University Press, 1973), p. 84.

23. As I assumed in discussing Lewis's views in *The Nature of Necessity*, pp. 102–14.

24. *On the Plurality of Worlds* (Oxford: Basil Blackwell Ltd., 1986), p. 2. (Hereafter "*Plurality*"; unless otherwise noted, page references in the text will be to this work.)

25. There is a more detailed account of Lewis's conception of possible worlds in Peter van Inwagen's "Two Concepts of Possible Worlds," *Midwest Studies in Philosophy* XI (1986), pp. 185–92, along with powerful criticism of this conception.

26. In *Plurality* as opposed to "Counterpart Theory and Modal Logic" Lewis allows that an object may have a counterpart in its own world.

27. A complication we may here ignore: Lewis holds that here are different counterpart relations appropriate to different contexts, so that an object may be my counterpart under one but not another of them.

28. " 'Property', and the rest/e.g., 'proposition' "—AP/, are names associated in the first instance with roles in our thought. It is a firm commitment of common sense that there are some entities or other that play the roles and deserve the names, but our practical mastery of uses of the names does not prove that we have much notion what manner of entities those are. That is a question for theorists." (Plurality, 189)

29. According to Richard Cartwright, "Moore is reported to have once had a nightmare in which he was unable to distinguish propositions from tables" ("Propositions," in R. J. Butler, ed., *Analytical Philosophy* [New York: Barnes & Noble, Inc., 1962], p. 103).

30. Lewis, of course, would disagree; indeed, he suggests that a concrete object—another person, e.g.—can represent me as being thus and so; it can represent me as being *it*: "It is not some other world, differing haecceitistically from ours, which represents *de re* of me that I am Fred; it is Fred himself, situated as he is within our world" (p. 232).

31. But things are not quite so simple; Lewis speaks of individuals and set-theoretic constructions on them as the things he is "most committed to"; and he is also sympathetic to the idea that there are immanent universals or tropes (but presumably not both) (pp. 64–69).

32. Gordon Kaufman, *Theology for a Nuclear Age* (Manchester: Manchester University Press, 1985), p. 43. (Of course I don't mean to suggest any real kinship between Lewis's thought and contemporary liberal theology.)

33. Strictly speaking, this argument requires the additional (and uncontroversial) premise that if the property of being a donkey is the set of donkeys, then the set of donkeys is essentially nonempty only if the property of being a donkey is essentially exemplified.

34. See note 4 of van Inwagen's "Two Concepts of Possible Worlds."

35. Purists may wish to state the above argument, not in terms of possible worlds and maximal objects, but in terms of the properties **being a possible world** and **being a maximal object**.

36. See Ernest Sosa's "Classical Analysis," *Journal of Philosophy*, vol. LXXX, no. 11 (November 1983).

37. G. E. Moore in "A Defense of Common Sense," *Philosophical Papers* (London:

George Allen and Unwin Ltd., 1959), p. 36: "Some philosophers use the expression
'The earth has existed for many years past' to express, not what it would ordinarily
be understood to express, but the proposition that some proposition, related to
this in a certain way, is true; when all the time they believe that the proposition,
which this expression would ordinarily be understood to express, is, at least partially,
false."

38. "Attitudes *de dicto* and *de se*," *Philosophical Papers* I, pp. 134–35. On Lewis's view
not everything that has properties is a *possibile* (for example, sets, or the mereological
sum of a couple of maximal objects, or of parts of a couple of such objects); in *Plurality*
he therefore takes properties to be sets of any kind, not just sets of possibilia.

39. And hence it is not clear to me whether or not he is what above I called a
*semantical* reductionist.

40. Nor any set theoretical construction on concrete individuals. Objection: "you
say that no concrete objects or sets have that intentional property you attribute to
propositions and states of affairs: the property of representing things as being thus
and so, of being a thing x such that according to x things stand thus and so. But isn't
this clearly mistaken? Surely *sentences of natural languages* are true or false, and thus
such that according to them things stand a certain way; and sentences are sets: sets
of sounds or shapes. Furthermore, sentences aren't the only things that represent: a
scale model of the *Titanic*, for example, can represent it as having four smokestacks,
and a topographical map of the North Cascades can represent Mt. Baker as being
more than 10,700 feet high."

Reply: stipulate for purposes of argument that sentences are sets. The important
point is that a sentence *in itself* does not have any such intentional property at all;
rather sentences are *used* by speakers and writers to *express* the things that do have the
relevant intentional property. The sequence of shapes "Socrates is wise" does not
represent Socrates as being wise; instead, speakers of English use that sequence of
shapes to express the proposition that Socrates is wise. Similarly for maps and models;
the map doesn't (except in a derivative sense) represent Mt. Baker as being more
than 10,700 feet high; instead, the *cartographer* uses the map to make that representation, that is, to communicate that proposition. Similarly for models: an object that
looks like a small *Titanic* isn't *in itself* any claim at all as to what the *Titanic* is like; but
if I assert that it is a scale model of that ship, then *I* use it to make claims or assertions
about what the *Titanic* is like—I use it, that is, to express propositions.

41. He might say something even more exciting: "God is the name of that center
which is everywhere, but it is everywhere only by being nowhere where it is only itself,
and therefore nowhere in the absence or silence of consciousness or speech." Thomas
J. J. Altizer, "History as Apocalypse" in *Deconstruction in Theology* by Thomas J. J. Altizer,
Max A. Myers, Carl A. Raschke, Robert P. Scharlemann, Mark C., Taylor, and Charles
E. Winquist (New York: Crossroad Publishing Co., 1982), p. 155.

42. See above, p. 210.

43. See, for example, Allen Hazen, "Counterpart-theoretic Semantics for Modal
Logic," *Journal of Philosophy*, vol. 76 (1979), p. 323.

44. ". . . what Plantinga disparages as a merely verbal agreement about the truth
value of the sentence 'Socrates could have been unwise' is the only agreement that
can be demanded from the counterpart theorist: it is the only agreement that matters.
Our logical intuition about such sentences of our ordinary modal language are the
evidence that both Plantinga and the counterpart theorist must appeal to and explain.
What proposition is expressed by such a sentence . . . is a matter of theory. . . ." *loc.
cit.*, p. 323.

45. *Counterfactuals*, p. 86.

46. As Lewis suggests in a different context (Lewis, *Plurality*, p. 247), it may still
do *something*. Perhaps it is more obvious that the words 'there could have been nothing
that had the property of being a donkey' express a truth than that it is false that the

proposition expressed by those words is really the proposition that there are maximal objects in which there are no members of the set of this- and otherworldly donkeys; then to claim the latter is less outrageous than to deny the former.

47. Again, I do not mean for a moment to suggest that semantical reductionism shares the devious and deplorably deceptive character sometimes attaching to such theology.

48. I take this opportunity to record my gratitude to many—in particular David Lewis, Peter van Inwagen, Philip Quinn, Del Ratzsch, Nicholas Wolterstorff and the members of the Calvin Colloquium—for stimulating discussion and incisive criticism. I should also like again to call attention to van Inwagen's penetrating discussion of allied matters in "Two Concepts of Possible Worlds" (above, note 25).

## REFERENCES

Adams, Robert. "Theories of Actuality" in (14).

Adams, Robert. "Actualism and Thisness," *Synthese* (49) 1981.

Altizer, Thomas J. J. "History as Apocalypse," *Deconstruction in Theology* by Thomas J. J. Altizer, Max A. Myers, Carl A. Raschke, Robert P. Scharlemann, Mark C. Taylor, and Charles E. Winquist (New York: Crossroad Publishing, 1982), p. 155.

Cartwright, Richard. "Propositions" in R. J. Butler, ed., *Analytical Philosophy* (New York: Barnes & Noble, 1962).

Fine, Kit, and Prior, Arthur. *Worlds, Times, and Selves* (Amherst: University of Massachusetts Press, 1977).

Fine, Kit. "Plantinga on the Reduction of Possibilist Discourse" in (28).

Hazen, Allen. "Counterpart-theoretic Semantics for Modal Logic," *Journal of Philosophy*, vol. 76 (1979).

Kaufman, Gordon. *Theology for a Nuclear Age* (Manchester: Manchester University Press, 1985).

Lewis, David. "Counterpart Theory and Quantified Modal Logic," *Journal of Philosophy* (1968), pp. 114–15. Reprinted with postscript in (10).

Lewis, David. *Philosophical Papers I* (Oxford: Oxford University Press, 1983).

Lewis, David. *Counterfactuals* (Cambridge, Mass.: Harvard University Press, 1973).

Lewis, David. *On the Plurality of Worlds* (Oxford: Basil Blackwell Ltd., 1986).

Lewis, David. "Attitudes *de dicto* and *de se*," *The Philosophical Review* 88 (1979). Reprinted in (10).

Loux, Michael. *The Possible and the Actual* (Ithaca: Cornell University Press, 1976).

Moore, G. E. "A Defense of Common Sense," *Philosophical Papers* (London: George Allen and Unwin Ltd., 1959).

Plantinga, Alvin. "How to Be an Anti-Realist," *Proceedings of the American Philosophical Association*, vol. 56.

Plantinga, Alvin. *The Nature of Necessity* (Oxford: Clarendon Press, 1974).

Plantinga, Alvin. "On Existentialism," *Philosophical Studies*, vol. 44 (1983).

Plantinga, Alvin. "Actualism and Possible Worlds," *Theoria* 42 (1976). Reprinted in (14).

Pollock, John. "Plantinga on Possible Worlds" in (28).

Prior, Arthur. *Worlds, Times, and Selves* (Amherst: University of Massachusetts Press, 1976).

Prior, Arthur. "Modal Logic and the Logic of Applicability" in (21).

Prior, Arthur. "Supplement to 'Modal Logic and the Logic of Applicability' " in (21).

Prior, Arthur. *Papers in Logic and Ethics* (Amherst: University of Massachusetts Press, 1976).

Prior, Arthur. "The Possibly True and the Possible" in (24).

Sosa, Ernest. "Classical Analysis," *Journal of Philosophy*, vol. LXXX, no. 11 (November, 1983).

Tomberlin, James, and van Inwagen, Peter. *Alvin Plantinga* (Dordrecht: D. Reidel Publishing Co., 1985).

van Inwagen, Peter. "Two Concepts of Possible Worlds," *Midwest Studies in Philosophy*, vol. XI (1986).

# 11

# Why Propositions Cannot Be Concrete

I should next like to offer an argument for the conclusion that propositions (the things, whatever their nature, that can be believed or disbelieved, are true or false, and stand in logical relations) cannot be concrete objects of *any* sort—at any rate, they can't be concrete objects that do not exist necessarily.[1] We can see this as follows. For definiteness, suppose propositions are human mental acts or perhaps brain inscriptions. It follows that if there had been no human beings, then there would have been no propositions. But doesn't that seem wrong? If there had been no human beings, one thinks, then it would have been true that there are no human beings—that is, *that there are no human beings* would have been true—in which case there would have been at least one truth (and thus one proposition): that there are no human beings.

The concretist, of course, will retort that as *she* sees the matter,

(a) If there had been no human beings, then it would have been true that there are no human beings—that is, *that there are no human beings* would have been true

is false. She will therefore have to reject

(b) Necessarily, there are no human beings if and only if it is true that there are no human beings

More specifically, she will be obliged to reject the left-to-right conjunct of (b):

(c) Necessarily, if there are no human beings, then it is true that there are no human beings

229

for (c) entails (a). She is therefore committed to

(d)  Possibly (there are no people and it is not true that there are no people).

But here we strike a problem: what does she mean, here, by 'possibly'? Not, presumably, 'possibly true' or 'could have been true'. For consider the proposition (d) says is possible: if it is possible, then so is its first conjunct. But on the concretist position, the first conjunct, clearly enough, could not have been true. For if it had been true, there would have been no people, in which case there would have been no propositions, in which case the proposition *There are no people* would not have existed, in which case that proposition would not have had the property of being true.[2] So that proposition could not have been true after all. But what, other than 'could have been true', could the concretist possibly mean by 'possible'?

This leads us to a more general problem. Most of us think that among the true propositions, there are some that are necessary: true, and such that they could not have failed to be true. But the concretist cannot concur; she cannot agree that there are propositions that could not have failed to be true. For propositions, on her view, are contingent beings: that is, they are contingently *existing* beings; they could have failed to exist. But then any given proposition could have failed to be true, for it could have failed to exist, in which case it would have failed to be true. Not that it would have been *false*, of course; if a proposition—*Socrates is wise*, let's say—had not existed, then there simply would have *been* no such proposition at all; so it would not have had the property of being false. (If you had failed to exist, then you would not have had the property of living on earth; but it does not follow that you would have lived somewhere else.) On the concretist view, therefore, no proposition is such that it could not have failed to be true. That is because each proposition could have failed to exist, and would have failed to be true if it had failed to exist. But then what can the concretist mean when she joins the rest of us in supposing that some propositions are necessary and others are not?

Well, perhaps she might suggest that we are asking too much when we ask that a necessary proposition be *strongly* necessary—that is, such that it could not have failed to be true. She may want instead to maintain that for a proposition to be necessarily true is for it to have the property of being true *essentially*. But that, she adds, does not require that the proposition in question be such that it can't fail to be true. What it requires is that it can't both *exist* and fail to be true: alternatively, what it requires is that it could not have been false. Compare: for me to have a property essentially, it is not necessary that I be such that I could not have lacked the property. After all, *no* property is such that I could not have lacked it; I could have failed to exist, in which case I would have had no properties at all. What is required is only that it be impossible that I *exist* and lack the property, or (equivalently) impossible that I have the *complement* of the property in question. So if I am essentially a person, then it is impossible that I be a nonperson, although it is not impossible that I fail to be a person. And the concretist suggests that we say something similar here: for a proposition *p* to be necessary, it is not required that *p* be such that it could not have failed to be true: all that's required is *weak* necessity: that *p* be such that it could not have been false.

But this suggestion has its own problems. Suppose the concretist thinks propositions are brain inscriptions: then the proposition *There are brain inscriptions* obviously enough will be such that it could not have been false. It is therefore necessary that there are brain inscriptions, and hence necessary that there are brains; what we have here is a sort of ontological argument for the existence of brains and brain inscriptions. On this account far too many propositions turn out to be necessary. And given that necessity and possibility are related as duals, we expect, of course, that the same difficulties will arise for possibility. The concretist can't say that a proposition is possible just in case it could have been true (the dual of weak necessity): for then far too few propositions are possible. It is possible, for example, that there be no human beings and no brain inscriptions; but on the concretist view, of course, this proposition could not have been true. She might therefore try retreating to the suggestion that a proposition is possible when (like *There are no human beings*) it *could have failed to be false* (the dual of strong necessity); but then on her view every proposition, including the most blatant contradiction, is possible. For take any proposition you like: it could have failed to exist, in which case it would have failed to be false. The conclusion, I think, is that propositions can't be concrete, contingently existing objects such as human mental acts, or brain inscriptions or other arrays of neural material, or sentence tokens, or anything else of that sort.

## BACK TO THE CAUSAL REQUIREMENT

If the causal requirement implies that what we know and believe are concrete representations in our brains or elsewhere, then what we have is less a remarkable discovery than a *reductio*. Here we should reason by *modus tollens* rather than *modus ponens*. But of course the causal requirement is open to many interpretations; the phrase 'the causal requirement' really hides a vast horde of possible principles. Taken vaguely, the principle certainly seems to have at least some initial intuitive support; *some* version of it, it seems, is likely to be true. But what kind of causal connection between object of knowledge and knower is required?

Could I know truths about abstract sets of concrete objects—for example, that the union of a pair of sets can't have fewer members than either of the pair—by way of standing in causal relations with their concrete members? Would *that* be enough of a causal connection with the sets? Further, sets of contingent objects are ontologically dependent[3] upon their members (more exactly, the members of their transitive closures) in that no set could have existed if one of its members had not existed. (If Quine had not existed, there would have been no such thing as his unit set.) Still further, no set could have existed at a time *before* its members exist. So in a way the fortunate event of Quine's coming into existence brings about, or causes, or produces, or is at any rate sufficient for the existence of his unit set. Is this sort of bringing about sufficient to satisfy the causal requirement? Can I know that Quine is a member of his unit set by virtue of standing in causal relation to Quine, whose existence in turn brings about the existence of that set? Aristotle thought I could grasp or apprehend a property (redness, for example) by standing in an appropriate causal relation to *exemplifications* of it (a red silo, for example): was he right? Can I grasp properties logically related to properties I grasp? If I grasp a given property $P$, is that sufficient (so far as the causal requirement is concerned) for grasping its complement $\bar{P}$, or must I also stand in the appropriate causal relation to some example of $\bar{P}$? (In some cases—cases of properties that are necessarily exemplified—this will be difficult to arrange.) And if I grasp the properties *humanity* and *mortality*, will that suffice, so far as the causal requirement goes, for grasping the proposition *All men are mortal?* Or must I stand in some causal relation with the proposition itself, as opposed to those properties?

But perhaps the fundamental question is really this: why think propositions, properties, sets, states of affairs, and their like cannot stand in causal relations? The notion of an abstract object, after all, comes from the notion of *abstraction*; it is in origin an *epistemological* rather than an ontological category. According to the tradition, it is *properties* that are abstracted in this way; Aristotle and many others have held that when we perceive an object of a certain sort, we are able to abstract and thus grasp some of its properties.[4] So an abstract object is the sort of object we grasp by abstraction: but of course that leaves open the question what sort of a thing an abstract object *is*. One traditional view is that the things we thus abstract are outside space and time and incapable of standing in causal relations. We are told that Plato held this view; if so, he didn't hold it clearly and consistently. Plato speaks of the idea of the good as *primus unter pares* among the ideas; it is an idea par excellence; but he also speaks of it as if he thinks it has causal powers of great significance.

And in any event, the view in question—that propositions, sets, properties, and their like are outside space and time and cannot stand in causal relations—is only one view among others. Theists, for example, may find attractive a view popular among medieval philosophers from Augustine on: the view that abstract objects are really divine thoughts. More exactly, propositions are divine thoughts, properties divine concepts, and sets divine collections.[5] But then these objects can enter into the sort of causal relation that holds between a thought and a thinker, and we can enter into causal relation with them by virtue of our causal relation to God. It is therefore quite possible to think of abstract objects as capable of standing in causal relations, and in causal relations with us; hence the causal objection to *a priori* knowledge can be easily sidestepped.

NOTES

1. For a development of this objection, see my "Two Concepts of Modality," in *Philosophical Perspectives, 1, Metaphysics,* 1987, ed. James Tomberlin (Atascadero, Calif.: Ridgeview, 1987), pp. 296ff.

2. Here I assume *serious actualism:* the view that no object could have had a property without existing. Serious actualism is a consequence of actualism *tout court:* the view that it is impossible that there be things that do not exist. See *Alvin Plantinga,* pp. 130–34 and 316–23. See chapter 9 of this volume.

3. See my "Actualism and Possible Worlds," *Theoria* (1977). See chapter 5 of this volume.

4. You may object that it is hard to conceive of this in neural terms; I reply that it is equally hard to conceive of thinking of the moon in neural terms, or to see how it is, in neural terms, that we are able to think about the null set, or the unit set of Quine. But then how exactly *does* this work? What happens when we grasp a property, and how does it happen that we can do that? Here perhaps the best answer is Aristotle's: "The soul is so constituted as to be capable of this process." *Posterior Analytics,* II, 19 100a14

5. See my "How to Be an Anti-Realist," *Proceedings and Addresses of the American Philosophical Association* (1982); see also Christopher Menzel, "Theism, Platonism and the Metaphysics of Mathematics," *Faith and Philosophy* 4, no. 4 (October 1987), reprinted in *Christian Theism,* ed. Michael Beaty (Notre Dame: University of Notre Dame Press, 1990); and Christopher Menzel and Thomas Morris, "Absolute Creation," *American Philosophical Quarterly* 23 (1986), reprinted in T. V. Morris, *Anselmian Explanations* (Notre Dame: University of Notre Dame Press, 1987). Suppose you find yourself convinced that (1) there are propositions, properties, and sets; (2) that the causal requirement is indeed true; and (3) that (due to excessive number or excessive complexity or excessive size) propositions, properties, and sets can't be *human* thoughts, concepts, and collections. Then you have the materials for a theistic argument.

# Index

α (as actual world), 96
aboutness, 154
abstract objects, 110, 141, 161, 188, 232–33
accidental properties, 193–94, 209–10
Ackerman, Diana, 126
actualism, 11–13, 145–46, 198–203
  Adams and, 106, 145, 171
  existentialism and, 13
  frivolous, 179, 201
  nonexistent objects and, 161, 167
  Pollock and, 176–78, 181
  possible worlds and, 106–20, 148
  serious actualism and, 16, 19, 20, 146, 155, 161, 167–70
actualist semantics, 120n.4
Adams, Robert
  actualism and, 106, 145, 171
  thisness and, 158–59, 161–62
alethic modality 167, 171, See also truth
Analogical Argument, 27–28
anti-existentialism, 165–71, 174. See also existentialism
anti-Fregeanism
  proper names and, 126–27, 130–31, 134
  See also Fregeanism
antirealism, 207, 212, 222
  existential, 192
Aquinas. See Thomas Aquinas
Aristotle, 25, 139, 232
Arnauld, Antoine, 67, 74–75

α-transform, 15
  essence and, 111–14, 128
  existentialism and, 150
  proper names and, 137
  attribution. See essential attribution

Blanshard, Brand, 194
Boethianism, 13, 15, 128–37
Boethius, 111
  individual essence and, 139, 140
  proper names and, 128
book (on a world), 5
  possible worlds and, 73
  as superproposition, 48
Buridan, Jean, 151, 156
  sentence tokens and, 174

Canonical Conception
  of modal metaphysics, 12
  possible worlds and, 103–6, 109, 110
  sets and, 115
Castañeda, Hector-Neri, 177, 206
causal requirement, 231–33
Chisholm, Roderick, 16, 139–45
  on properties, 137, 140
  Theory of World-bound Individuals and, 73
Classical Argument, 90, 92–93
cluster theory, 15–16
complete states of affairs, 107
concept. See individual concept

235